TRIVIA TRACKDOWN
It's a game in a book!

• At what college does Indiana Jones teach?
• Is a koala a bear?
• Can peanuts be used to make dynamite?

If you can answer questions like these, you'll rack up big points as you move from page to page in TRIVIA TRACKDOWN!

But watch out! There are traps and tricks along the way: Sudden Death! Double or Nothing! Killer Questions!

They're all ready for you inside TRIVIA TRACKDOWN. But are *you* ready for TRIVIA TRACKDOWN? Turn the page and find out!

Trivia Trackdown
GAMEBOOK #1

Nancy E. Krulik

Random House ⌂ New York

For my mom and dad

ISBN: 0-394-87526-5

Manufactured in the United States of America

1 2 3 4 5 6 7 8 9 0

Published by arrangement with
Parachute Press

THE RULES

Trivia Trackdown can be played by one or two players, or by two teams. There are many different Trivia Tracks to explore, making the game different each time you play.

Whether you play against a friend, by yourself, or as part of a team, the object of the game is the same—to move successfully through the Trivia Tracks, scoring points by answering questions correctly. There are many traps and sudden-death surprises along the way, and your strategy skill will be challenged along with your trivia knowledge.

First player or team to reach a score of 500 points is the winner. To play, follow these rules:

FOR ONE PLAYER

1. Select a Skill Level—Trivia Tracker or Trivia Master. The Trivia Tracker questions are easier; the Trivia Master questions are worth more points.

2. Begin the game on one of the *It's Your Move!* pages. These pages will get you started through a Trivia Track.

3. Follow the directions on each page you come to. You will be told how many questions you need to answer on each page—and how many points each will be worth.

4. After you have come up with your answers, check them. Answers are upside down on each page.

5. Keep a running tally of your score on the scoresheets provided in the back of the book. (You'll want to make extra copies too.) You always start out with 100 points. After you check your answers, add or subtract your points, and place the total on your scoresheet.

6. At the bottom of each page, you will find directions for where to go next. Many pages offer you a choice. You may come to a *Bonus Break!* page (which leads to the high-scoring *Bonus Questions*), or a *Double or Nothing!* page (where you can gamble and double your points!). Watch out, you may find yourself on a *Sudden Death!* page, where a single answer will determine whether you are still in the game or not!

You may also find yourself on a *Trivia Trip!* page. These pages allow you to trip from the track you're on to an easier or harder track.

7. You are a winner if you score a total of 500 points before you reach the end of your Trivia Track. Keep a record of your scores. See if you can reach the winning total in fewer and fewer moves, or keep going past 500 and see just how high you can score.

FOR TWO PLAYERS

1. Each player selects a Skill Level—Trivia Tracker or Trivia Master. It is not necessary for both players to play on the same Skill Level. One player may prefer the Trivia Tracker questions because they are easier; the other player may prefer to try for higher points with the harder Master questions.

2. Begin the game on one of the *It's Your Move!* pages. One player plays on the *even*-numbered pages; the other player plays the game on the *odd*-numbered pages.

3. Player #1 reads the questions for player #2 and then checks player #2's answers. Player #1 then reads the instructions on the bottom of the page to player #2. Player #2 fills in his or her scoresheet, adding the total and writing down which page he or she will play on his/her next turn. Then player #2 takes the book, turns to the page for player #1's next turn, and reads the questions.

4. Follow the rest of the directions for one player. Each player starts out with 100 points. Whoever reaches a score of 500 points first is the winner. If the game ends before either player has scored 500 points, the player with the highest point total wins.

FOR TWO TEAMS

1. Follow the rules for two players. One team plays on the *even*-numbered pages; the other team plays on the *odd*-numbered pages.

2. Players on each team take turns answering the questions each time their team has a turn. (You must decide before the game begins if you will allow teammates to discuss answers among themselves.)

3. Each team starts out with 100 points. First team to reach a total of 500 points wins the game. If neither team has 500 points at the end of the game, the team with the highest point total wins.

READY, SET, PLAY!

Start your game on one of the *It's Your Move!* pages—they're your first stop on your way through the exciting, fast-paced game of *Trivia Trackdown*.

You'll find the *It's Your Move!* pages on 32, 43, 68, and 121.

Pick one of those pages, then just follow the instructions you find there.

Sports Shorts

Here are four ball-game bafflers for you. You must try to answer all four. Give yourself 15 points for each right answer. Deduct 10 points for each wrong answer. Good luck—and remember, be a good sport!

1. What was Babe Ruth's real name?
2. In which sport do you hit a birdie with a racket?
3. What is the highest possible score you can get in a single bowling game?
4. In which popular sport is a ball made of horsehide generally used?

Tally your points. Now go on to page 91.

Tally your points. Now go on to page 91.

Answers: 1. George Herman Ruth. 2. Badminton. 3. A perfect bowling game of 12 strikes will earn the bowler 300 points. 4. Baseball.

DOUBLE OR NOTHING!

Here are two questions. Each one is worth 20 points—if you get them right. You don't lose any points if you get them wrong . . . unless you feel reckless enough to try some gambling.

You can get 40 points for each right answer if you choose to double. But here's the bad news—if you do choose to double, and you get a question wrong, you lose 40 points.

Which will it be? First you have to decide, and then you can go to the questions.

1. What video game forces you to help Dirk the Daring rescue the beautiful Princess Daphne?

2. Can a horse sleep standing up?

Add or subtract your points. Then go to page 12.

KILLER QUESTION!!!

Still feeling up to the challenge? You have to choose now—you have to face it! Remember, you get 50 points for a right answer, and you must take away 30 points if you answer wrong.

Get ready, here it comes—your Killer Question!!!

In the comic strip "Peanuts," what is Lucy and Linus's last name?

Total your points. Then move to page 17.

Answer: Van Pelt.

TRIVIA TRIP!

Attention, All Players

Trivia Trackers

Are you ready for a greater challenge? Here's your chance to move on up to the Trivia Master game on *page 90*. Remember, the points add up faster on the Master track—but the questions are harder and the risks greater!

So if you want to stay on the Tracker course, go to *page 144*.

Trivia Masters

Feel like giving yourself a little break? Then why not try some Tracker questions for a while? If you want to join the Tracker game, go to *page 144*.

If you want to keep mastering the Masters, move to *page 90*.

Terrifying Trivia

These questions are truly and terrifically tricky. Tough luck—you must try all three anyway! You get 60 points for each right answer—but you also lose 60 points for each wrong one!

1. What is the only U.S. state whose name has only one syllable?
2. Who was the first head of a U.S. post office?
3. As a boy, George Washington chopped down a cherry tree and said "I cannot tell a lie" when his father questioned him about it. True or false?

Add up your points and then trip over to page 47.

Answers: 1. **Maine.** 2. **Benjamin Franklin.** 3. **False.** He said "We cannot tell a lie." But it never really happened—the story is a legend made up by a man named Parson Mason L. Weems.

KILLER QUESTION!!!

This question *is* a killer. But hang in there. You can really roll up big points—a right answer gives you 75 points. But if you get it wrong, you have to take 50 points away from your score.

Okay, get ready. Here comes your Killer Question!!!

Who is George O'Dowd?

Add or subtract your points, then move to page 170.

Add or subtract your points, then move to page 170.

Answer: George O'Dowd is the real name of singer Boy George.

DOUBLE OR NOTHING!

These two questions are worth 50 points each—if you come up with right answers. And you don't lose anything for wrong answers. That is, unless you want to fling caution to the winds and gamble a little.

If you choose to double, you'll get 100 points for each correct answer. However, if you double and then miss a question, you lose 100 points.

Will you be careful or will you be brave? Decide first! Then go on to the questions.

1. What did Louis Braille invent?
2. What is the most commonly used word in the English language? (a) I (b) the (c) a

Add up your points, then move to page 33.

Add up your points, then move to page 33.

Answers: 1. He invented Braille, a system of reading and writing for the blind which uses raised dots. **2.** (c) That small word—the article "a"—is the word we use most often.

Mixed Bag

This mixed bag of questions may leave you mixed up, but you're stuck with it. Each right answer is worth 40 points, and you could lose 25 points for each wrong answer.

First decide if you want to answer one question, or some, or all of them. Whatever you decide, you must start at the top and take them in order!

1. In the comic strip "Nancy," what is Nancy's boyfriend's name?

2. What is the name of Captain Kirk's spaceship?

3. In a normal person, which lung takes in more air, the left or the right?

4. What do Opie Taylor and Richie Cunningham have in common?

5. What is the most expensive property on the Monopoly board?

Tally your score. Then move to page 36.

Answers: 1. Sluggo. 2. The USS *Enterprise.* 3. The right. 4. Opie Taylor on *The Andy Griffith Show* and Richie Cunningham on *Happy Days* were both played by Ron Howard. 5. Boardwalk.

BONUS BREAK!

This is your chance to break loose and try a tough Bonus Question, which could earn you 75 points. But remember, if you get it wrong, you lose 75 points. Is the risk worth taking? If so, pick a number from 1 to 10. That's the number of the question you'll answer, and you'll find it on *page 183*.

If you're not in a risk-taking mood, stay right here with these four cartoon-crazy questions. Give yourself 10 points for each correct answer.

1. Which Walt Disney movie stars Mowgli, Baloo the Bear, and Shere Kahn the Tiger?

2. What is the amazing Spider-Man's real name?

3. Where do Yogi Bear and Boo Boo live?

4. What is the name of the goldfish in Disney's *Pinocchio*?

Tally your score and turn to page 133.

Answers: 1. *The Jungle Book.* 2. Peter Parker. 3. Jellystone Park. 4. Cleo.

Danger: Tricky Trivia Ahead

You get 20 points for each one you get right. You lose 15 points for each one you get wrong.

1. How many cards are there in a regular deck of playing cards?

2. A duck will lay eggs only in the morning. True or false?

3. When is April Fool's Day?

4. From what part of your body do you lose most of your body heat?

5. How did the first airmail letter travel? (a) plane (b) zeppelin (c) balloon

Tally your score and then move to page 42.

Tally your score and then move to page 42.

Answers: 1. 52. 2. True. 3. April 1. 4. From your head. 5. (c) balloon.

DOUBLE OR NOTHING!

Here are two questions. Each one is worth 25 points to you if you get them right. If you get them wrong, you don't lose any points.

But if you're feeling lucky, gamble a little and go for double points! Now you'll get 50 points for each right answer, but you'll also lose 50 points for each wrong answer.

Is it your lucky day? When you've made up your mind, go on to the questions.

1. On what hand does Michael Jackson wear his glove?

2. What did Prince Charles and Princess Diana name their first child?

Tally your score and go to page 157.

Answers: 1. On his right hand. 2. Prince William.

It's a Question!
It's a Chance!
IT'S SUPERMASTER!

Step right up—we're offering all Masters a chance to rack up some points! All you have to do is answer a really hard Killer Question! It's worth 100 points to you if you get it right; get it wrong and you lose 75 points. Want to take us up on our offer? Then go over to *page 22.*

If not—play it safe and stay right here with these questions. They're worth only 25 points each, but then you lose only 10 points for each wrong answer.

1. What shows you your place on a computer screen?

2. How do the nomads of the Sahara carry their supplies?

3. How often does Halley's Comet pass Earth?

Total your points, then move to page 44.

Answers: 1. The cursor. 2. On the backs of their camels. 3. Every 76 years.

Trivia Toughies

You may try as many of these tough little trivia puzzlers as you wish, taking them in order from 1 to 5—but as soon as you miss one, that's the end of your chance to earn points on this page! Each right answer will get you 50 points.

1. What track star ran barefoot in the 1984 Olympics?

2. What is the name of Paul Bunyan's blue ox?

3. Which continent surrounds the South Pole?

4. Who is Miss Grundy?

5. What were the Turtles, Strawberry Alarm Clock, Vanilla Fudge, and Herman's Hermits?

Add up the points for your correct answers. If you got them all right, give yourself a bonus of another 50 points. Then go to page 175.

KILLER QUESTION!!!

You may have a really hard time answering this question, but if you get it right, it's worth 100 points. You lose 75 points if you give the wrong answer.

Get set! Here comes your Killer Question!!!

In what town was Superboy brought up by his foster parents, the Kents?

Add up your score. Then move to page 174.

Add up your score. Then move to page 174.

Answer: Smallville, U.S.A.

Frightening Facts

These questions are ferocious—but you can't run away. You have to stay where you are and try them all!

1. Cavemen ate dinosaur meat. True or false?

2. How many female Smurfs are there?

3. How many lungs do people have?

4. Who are Snake-Eyes, Gung-Ho, and Duke?

5. What color is Clifford, the giant story-book dog?

If you got all five right, give yourself 60 points and move to page 51.

If you got three or four right, give yourself 40 points and move to page 49.

If you got only one or two right, take away 20 points and move to page 25.

Answers: 1. False. Dinosaurs were extinct long before cavemen appeared. 2. One—Smurfette. 3. Two. 4. Members of the G.I. Joe Team. 5. Red.

Animal Crackers

These animal questions could drive you wild! They're worth 15 points for each right answer. But you lose 10 for each wrong one!

1. What basketball team once had a Goose and a Meadowlark playing for it?

2. Can an owl see in the daytime?

3. What type of animal is Babar?

4. Swans cannot make sounds. True or false?

Add or subtract your points. Then move to page 134.

Answers: 1. The Harlem Globetrotters had players "Goose" Tatum and "Meadowlark" Lemon. **2.** Yes. **3.** An elephant. **4.** False. Some swans are mute, but others like the trumpeter swan can make sounds.

KILLER QUESTION!!!

This extra-tough question may kill you, but it's worth it—75 points' worth, if you get it right. Get it wrong and you lose 50 points.

Are you ready? Here comes the Killer Question!!!

A five-star general is called a general of the army. What do you call a one-star general?

Do your addition or subtraction and then move to page 19.

Do your addition or subtraction and then move to page 19.

Answer: A brigadier general.

The Numbers Game

These four questions are really hard. So hard that each correct answer will earn you a whopping 40 points. But each wrong answer will cost you 25 points.

How many questions are you willing to risk answering? Decide first. Then go on to the questions. Start with the first one and take them *in order* (no skipping around, gang)!

1. A quintet is made up of how many instruments playing together?

2. How many keys are there on a piano?

3. How long would you have to swim to work off all the calories from an ice cream soda? (a) 41 minutes (b) 20 minutes (c) 57 minutes

4. How many advertisements does the average person see and hear in one day? (a) 115 (b) 560 (c) 1,025

Total up your new score. Then move to page 170.

Total up your new score. Then move to page 170.

Answers: 1. Five. **2.** 88. **3.** (a) It takes 41 minutes to work off the 350 calories in the average ice cream soda. **4.** (b) 560.

SUDDEN DEATH!

You must get *both* of these questions right to stay in the game.

1. What is the name of Little Orphan Annie's guardian?
2. Where would you find the Golden Gate Bridge?

If you got both of these questions right, give yourself 40 points and move to page 103.

If you missed one, you're out. Better luck next time!

It's a Small World, After All

These world-class questions are earth-shaking. Even so, you have to give all of them a try. We'll give you 20 points for each one you get right. And we'll take away 25 points for each one you miss.

1. In what country will you find the Taj Mahal?

2. Where is the Miss America Pageant held each year?

3. Who lives "over the river and through the woods," according to a well-known old song?

4. True or false: Ancient Egyptians slept on pillows made of stone.

Figure up your new score and then move to page 16.

Answers: 1. India. The white marble Taj Mahal is really a mausoleum. India's Emperor Shah Jahan had it built as the burial site for his favorite wife and himself. 2. Atlantic City, NJ. 3. Grandmother. 4. True.

Off and Running

Be very careful how you answer these questions. They are worth 30 points each. And on top of that, how well you do on them determines which game track you start out on!

1. At what college does Indiana Jones teach?
2. In what town is the Rose Bowl game played?
3. What is another word for "epidermis"?
4. How many items are there in a "baker's dozen"?

Add up the points for your correct answers.

If you got all four of them, move to page 21.

If you got three right, move to page 131.

If you got only one or two right, move to page 159.

If you got all four of them, move to page 21.
If you got three right, move to page 131.
If you got only one or two right, move to page 159.

Answers: 1. Marshall College 2. Pasadena, CA. 3. Skin. 4. 13.

Brainbusters

Here are four real brainbusters. You've got no one to call; you must answer them all! Give yourself 35 points for each right answer. Take away 35 points for each wrong answer.

1. Is a shooting star really a star?
2. What English word is based on Greek words meaning "write with light"?
3. What are the two end players called in a tug-of-war?
4. What was the first position in training to be a knight? (a) page (b) squire (c) kitchen boy

Total up your points. Then move your brain on over to page 58.

Answers: 1. No, a shooting star is not a star at all. It's a meteor, which is actually a bit of dust traveling through space at a very fast speed. When it hits Earth's atmosphere, it gets so hot it glows! That trail of glowing dust is what we call a shooting star. **2.** Photography. **3.** They're called the anchors. **4.** (a) page.

THE END OF THE TRACKS!

You have come to the end of this round of *Trivia Trackdown*. Total up the final scores. Declare a winner.

And as soon as you're rested and ready, go to another *It's Your Move!* page for your next game of *Trivia Trackdown*.

IT'S YOUR MOVE!

Okay, gang, here it is—your first big decision. Do you want to build up points (fairly safely) on the Trivia Tracker track? Or do you want to go for the big points (and the big risks) on the Trivia Master track? Think carefully! Which will it be . . .

If you choose the Tracker track, turn to page 18.

If you choose the Master track, turn to page 60.

The Name Game

Are you good at names? Then test your memory on these questions, starting with the first one and working through them in order. As soon as you miss one, stop right there— your turn is over! Give yourself 50 points for each one you get right.

1. What doctor could talk to animals?
2. In the film *Rumblefish*, what was the nickname of Rusty James's older brother?
3. Who wrote *Poor Richard's Almanack*?
4. What are the Hardy Boys' first names?
5. Who wrote *Gulliver's Travels*?
6. Who was Secretariat?

Total up the points for your correct answers. Did you get them all right? If so, give yourself an extra 50 points as a bonus. Then move to page 55.

Answers: 1. Dr. Dolittle. 2. Motorcycle Boy 3. Benjamin Franklin. 4. Joe and Frank. 5. Jonathan Swift. 6. A famous racehorse.

SUDDEN DEATH!

You must get *both* questions right to stay in the game!

1. How quick is a wink? (a) .28 to .1 second (b) .12 to .30 second (c) 1 second
2. Which city is farther west—Los Angeles or Reno?

If you got two correct answers, give yourself 40 points and move on to page 78.

If you got one wrong answer, you're out! Better luck next time you play the game.

Answers: 1. (a) .28 to .1 second. 2. Reno (look it up!).

BONUS BREAK!

Here's your chance to break away and go for a big Bonus Question worth 90 points—for a right answer, of course. A wrong answer will cost you 50 points. Want to try? Think of a number between 1 and 10. That's the number of your question, and you'll find it on *page 186*.

If you'd rather not risk it, stay here with these two questions, which are worth 20 points each.

1. What musical instrument has been nicknamed the licorice stick?
2. True or false: The best diamonds are colorless.

Tally your score and go to page 81.

Answers: 1. The clarinet. 2. False. The best diamonds are blue-white in color.

It's a Question!
It's a Chance!
IT'S SUPERMASTER!

Here's your chance, all you Masters, to give your score a big boost. All you have to do is come up with the right answer to a Killer Question!!! The right answer gets you 100 points, but you risk losing 75 points if you get it wrong. The question is lying in wait for you on *page 110.*

Not in the mood for risks? Stay here and answer these three trivia toughies. They're worth 30 points each. And you lose only 20 points if you miss.

1. What made Popeye strong?
2. What are the colors in the rainbow?
3. True or false: Peanuts can be used to make dynamite.

Add or subtract your points. Then move to page 56.

Answers: 1. Spinach. 2. Red, orange, yellow, green, blue, indigo, and violet. 3. True.

Brainbusters

These five questions will bust your brain. But you can't call for help—you have to bust them yourself. You get 25 points for each right answer, and you lose 25 points for each wrong one.

1. Who is Charlotte A. Cavatica?
2. Who were Zeus, Apollo, Aphrodite, and Athena?
3. What is the tallest animal on Earth?
4. Which of the Chipmunk brothers wears glasses?
5. Do baby sea lions know how to swim when they're born?

Add or subtract your points. Then move to page 85.

Answers: 1. The spider that saves Wilbur's life in *Charlotte's Web.* 2. Greek gods and goddesses. Zeus was the chief god. Apollo was the god of light and youth. Aphrodite was the goddess of love and beauty, and Athena was the goddess of wisdom. 3. The giraffe. 4. Simon. 5. No, they have to be taught.

Movie Mania

You can practically smell the popcorn on these questions! By the way, this is a triple feature. You have to answer all three. If you do, you get 60 points. If you don't, you get zero!

1. Where does the Wizard of Oz live?
2. Who sang "On the Good Ship Lolli-pop"?
3. Who is Luke Skywalker's father?

Total your score and move to page 98.

Answers: 1. In the Emerald City **2.** Shirley Temple. **3.** Darth Vader.

TRIVIA TRIP! ◆

Attention, All Players

Trivia Trackers

Are you ready for a greater challenge? Here's your chance to move on over to the Trivia Master game on *page 103*.

But if you want to stay on the Tracker course, turn to *page 9*.

Trivia Masters

Is your brain getting tired? Want to try some Tracker questions for a while? Then why not move to *page 9* and pick up the Trivia Tracker track?

If you'd rather keep mastering the Masters, move on to *page 103*.

KILLER QUESTION!!!

This one really is a killer, but you can rack up a big score if you get it right—it's worth 75 points. But if you get it wrong, deduct 50 points from your score!

Take a deep breath, get ready, here it comes—your Killer Question!!!

On which United States national treasure are the words "Proclaim liberty throughout the land and unto all the inhabitants thereof"?

When you've figured up your new score, move to page 122.

When you've figured up your new score, move to page 122.

Answer: These words are inscribed on the Liberty Bell, which is in Philadelphia.

It's a Question!
It's a Chance!
IT'S SUPERTRACKER!

Okay, Trackers, here's the chance of a lifetime to rack up big points. You can do it by answering a Killer Question!!! The right answer will give you 75 points. But if you get it wrong, you lose 50 points. Feel brave? Make tracks to *page 95*.

Or if you'd rather play it safe, stay here and answer these questions. Give yourself 10 points for each one you answer correctly.

1. Which rock star is known as the Boss?
2. Which law of nature did Sir Isaac Newton discover when an apple fell from a tree and landed on his head?
3. In circus slang, what animal is known as a "stripe"?
4. Can cats see in pitch dark?

Total your points. Then move to page 83.

Answers: 1. Bruce Springsteen. 2. The law of gravity. 3. The tiger. 4. No. They have good night vision, but they can't see if it is absolutely dark.

Those Amazing Aliens

Here are five questions about some really far-out folks! You get 25 points for each right answer. You lose 15 points for each wrong one.

1. Who is the enemy of the evil Gobot Cy-Kill?

2. What was the name of Mork's leader from Ork?

3. Who played Lando Calrissian in *The Empire Strikes Back* and *Return of the Jedi*?

4. What did Yoda teach Luke Skywalker to become?

5. Who is Megatron?

If you got three or more questions correct, move to page 54.

If you got two or less correct, go to page 24.

(Don't forget to total up your new score.)

Answers: 1. Leader **2.** Orson. **3.** Billy Dee Williams. **4.** A Jedi knight. **5.** Leader of the Transformer Decepticons.

IT'S YOUR MOVE!

Okay, gang, here comes your first big decision. Do you want to build up points—fairly safely—on the Trivia Tracker track? Or do you want to go for the big points—and the big risks—on the harder Trivia Master track? It's up to you . . . !

If you choose the Tracker track, turn to page 23.

If you choose the Master track, turn to page 29.

BONUS BREAK!

Give yourself a break, and add some big bonus points to your total score. You can do it by deciding to try one of the Bonus Questions, which will be worth 150 points to you if you come up with the right answer. Get it wrong, though, and you lose 100 points. Will you try it? Pick a number between 1 and 10—that's the number of the question you must answer on *page 184*.

If you think you'd better not try it, stay here and answer these six questions. Each right answer earns you 25 points. Each wrong answer costs you 20 points.

1. What was Florence Nightingale's profession?
2. What was the name of Samantha's mother on *Bewitched*?
3. In *Star Wars*, what is Princess Leia's home planet?
4. In short-order cook slang, what is a "tuna down"?
5. What do we call the colored light reflected through raindrops in the air?

Add or subtract your points and move to page 160.

Add or subtract your points and move to page 160.

Answers: 1. She was a nurse. 2. Endora. 3. Alderaan. 4. A tuna sandwich on white toast. 5. A rainbow.

THE END OF THE TRACKS!

You have come to the end of this round of *Trivia Trackdown*. Add up the final scores. Declare a winner.

Now—or as soon as you feel like it again—go to another *It's Your Move!* page and take up the challenge of another *Trivia Trackdown* game.

These Will Really Bug You!

These pesty questions are worth 10 points each if you get them right. But you lose 10 points for every question you get wrong.

1. Bees don't have which of the following senses? (a) touch (b) smell (c) hearing

2. True or false: Moths can chew holes in sweaters.

3. How many times a minute can a fly flap its wings? (a) 60 (b) 18,000 (c) 1,000,000

4. What is the only U.S. state with no houseflies?

Total up your points.

If you got three or more answers right, move to page 162.

If you got two or less right, move to page 104.

Answers: 1. (c) hearing. **2.** False. The *larvae* are the ones that eat wool. **3.** (b) 18,000. **4.** Alaska. The weather is too cool for flies to live.

Brain-Bungling Questions

Try not to bungle these. They are worth 40 points each if you get them right. Unfortunately, you lose 20 points for each wrong answer.

1. Which is heavier, hot water or cold water?
2. True or false. Minnows have teeth in their throats.
3. Who played C-3PO in *Star Wars*? (a) Anthony Daniels (b) Mark Hamill (c) Jason Bateman
4. Does the sun affect the tides?
5. What word in the English language has the most meanings? (a) see (b) set (c) cut

Add up your points. Now, to move on, you must make a choice.

Want to try a really fast track? Move to page 115.

Want to try a little less risky track? Move to page 109.

Answers: 1. Hot water. 2. True. 3. (a) Anthony Daniels. 4. Yes. The moon is closer, so it has a greater effect, but the sun does affect the tides. 5. (b) set.

Rainbow Riddles

These rainbow riddles might make you see red, but you've got to answer them all anyway! You get 30 points for each right answer, and you lose 35 points for each wrong one.

1. What are the two colors of a giant panda?

2. What color are robin's eggs?

3. What are the primary colors?

4. Puce is a greenish color. True or false?

Tally your new point score.

If you answered two or more questions correctly, move to page 26.

If you got less than two right, move to page 96.

If you answered two or more questions correctly, move to page 26.

If you got less than two right, move to page 96.

Answers: 1. Black and white. **2.** Blue. **3.** Red, yellow, and blue. **4.** False. It's a reddish color.

Those Amazing Animals

These four questions are beasts, but you have to try to trap all of them. Give yourself 30 points for each question you get right. Take away 20 points for each wrong answer.

1. A koala is a bear. True or false?
2. What was the name of Roy Rogers' horse?
3. What animal lives the longest?
4. What mammal can read and write?

Total your new point score. Then escape to page 101.

Answers: 1. False. A koala is a marsupial. The marsupial family includes most pouched animals; probably the most familiar one is the kangaroo. **2.** Trigger. **3.** The tortoise. **4.** The human.

DOUBLE OR NOTHING!

Here are two questions. You must answer them both. Each one is worth 20 points—if you get them right. There's no loss of points if you get them wrong. Unless you feel daring enough to gamble a little. You can get 40 points for each question if you decide to take a chance on a double score. But you'll also lose 40 points for each wrong answer!

Want to play it safe or risk being sorry? First decide, then go to the questions.

1. What is Batman's real name?
2. Who is famous for saying "Elementary, my dear Watson"?

Total up your points and move to page 172.

Total up your points and move to page 172.

Answers: 1. Bruce Wayne. 2. Sherlock Holmes. (Actually, Holmes never did say it in any of the stories, but he *is* famous for it.)

It's a Question!
It's a Chance!
IT'S SUPERTRACKER!

If you decide to take this chance, Trackers, you'll be challenging yourself to some big points. How do you do it? By trying to answer a Killer Question!!! It's worth 50 points if you get it right, but you lose 30 points if you get it wrong.

If you're feeling brave, go for it on *page 11*.

If you're not feeling very adventurous, stay here and answer the two questions below. They're worth 10 points each if you get them right.

1. Whose face is on the one-dollar bill?
2. What are Moodies, Puffies, and Smellies?

Total your points, then move to page 161.

Hardworking Trivia Questions

Each of these questions is worth 60 points. But we're making you work hard for them. You must answer *all three* of these questions, *and* you must subtract 100 points for each question you miss.

1. On TV's *The Odd Couple*, what did Oscar Madison do for a living?
2. Who was the captain of the *Millennium Falcon*?
3. Before he ran for office, what did Abraham Lincoln do for a living?

Figure up your new score.
If you got two or more correct answers, move to page 126.
If you got less than two right, move to page 108.

If you got two or more correct answers, move to page 126.
If you got less than two right, move to page 108.

Answers: 1. He was a sportswriter. **2.** Han Solo. **3.** He was a lawyer.

Who Dunnit?

For each of these four questions, figure out who dunnit! Give yourself 10 points for each correct answer.

1. Who is credited with sewing the first American flag?

2. Who was the first woman to be appointed to the United States Supreme Court?

3. Who killed Abraham Lincoln?

4. Who was comedian Jerry Lewis's partner in the 1950s?

Total your score. Then move along the track to page 73.

Total your score. Then move along the track to page 73.

Answers: 1. Betsy Ross. 2. In 1981, Sandra Day O'Connor became the first woman to be a justice of the U.S. Supreme Court. 3. John Wilkes Booth. 4. Dean Martin.

The Numbers Game

Each of these questions can be answered with a number. But your points are numbered too. Give yourself 30 points for each right answer, and take away 20 points for each one you get wrong.

1. How many times does a telephone ring in one minute? (a) 60 (b) 15 (c) 10

2. In football, how many points is a safety worth?

3. How many fingers does Mickey Mouse have on each hand?

Add up the points and count on moving over to page 62.

Add up the points and count on moving over to page 62.

Answers: 1. (c) 10. **2.** Two. **3.** Mickey has four fingers on each hand. Why? To save money. It would have cost the Disney studio a great deal more to animate five fingers.

Monkey Madness

These four questions will drive you ape! You have to monkey around with them and find the answers anyway. Give yourself 25 points for each one you get right.

1. Is there such a thing as a man-eating ape?

2. What is the name of the chimp that starred in a 1951 film with Ronald Reagan?

3. In the remake of the film *King Kong*, the mighty ape's roar was made by playing a recording of a lion's roar backward and slower. True or false?

4. Who is Cheetah?

Add up your score and swing over to page 171.

Add up your score and swing over to page 171.

Answers: 1. No. Members of the ape family are vegetarians. 2. Bonzo, star of *Bedtime for Bonzo*. 3. True. 4. Tarzan's chimp.

Some Far-Out Folks!

Here are four out-of-sight questions about some really far-out people. Answer as many as you can. Start with the first one and take them in order. As soon as you get a question wrong, your turn is over. Each right answer is worth 45 points.

1. Who is Optimus Prime?
2. Who is Kara Zor-El?
3. On what TV show did Mork from Ork first appear?
4. What is Wonder Woman's most powerful weapon?

Add up the points for your correct answers. If you got them all right, give yourself an extra 45 points as a bonus. Move on to page 64.

Move on to page 64.

Answers: 1. He is the leader of the Autobot Transformers. 2. Supergirl. 3. *Happy Days.* 4. Her golden bracelets.

KILLER QUESTION!!!

You're taking a big chance with this question. Is it worth it? Yes—125 points if you get it right! Get it wrong and you lose 75 points. But you can't back out now.

So get ready, because here it comes—your Killer Question!!!

If you are in a restaurant and a waitress serves you a Coney Island chicken, what are you getting?

Add up your score. Then move to page 75.

Answer: A frankfurter. "Coney Island chicken" is part of the special luncheonette lingo used by waiters and waitresses to speed up service.

It's a Question!
It's a Chance!
IT'S SUPERMASTER!

The question for you Masters is, will you take this once-in-a-lifetime chance? You can really roll up your score if you're willing to tackle a Killer Question!!! Get it right and you get a super 95 points. Get it wrong, though, and you lose 75 points. If you want to give it a shot, get on over to *page 92*.

If not—if you'd rather play it safe—stay here and answer these two questions. Each right answer will give you 20 points.

1. Name the seven dwarfs in Walt Disney's *Snow White*.
2. What trees do acorns come from?

Add up your score and move to page 128.

DOUBLE OR NOTHING!

You have to answer both of these questions. They're worth 25 points each if you get them right. If you get them wrong, you don't lose any points.

But maybe you'd like to live dangerously. You could try to double your score. You'd get 50 points for each correct answer. But you'd also lose 50 points for each wrong answer.

Will you be courageous or cautious? First make up your mind. Then go on to the questions.

1. Name two sports that use the term "strike."

2. What is the main ingredient in glass?

Total your points and move to page 93.

Total your points and move to page 93.

Answers: 1. Baseball and bowling. 2. Sand.

Traveling Toughies

These worldwide questions are really tough, but you've got to try them all! Start at the first question and work your way around the world. Give yourself 35 points for each correct answer. Take away 20 points for each incorrect answer.

1. What is the southernmost state in the U.S.? (a) Texas (b) Florida (c) Hawaii

2. What country's flag has a maple leaf on it?

3. What would you use to make an origami sculpture?

4. In what country would you find a sphinx?

5. What country has the largest population in the world?

Total up your points for your new score.

If you got three or more questions right, move to page 140.

If you got less than three right, move to page 124.

Answers: 1. (c) Hawaii **2.** Canada's **3.** Paper. **4.** Egypt **5.** China.

SUDDEN DEATH!

You must get both—we repeat, both—of these questions right to stay in the game!

1. Name the railroads on a Monopoly board.

2. What U.S. landmark is built 555 feet straight up, is made of white granite, and is dedicated to a national hero?

If you got both of these questions right, give yourself 40 points and move on to page 67.

If you missed either one, you're out. Better luck next time you play the game!

Answers: 1. The Reading, B&O, Shortline, and Pennsylvania railroads. 2. The Washington Monument (in Washington, DC).

It's a Question!
It's a Chance!
IT'S SUPERTRACKER!

Trackers, here's the chance of a lifetime to chase after a big score by answering a Killer Question!!! You win 75 points if you get it right, but you lose 50 points if you get it wrong. Do you dare to try it? It's waiting for you on *page 40.*

If you'd rather play it safe, stay here and answer these 10-point questions.

1. Which type of egg will spin—a hard-boiled one or a soft-boiled one?
2. How many stripes are there on the American flag ?
3. Is an adult human skull one bone or many bones?
4. Leonardo da Vinci kept his notes in reverse writing. True or false?
5. Langston Hughes is a U.S. senator. True or false?

Add up the points for your correct answers and move to page 156.

Answers: 1. A hard-boiled one. Neither a soft-boiled nor a raw egg will spin. **2.** 13—one for each of the original colonies. **3.** An adult human skull (the cranium) is one bone. **4.** He did. Reverse writing goes from right to left and can be read in a mirror. **5.** False. Hughes was a famous poet, playwright, and novelist who wrote about black urban American life. He died in 1967.

Mixed-Up Bag of Tough Trivia

Each of these questions is worth 35 points if you get it right. But you lose 30 points for each one you get wrong.

You don't have to answer all of them—so first decide how many you want to tackle. Even if you decide to try only one—or two or three—you have to start with question 1 and proceed in order!

1. Does a record turn clockwise or counterclockwise on the turntable? (No getting up to check, gang!)
2. How many points are there on the Statue of Liberty's crown?
3. What letters do *not* appear on a telephone?
4. What do Granny Smith, Rome, and McIntosh all have in common?

Total up your new score. Then move to page 147.

Answers: 1. Clockwise. 2. Seven. 3. Q and Z. 4. They are all types of apples.

TRIVIA TRIP!

Attention, All Players

Trivia Trackers

Are you ready for a greater challenge? Here's your chance to move on over to the Trivia Master game on *page 74.*

If you want to stay on the Tracker track, pick it up on *page 166.*

Trivia Masters

Brain getting a little tired? Then why not try some Tracker questions for a while? If you want to join the Tracker game, go to *page 166.*

If you want to keep mastering the Masters, move to *page 74.*

Stop the World!

These four questions are world-class toughies. Each correct answer will earn you 30 points. Each wrong answer will cost you 35 points!

How many of these worldly questions do you want to try? Decide first—and remember, whatever number you decide on, you must start with the first question and go in order. (You can't just pick out the easy ones!)

1. What is Persia called today?
2. True or false: In the Tokyo subway, some workers are hired just to squeeze passengers into crowded cars.
3. Where is the Football Hall of Fame?
4. Which ocean is the largest?

Add or subtract your points. Then move to page 107.

Then move to page 107.

Answers: 1. Iran. 2. True. 3. Canton, OH. 4. The Pacific Ocean.

KILLER QUESTION!!!

Here it comes. One Killer Question!!! Get it right and you get 75 points. Get it wrong and you lose 50 points.

Ready, set, go!

According to his hit song, which girl does Rick Springfield want? (a) Sweet Caroline (b) Jesse's Girl (c) Nancy with the Laughing Face.

Add up your score. Then move to page 82.

Answer: (b) Jesse's Girl.

Animal Crackers

You can bet on it—these animal questions will drive you crackers. You must start at the first one and take them in order. As soon as you miss one, your turn is over—you can't earn any more points on this page. Give yourself 50 points for each one you get right.

1. What kind of bird is a budgerigar?
2. What do the ostrich, the emu, the penguin, and the kiwi all have in common?
3. What is the name of Dr. Dolittle's mythical two-headed llama?
4. True or false: Butterflies taste with their feet.

Add up your points. If you got all the questions right, give yourself a 50-point bonus! Then get cracking over to page 31.

Answers: 1. A budgerigar is a parakeet. 2. They are all birds that cannot fly. 3. Pushmi-Pullyu. 4. True. A butterfly's taste buds are on the bottoms of its feet.

IT'S YOUR MOVE!

Okay, gang, here's where you decide how you want to play the game. Do you want to build up points on the fairly easy Trivia Tracker track? Or do you want to go for the big points—and the big risks—on the Trivia Master track? Make up your mind . . . now!

If you choose the Tracker track, move to page 46.

If you choose the Master track, move to page 146.

The Fierce Foursome

These four questions are tough ones. (But so are you—right?) Give yourself 20 points for each one you get right. You must also take away 10 points for each one you miss.

1. What mythical animal looks like a horse or a goat, but has a single horn growing from the center of its forehead?
2. In a computer, what function do the RAM and the ROM control?
3. In what city were all of the Beatles born?
4. What is Mr. T's hometown?

Total your points and go on to page 19.

Total your points and go on to page 19.

Answers: 1. A unicorn. 2. The memory 3. Liverpool, England. 4. Chicago.

TRIVIA TRIP!

Attention, All Players

Trivia Trackers

Are you ready for a greater challenge? Here's your chance to move on over to the Trivia Master track on *page 136*.

If you want to stay on the Tracker track, move to *page 166*.

Trivia Masters

Brain getting a little tired? Then why not try some Tracker questions for a while? If you want to join the Tracker game, go to *page 166*.

If you want to keep mastering the Masters, move to *page 136*.

SUDDEN DEATH!

You must get both of these questions right to stay in the game!

1. Who was the first star to have his picture on the front of a lunchbox? (a) Roy Rogers (b) Lassie (c) Mark Hamill

2. What was the first video game ever invented?

If you got both questions right, give yourself 40 points and move to page 77.

If you missed either one, you're out. Better luck next time you play!

Answers: 1. (a) Roy Rogers. **2.** Pong (a video Ping-Pong game invented by Nolan Bushnell).

Common Questions

In each of the two sets of questions below, tell what the members of the set have in common.

1. What do the Stray Cats, Billy Joel, and Dee Snyder have in common? (a) They all play Ibanez guitars. (b) They all grew up on Long Island, NY. (c) They all wrote songs for Frank Sinatra.

2. What do Richard Nixon, Gerald Ford, Walter Mondale, and Theodore Roosevelt have in common? (a) They were all president of the United States. (b) They were all born in Nebraska. (c) They were all vice-president of the United States.

Give yourself 25 points for each question you got right and move to page 170.

Careful—Tricky Trivia Ahead

But we don't want to trick you into answering more than you want to. You can try just one, or two, or three—or all of them, if you're feeling bold. Each one is worth 20 points, but be careful. Each one you get wrong costs you 15 points!

1. Where are you if you are celebrating Christmas by breaking a candy-filled clay sculpture called a piñata?

2. What is the name of the car driven by Bo and Luke Duke on *The Dukes of Hazzard*?

3. Lassie is really a male dog. True or false?

4. In which country was spaghetti invented?

Add or subtract your points and head on over to page 45.

Add or subtract your points and head on over to page 45.

Answers: 1. Mexico. **2.** The General Lee. **3.** True. Lassie has always been played by male dogs, even though in the story Lassie is a female. Male collies are easier to work with. **4.** China.

It's a Dog's Life

These questions prove that it's a dog-eat-dog world out there. And doggone it—you have to answer all of them. They're worth 30 points apiece. But you lose 15 points for each wrong answer.

1. What is the name of the dog in the comic strip "Garfield"?
2. True or false: Pets have their own national holiday.
3. What is the name of the Brady Bunch's dog?
4. What is the name of Dorothy Gale's dog?
5. Which of the following is *not* a breed of dog? (a) Pomeranian (b) Norwegian elkhound (c) Russian spaniel

Tally your score and then lead yourself over to page 34.

Answers: 1. Odie. 2. True. In the U.S., National Pet Week is the first week in October (not really a holiday, but definitely a national observance). 3. Tiger. 4. Toto. 5. (c) Russian spaniel.

DOUBLE OR NOTHING!

Each of these two questions is worth 50 points to you if you answer them correctly. You won't lose anything if you guess wrong.

But maybe you're in the mood to gamble. You can get 100 points for each correct answer if you feel like doubling. But if you double and you get the wrong answer, you lose 100 points.

What are you in the mood for? First decide, and then go to the questions.

1. Are monkeys colorblind?
2. Would you find page 43 on the right or the left side of a book?

Add or subtract your points. Then move to page 31.

Add or subtract your points. Then move to page 31.

Answers: 1. No. They can see all the colors we do. 2. On the right side. Odd-numbered book pages traditionally appear on the right.

KILLER QUESTION!!

This question is more than really tough! But it's worth 75 points if you get it right. The trouble is, if you guess wrong you lose 40 points.

Are you ready? Get set, because here comes your Killer Question!!!

What kind of car is pictured on the back of a $10 bill?

Add up your score. Then move to page 26.

Answer: It's a Hupmobile, a car that dates back to the 1920s.

It's a Question!
It's a Chance!
IT'S SUPERMASTER!

We're giving you masters a once-in-a-life-time chance at some really big points. All you have to do is try to answer a big Killer Question!!! That question is worth—are you ready for this?—125 points. But watch out—if you get it wrong, you lose 75 points! Feeling lucky? Then go to *page 57*.

If you aren't feeling especially lucky, just stay here and try these questions. They're worth 40 points each, and you lose 25 points for each wrong answer.

1. What sport are you watching if you see a left hook, a right cross, and clinching?
2. According to the song, what is the name of the Magic Dragon?
3. Is cellophane made of plastic?
4. Half of Earth's surface is covered by glaciers. True or false?

Tally your score. Move to page 61.

Answers: 1. Boxing. 2. Puff. 3. No. Cellophane is made from plant fibers. 4. False. Only a tenth of Earth's surface is covered by glaciers.

Three at Last

These three questions are very threatening. Even if you're not sure you can face up to them, you have to try them all! Each right answer is worth 25 points to you. Each wrong answer costs you 20 points.

1. Name two professional major-league baseball teams whose names do not end in *s*.

2. What is the largest country in the world?

3. What is Francis Scott Key famous for?

Figure up your new score and run over to page 168.

Figure up your new score and run over to page 168.

Answers: 1. The Boston Red Sox and the Chicago White Sox. 2. The Union of Soviet Socialist Republics. 3. He composed the words of "The Star-Spangled Banner."

BONUS BREAK!

Here's a chance to break into the world of high scores by choosing to skip this page and go on to a Bonus Question. It's worth 85 points, but you could also lose 40 points if you miss it. Think it's worth a try? Pick a number from 1 to 10. That's the number of your question, and you'll find it on *page 186*.

If you don't feel like making the move, stay here and answer these three questions. They are worth 20 points each.

1. What do the letters ESP stand for?
2. True or false: You can't sneeze with your eyes open.
3. Which bear is the fastest swimmer? (a) grizzly bear (b) polar bear (c) teddy bear

Add up your points, then move to page 87.

Answers: 1. Extrasensory perception. **2.** True. **3.** (b) polar bear.

BONUS BREAK!

We're giving you a chance to break loose and go for a big score—by trying a tough Bonus Question. It'll be worth 75 points to you. But if you get it wrong, you'll lose 50 points. Want to go for it? Think of a number between 1 and 10—that's the number of the question you must answer, on *page 180*.

Or would you rather stay here? Then try to answer all four of these questions. They're worth 15 points each.

1. What is Narnia?
2. What do the opposite sides of a dice cube add up to? (No looking to find out!)
3. Are peanuts really nuts?
4. Does warm air rise or sink?

Add the points for your right answers to your score and move to page 70.

Answers: 1. Narnia is the magic land in the fantasy series by C. S. Lewis. *The Lion, the Witch and the Wardrobe* is the first book. **2.** 7 (1 and 6; 2 and 5; 3 and 4). **3.** No, they are a legume—a kind of vegetable (other legumes are beans and peas). **4.** It rises.

Rough and Rocky Trivia

These rock 'n' roll questions are really heavy! Give yourself 25 points for each right answer. Take away 10 points for each one you can't answer.

1. What band was Lionel Richie a member of before he became a solo performer?

2. What part does wrestler Lou Albano play in Cyndi Lauper's video *Girls Just Want to Have Fun?*

3. What singer is known as the King of Rock 'n' Roll?

4. What is the name of Rick Springfield's dog, who appears on the cover of *Working Class Dog?*

Tally your score.

If you got three or more correct answers, move to page 139.

If you got two or less correct, move to page 79.

Heroic Trivia

Super questions about superheroes! They are worth a super 30 points each.

1. What word will turn Billy Batson into the daring Captain Marvel?
2. Where does Supergirl come from?
3. What gives the Green Lantern his power?
4. Whose job is it to protect Castle Grayskull?

Add the points for your correct answers to your score.

If you got two or more questions right, move to page 114.

If you got less than two right, turn to page 116.

Answers: 1. Shazam. **2.** Argo City. **3.** His ring, which he lights on the lantern given to him by the guardians of the universe. **4.** He-Man's.

Multiple Miseries

Will these multiple-choice questions make you miserable? Not if you get the right answers. Each one is worth 50 points. A wrong answer costs you 35 points. How many will you risk answering? There's no right or wrong answer—the choice is strictly up to you! But you must start with the first question and take them in order.

1. How many times must you frown to make a wrinkle? (a) 1,000 (b) 5,000,000 (c) 200,000

2. Mosquitoes are attracted to one color more than to any other. What is it? (a) blue (b) red (c) yellow

3. What can't cats taste? (a) bitter things (b) sweet things (c) minty things

4. Which country has the mark as a unit of money? (a) Israel (b) Germany (c) England

Tally your score and move to page 59.

Tally your score and move to page 59.

Answers: 1. (c) 200,000. 2. (a) blue. 3. (b) sweet things. 4. (b) Germany.

DOUBLE OR NOTHING!

These two questions give you 40 points each if you get them right. And you don't lose points if you get them wrong . . . unless you want to gamble a little.

You can get 80 points for each right answer if you decide to double. But if you double and you get a wrong answer, you also lose 80 points for each one!

Decide now whether you want to gamble or stick to the sure thing. Then go on to the questions.

1. How many newborn opossums could you fit onto one tablespoon? (a) 20 (b) 1 (c) 100

2. What is the baby's name in the "Popeye" cartoons?

Add up your points and go to page 102.

Add up your points and go to page 102.

Answers: 1. (a) 20. **2.** Swee' Pea.

It's a Question!
It's a Chance!
IT'S SUPERTRACKER!

Hey, all you Trackers, we're offering you a really great chance to rack up some big points. If you want to take us up on it, you can try your luck with a Killer Question!!! Get it right, and you get 75 big points. Get it wrong, though, and you lose 50 points. Want to give it a try? Then go to *page 117*.

If you're not feeling all that lucky, stay here and answer these two questions. They're worth 25 points each. And you only lose 10 points for each wrong answer.

1. Name the four Beatles.
2. How many planets are there in our solar system?

Add up your points and move to page 143.

Answers: 1. John Lennon, Paul McCartney, George Harrison, and Ringo Starr. 2. Nine.

SUDDEN DEATH!

You must get both of these questions right to stay in the game!

1. What is the first word of the U.S. Constitution?

2. Does it take more muscles to smile or to frown?

If you got both of these questions right, give yourself 40 points and move to page 64.

If you got either one wrong, you're out. Better luck next time!

SUDDEN DEATH!

You must answer both of these questions correctly to stay in the game.

1. Do turtles have teeth?
2. In the Walt Disney film *Snow White*, which dwarf doesn't have a beard?

If you got either question wrong, you're out! Better luck next time you play the game.

If you got both of them right, give yourself 30 points. Then move to page 65.

Then move to page 65.

Answers: 1. No, but snapping turtles do have strong jaws that snap and function like teeth. 2. Dopey.

KILLER QUESTION!!!

The question on this page is a toughie, but you chose to come here, so now you're stuck with it. But if you get it right, you can add 100 points to your score. Miss it, and you take 70 points off your score. Are you ready?

Take a deep breath, because here comes the Killer Question!!!

Where did Duran Duran get its name?

Tally your score. Move to page 116.

Tally your score. Move to page 116.

Answer: From Durand-Durand, a character in the film *Barbarella* (a 1960s movie that starred Jane Fonda).

Food, Glorious Food

Here are some mean questions about munchies. You must chew over all three of them. Give yourself 50 points for each right answer; subtract 40 points for each wrong one.

1. What was the first food manufactured (not grown) by human beings?

2. True or false: It is illegal to peel a lemon in a hotel room in California.

3. How many cacao beans does it take to make a pound of chocolate? (a) 400 (b) 5,000 (c) 65

Add up your points and move to page 129.

Some Beastly Questions

These animal questions might make you growl—but you have to try them all anyway! Give yourself 35 points for each right answer. Take away 35 points for each one you miss.

1. An octopus has three hearts. True or false?

2. Does an elephant have *more* or *less* than 30,000 muscles in its trunk?

3. Jellyfish see better at night. True or false?

4. What is a wallaby?

Add up your points.

If you got three or more questions correct, move to page 112.

If you got two or less correct, move to page 142.

Answers: 1. True. 2. More. The elephant has 40,000 muscles in its trunk! 3. False. Jellyfish can't see at all. 4. A wallaby is a marsupial found in Australia and adjacent islands. It is smaller than its relative, the kangaroo, and usually brightly colored.

BONUS BREAK!

How about a chance to break loose and try a tough Bonus Question? It's worth 75 points! But you'll lose 50 points if you get it wrong. Feel brave enough to try it? Pick a number between 1 and 10. That's the number of the question you must answer. Now go to *page 181*.

Don't want to risk it? Then stay right here and answer these two questions. Give yourself 10 points for each correct answer, and take away 5 points for a wrong answer.

1. True or false: A pony is a baby horse.
2. Are there really such things as flesh-eating plants?

Total up your new score, then move yourself on over to page 53.

Answers: 1. False. A pony is a small breed of horse. A baby horse (under one year old) is called a foal. A young male horse is a colt, and a young female is a filly. **2.** Yes. The Venus's flytrap, the bladderwort, and the pitcher plant all live off the flesh of insects.

KILLER QUESTION!!!

The question here is, will you get the answer right? If you do, it's worth 95 points to you. Or will you get it wrong? In that case you lose 75 points.

Ready to try it? Here it comes—the Killer Question!!!

How did rock star Gordon Sumner get the nickname Sting?

Total up your new score and turn to page 152.

Answer: While playing with the band Last Exit, Gordon liked to wear a yellow and black sweatshirt. It made him look a bit like a bumblebee—thus the nickname.

TRIVIA TRIP!

Attention, All Players

Trivia Trackers

Are you ready for a greater challenge? Here's your chance to move on over to the Trivia Master game on *page 71*.

If you want to stay on the Tracker track, move to *page 81*.

Trivia Masters

Brain getting tired? Then why not try some Tracker questions for a while? If you want to join the Tracker game, move to *page 81*.

If you want to keep on mastering the Masters, move to *page 71*.

Five Alive!

Here are five questions for you to try. They are worth 30 points each. But you lose 20 points for each question you miss. *You have to answer them all.*

1. Who is Colonel Steve Austin?
2. In one night, which uses up more electricity—the city of Troy, NY, or the World Trade Center in New York City?
3. James Audubon was a naturalist who studied birds. True or false?
4. Henry Ford once tried to buy the Eiffel Tower. True or false?
5. What famous Beatles song was once called "Scrambled Egg"?

Add up your points and move to page 72.

Answers: 1. He's TV's Six-Million-Dollar Man. 2. The World Trade Center. 3. True. 4. True. 5. "Yesterday."

KILLER QUESTION!!!

This incredibly tough question is just what we said it would be. If you get it right, you get 75 points. If you get it wrong, you lose 50 points.

Are you ready? Here comes the Killer Question!!!

What types of costumes were the colonists wearing at the Boston Tea Party?

Add up your score and move to page 143.

Add up your score and move to page 143.

Answer: They were dressed as Indians.

Four for You

These questions are worth 20 points each, and you'll lose only 10 points for each wrong answer.

1. Who lived in a place called Neverland and refused to grow up?
2. Which is bigger, the female or the male blue whale?
3. What fruit is grown in a vineyard?
4. Pittsburgh is the capital of Pennsylvania. True or false?

Add up your points. Now go to page 170.

Now go to page 170.

Answers: 1. Peter Pan. 2. The female. 3. Grapes. 4. False. The capital is Harrisburg.

Movie Madness

These movie questions are murder to answer! There are four of them—you get 40 points for each right answer, and you lose 40 points for each wrong one.

You don't have to try them all, so first decide how many questions you want to risk answering. But you must start with question 1 and take them in order (no fair picking out just the ones you think you can get right!).

1. What movie featured Kira, a gelfling, who escapes from the evil Skeksis?

2. Which of the following were *not* used to create Chewbacca's roar in *Return of the Jedi*—bears, seals, drums, walruses, badgers, or lions?

3. According to *Return of the Jedi*, Luke Skywalker and Princess Leia are brother and sister. True or false?

4. What did Gertie use to teach E.T. how to speak English?

Add or deduct your point score and move to page 163.

Add or deduct your point score and move to page 163.

Answers: 1. *The Dark Crystal.* **2.** Drums. **3.** True. **4.** Her Speak and Spell toy.

Troublesome Trivia

These questions will give you some trouble—we hope! They're worth 40 points each, but you'll make those points the old-fashioned way—you'll *earn* them! And you must subtract 40 points for each answer you miss!

1. What are the military press, the snatch, and the clean and jerk?

2. What athlete was the winner of two Olympic gold medals and one silver medal for track and field, was a champion golfer, and was named sportswoman of the half-century in 1950?

3. What Walt Disney film features young King Arthur and Merlin the Magician?

4. What symbol is traditionally on a pirate's flag?

5. What is the slogan on the salt container that features the little girl carrying a big umbrella?

Tally your score. Then move to page 170.

Answers: 1. They're basic lifts in Olympic weight-lifting. **2.** Babe Didrikson Zaharias. **3.** *The Sword in the Stone.* **4.** The skull and crossbones. **5.** "When it rains, it pours" (on Morton salt).

SUDDEN DEATH!

You must get two out of two questions correct in order to stay in the game.

1. In what book would you find Bilbo Baggins?

2. Who was the only U.S. president never elected to the office of either president or vice-president?

If you got one or both questions wrong, you're out of the game. Better luck next time you play.

If you got both questions right, give yourself 40 points and go to page 169.

Answers: 1. *The Hobbit*, by J.R.R. Tolkien. 2. Gerald Ford.

Historical Hysteria

Make history! Give yourself 25 points for each question you get right. Take away 10 points for each question you get wrong.

1. George Washington wore wooden false teeth. True or false?

2. In what city was the Declaration of Independence signed?

3. In what year did Columbus sail to the New World?

4. Who was the youngest president ever elected?

5. What was Paul Revere's occupation?

If you answered three or more questions correctly, move to page 138.

If you got two or less right, move to page 48.

(Don't forget to figure up your new score first.)

If you answered three or more questions correctly, move to page 138.

If you got two or less right, move to page 48.

Answers: 1. False. He wore teeth of ivory, made for him in 1795 by a dentist named John Greenwood. 2. Philadelphia, PA. 3. 1492. 4. John F. Kennedy, at the age of 43. 5. Paul Revere was a silversmith.

Really Rough Rerun Riddles

It's time to test your memory. Here are five questions based on TV reruns. Take them in order, and answer as many as possible. But as soon as you get one wrong, you have to stop right there—no more points for you on this page. Give yourself 20 points for each correct answer.

1. On *Star Trek*, what is Dr. McCoy's nickname?

2. Which part of his body did Mork use for drinking?

3. What was the number of the army hospital unit in *M*A*S*H*?

4. What are Laverne's and Shirley's last names?

5. What's the name of Ed Norton's wife on *The Honeymooners*?

Total up your points. Then go to page 113.

Answers: 1. Bones. 2. His forefinger. 3. 4077. 4. Laverne DeFazio and Shirley Feeney. 5. Trixie.

Tricky Trivia

We're up to our old tricks with these not-so-trivial trivia questions. We'll give you 15 points for each right answer. But you lose 20 points for each wrong one.

1. True or false: The biggest collection of baseball cards is in the Baseball Hall of Fame in Cooperstown, NY.

2. What does Marcie call Peppermint Patty?

3. When a pitcher balks, how is he penalized?

Add up your score. Then move to page 148.

Add up your score. Then move to page 148.

Answers: 1. False. It is in New York's Metropolitan Museum of Art. 2. Sir. 3. All runners advance one base.

The Numbers Game

If you're good with numbers, you'll be good at these questions, each of which can be answered with a number. Give yourself 30 points for a right answer; subtract 20 points for a wrong one.

1. How do you write the number 9 in binary numbers?

2. How many stars make up the Big Dipper?

3. How much money do you get when you pass GO in Monopoly?

Count up your points. Then move to page 99.

DOUBLE OR NOTHING!

Here are two questions. You have to try both of them. Each right answer is worth 40 points. And there's no loss of points for wrong answers—unless you want to try your luck at a little gambling.

You can get 80 points for each question you get right if you decide to go for double or nothing. But this time you lose 80 points for each wrong answer.

What will you do? Decide, then go on to the questions.

1. What character is the mascot of *Mad* magazine?

2. When must the members of the band Menudo leave the group?

Total up your points. Then move to page 86.

Answers: 1. Alfred E. Neuman. **2.** When their voices change or when they turn 16—whichever happens first.

KILLER QUESTION!!!

This one is a *real* killer, but you chose it, so now you're stuck with it. But get it right and you get 75 points! Miss it and you lose 50 points.

Are you ready? Here comes the Killer Question!!!

What color are the berries on a poison ivy plant?

Add up your score. Then move to page 137.

Add up your score. Then move to page 137.

Answer: White.

DOUBLE OR NOTHING!

Here are two questions. Try to answer both of them. Each right answer gives you 40 points. A wrong answer doesn't cost you any points . . . unless you want to try a little gambling.

You can get 80 points for each right answer if you choose to double. But if you do double and you get wrong answers, you lose 80 points for each one.

Decide first what you feel like doing. Now go to the questions.

1. What is the real name of TV's *Love Boat*?
2. Who found Curious George in the jungle and became his friend and guardian?

Total up your new score, then move to page 170.

Total up your new score, then move to page 170.

Answers: 1. The *Pacific Princess*. **2.** The man with the yellow hat.

What's in a Name? Points!

So you think you're a real name-dropper. Well, drop these names! Be careful—you get 25 points for each right answer, but you lose 35 for each wrong one.

1. Who ran for vice-president in 1984, when Walter Mondale ran for president?
2. What two brothers invented the airplane?
3. What was the name of Laura and Rob Petrie's son on *The Dick Van Dyke Show*?

Add up your score and move to page 135.

Sneaky Sports Shots

These four sneaky sports questions are worth 40 points each—if you get them right. Answer incorrectly, and you lose 30 points for each wrong guess. Be a good sport and take the questions *in order,* starting with the first one. But you don't have to tackle them all. Decide first how many you'll shoot for, and then go to the questions.

1. What is "double dutch"?
2. What ex–New York Jet was known as Broadway Joe?
3. Who kills the bull in a bullfight?
4. What is the Stanley Cup?

Total up your points and go on to page 170.

Total up your points and go on to page 170.

Answers: 1. It's a jump-rope game using two ropes. 2. Joe Namath. 3. The matador. 4. The Stanley Cup is the prize given to the National Hockey League team that wins the championship that season.

Whatchamacallit?

For each of the following, give a name to the . . . uh . . . whatchamacallit. You must start at the first question and go in order. As soon as you miss one, your turn is over—you have to leave this page. Give yourself 25 points for each correct answer.

1. What do you call the trophy that goes to the most outstanding college football player?

2. What is a polliwog?

3. What was a horseless carriage?

4. What is the only substance that can defeat Superman?

Add up the points for your right answers and move to page 63.

Add up the points for your right answers and move to page 63.

Answers: 1. The Heisman Trophy. **2.** A tadpole. **3.** That was the nickname given to the first automobiles. **4.** Kryptonite.

KILLER QUESTION!!!

This question will get you if you don't watch out! But if you get it right we'll give you 100 points. Get it wrong and we take away 75 points.

So get ready, because we're going to spring it on you—your Killer Question!!!

What is Captain Kirk's middle initial?

Total up your points and move to page 150.

Answer: T. His full name is James Thaddeus Kirk.

Some Beastly Questions

These animal questions may give you paws! They'll also give you 40 points for each right answer. You lose 20 points for each wrong one.

1. What is the only bird that has no wings? (a) kiwi (b) ostrich (c) turkey

2. What can the mudskipper do that no other fish can do? (a) eat mud (b) climb trees (c) change colors

3. Which is larger, a lion or a tiger?

4. What animal takes a shower by filling its nose with water and squirting it all over itself?

Figure up your wins and losses—then move to page 151.

move to page 151.

Answers: 1. (a) kiwi. **2.** (a) eat mud. **3.** A tiger. **4.** Elephant.

Who's Who

These questions are worth 60 points—for each *correct* answer. But each *wrong* answer will cost you 60 points.

You don't have to try all six questions—but no matter how many you decide on, you must start with the first one and take them *in order.*

1. Who is the friendly ghost?
2. Who is Christopher Robin's teddy bear?
3. Who was the first man to walk on the moon?
4. Who was the first woman to be featured on a U.S. coin?
5. Who is Gargamel?
6. Who was Gene Autry's horse?

Tally your score. Then move to page 98.

Tally your score. Then move to page 98.

Answers: 1. Casper. 2. Winnie-the-Pooh. 3. Neil Armstrong. 4. Susan B. Anthony, on the Susan B. Anthony dollar. 5. He is the evil wizard who hates the Smurfs. 6. Champion.

SUDDEN DEATH!

You must get both of these questions right to stay in the game!

1. What country is known as the Land Down Under?
2. On a centigrade thermometer, what is the freezing temperature? (a) 32° (b) 10° (c) 0°

Did you get both questions right? Add 40 points to your score and go to page 161.

Did you miss one question? You're out. Better luck next time!

Terrifying Threesome

Here are three tough questions. Each one you get wrong will cost you 25 points. Each one you get right will earn you 30 points.

You may choose to answer one, two, or three of them. But you have to decide first how many, *and* you have to start with the first question and take them in order.

1. What is philately?
2. In what part of the body will you find the retina?
3. Who is Agent 007?

Add up your points and move to page 130.

Add up your points and move to page 130.

Answers: 1. Stamp collecting. 2. In the eye. 3. James Bond.

Nature's Nasties

All of these questions about nature are very nasty. Don't be fooled into thinking they're easy! What's more, you get 40 points for each right answer—but you lose 50 points for each wrong one.

1. Which animal has the largest brain in proportion to the rest of its body? (a) human (b) ant (c) elephant

2. How can you tell how old a tree is?

3. True or false: The bark of the redwood tree is fireproof.

4. Which is hotter, a lightning bolt or the sun's surface?

Tally your score. Move to page 93.

Tally your score. Move to page 93.

Answers: 1. (c) elephant. **2.** By counting its rings. **3.** True. Fires in redwood forests start inside the trees, not on the bark. **4.** A lightning bolt is five times hotter than the sun's surface!

TRIVIA TRIP!

Attention, All Players

Trivia Trackers
Are you ready for a greater challenge? Here's your chance to move on over to the Trivia Master game on *page 52*.

If you want to stay on the Tracker course, go to *page 156*.

Trivia Masters
Brain getting a little tired? Then why not try some Tracker questions for a while? If you want to join the Trivia Tracker game, go to *page 156*.

If you want to keep mastering the Masters, move to *page 52*.

KILLER QUESTION!!!

This question is really a killer! If you get it right, give yourself 75 points. But if you get it wrong, you lose 50 points.

Are you ready? Take a deep breath. Here comes your Killer Question!!!

Where do you find the peanuts on a peanut plant?

Figure up your wins or losses and move to page 173.

move to page 173.

Answer: In the ground. The stalks of the peanut plant bend over as they grow and push into the soil, where they produce pods containing two or three seeds. The seeds then ripen into peanuts underground.

SUDDEN DEATH!

You must get both of these questions right to stay in the game!

1. What is the name of the newspaper Clark Kent works for?
2. In reference to record albums, what do the letters LP stand for?

If you got both questions right, give yourself 40 points and move to page 100.

If you got either one wrong, you're out! Better luck next time you play the game.

Come and Get It!

Come and get caught by these tricky trivia traps. Each question is worth 30 points—but first you've got to get them right. Right? And do you lose 10 points for each wrong answer? You bet.

1. Does a west wind blow *from* or *to* the west?
2. What is Nancy Drew's boyfriend's name?
3. Who was the first person to fly across the Atlantic alone in a plane?
4. Johann Sebastian Bach was an English composer. True or false?
5. What is Charlie Brown's sister's name?

Add or subtract your points.

If you got three or more answers right, move to page 37.

If you got only one or two right, move to page 41.

Answers: 1. *From* the west. 2. Ned. 3. Charles Lindbergh. 4. False. Bach was German. 5. Sally.

What's in a Name?

How good are you at naming names? Each name you get right earns you 20 points. Each name you get wrong costs you 10 points.

1. Stevie Wonder is the singer's real name. True or false?

2. What was the name of Tom Sawyer's girl friend?

3. What is the name of Mrs. Garrett's store on *The Facts of Life*?

4. What record-breaking football star's nickname is Sweetness?

5. What famous tough guy's real name was Marion Morrison?

Add or subtract your points, then move to page 116.

Add or subtract your points, then move to page 116.

Answers: 1. False. His real name is Steveland Morris. **2.** Becky Thatcher. **3.** Edna's Edibles. **4.** Walter Payton's. **5.** John Wayne's.

IT'S YOUR MOVE!

Okay, gang, it's time to make the first big decision. Do you want to build up points—fairly safely—on the Trivia Tracker track? Or do you want to go for the big points—and the big risks—on the Trivia Master track? Ready to decide . . . ?

If you choose the Tracker track, turn to page 119.

If you want to try the Master track, move to page 153.

Around the World in Four Questions

Here are four questions from around the world. Start on your journey, but try not to trip up—the ones you get right are worth 20 points, and the ones you get wrong will cost you 15 points each.

1. True or false: Deserts are always hot.
2. What do you call a baby kangaroo?
3. What is the name of the river that runs between Mexico and Texas?
4. Name the seven continents.

If you got three or more right, move to page 120.

If you got two or less right, move to page 10.

(But don't budge till you've figured out your new score.)

Answers: 1. False. Deserts get cold at night. 2. A baby kangaroo is called a joey. 3. The Rio Grande. 4. North America, South America, Australia, Europe, Asia, Africa, and Antarctica.

DOUBLE OR NOTHING!

These two questions are worth 40 points each if you get them right. And you won't lose any points if you get them wrong . . . unless you're a gambler.

You can get 80 points for each question you get right if you take a chance and try for double points. But if you get a question wrong, you lose 80 points.

Which will you choose? Decide first. Then go to the questions.

1. Neither fish nor snakes can blink. True or false?
2. Which Ghostbuster got slimed?

Total up your points and move to page 27.

Total up your points and move to page 27.

Answers: 1. True. 2. Dr. Venkman (played by Bill Murray).

Mixed Bag

Can you sort out this curious mixture of questions? Start with the first one and try to answer as many as you can. You have to take them in order, and you have to stop as soon as you miss one. Give yourself 30 points for each correct answer.

1. If you put a freshwater electric eel in salt water, it will electrocute itself. True or false?

2. According to *The Wizard of Oz*, what state was Dorothy from?

3. What was the name of the skunk in the film *Bambi*?

4. Who invented the lightbulb, the camera, and the phonograph?

5. What are the worm, the pop, the electric boogie, and the King Tut?

6. Which is heavier, milk or cream?

Tally up your score and move to page 84.

Tally up your score and move to page 84.

Answers: 1. True. 2. Kansas. 3. Flower. 4. Thomas Alva Edison. 5. Breakdancing moves. 6. Milk.

Sports Shorts

You have a sporting chance to answer these four questions. And to show you how sporting we are, we'll give you 50 points for each right answer, and you lose only 25 points for each one you get wrong.

You can try four questions, or one, or anything in between, but you have to start at the top and take them in order. Decide first how many, then go to the question.

1. How did basketball get its name?
2. What Olympic event involves the following activities: the 100-meter dash, the long jump, the shot put, the high jump, the 400-meter run, the 110-meter hurdles, the discus throw, the pole vault, the javelin throw, and the 1,500-meter run?
3. Where do the Dallas Cowboys play their home games?
4. What player on an ice hockey team never sits in the penalty box after he commits a penalty?

Add or subtract your points. Turn to page 123.

Answers: 1. The hoops were originally made from peach baskets. 2. The decathlon. 3. Irving, TX. 4. The goalie.

SUDDEN DEATH!

Want to stay in the game? Okay—but you must answer *both* of these questions or you're out.

1. On your television set, what do the letters VHF stand for?

2. According to the folk song, who is "lost and gone forever"?

If you missed either one, the game is over— better luck next time!

But if you got them both right, give yourself 40 points and then go to page 38.

Answers: 1. Very high frequency **2.** "My Darling Clementine."

KILLER QUESTION!!!

This is a trivia question, but it's not trivial! Now that you're here, you've got to try it. Give yourself 100 points if you get it right. Take away 50 points if you get it wrong.

Are you ready? Take a deep breath, because here comes your Killer Question!!!

Christopher Columbus used something you see every day to make the sails of the *Nina*, the *Pinta*, and the *Santa Maria*. What was the heavy material that he used?

Add or subtract your points and move on to page 97.

BONUS BREAK!

Here's a real chance for you to break loose and rack up 125 points by answering a Bonus Question. Of course, the answer has to be right, and if it's wrong, you lose 75 points. Do you feel like taking the chance? Then think of a number between 1 and 10—that will be the number of the question you'll answer on *page 185*.

If you'd rather play it safe, stay right here with these four questions. They're worth 20 points each. You lose 10 points for each wrong answer.

1. What happens to Pinocchio when he tells a lie?

2. What did Daniel Boone call his rifle?

3. What was on the U.S. penny before Abraham Lincoln was portrayed there?

4. When Washington, DC, had a major-league baseball team, what was it called?

Total up your new score. Then make tracks to page 148.

Answers: 1. His nose grows longer. **2.** The Tick Licker. **3.** An Indian's head. **4.** The Washington Senators.

BONUS BREAK!

If you want to break loose and rack up some big points, skip this page and go for a Bonus Question. It's worth 150 points if you get it right. The catch is that you lose 100 points if you get it wrong. If you decide it's worth the risk, then think of a number between 1 and 10. That's the number of the question you must answer, and you'll find it on *page 182*.

If you'd rather play it safe, answer the questions on this page instead. You get only 30 points for each one you get right, but then you lose only 15 points for each one you get wrong.

1. In what country was the Statue of Liberty built?
2. What is the Boy Scout motto?
3. What network TV show did Eddie Murphy get his start on?
4. The needle was invented during the Stone Age. True or false?

Add up your points and move to page 99.

Kiddie Questions

No kidding, can you answer these questions? Give yourself a big 25 points for each correct answer.

1. Mosquitoes bite kids more than adults. True or false?

2. Are babies born with a soft spot on their skull?

3. Who is Wally Cleaver's little brother?

Add up your score and move to page 156.

Add up your score and move to page 156.

Answers: 1. False. Mosquitoes bite adults more frequently. **2.** Yes. **3.** Beaver Cleaver.

Brainbusters

You may bust the blood vessels in your brain trying to think up the answers to these questions—but you have to try them all anyway. You get 35 points for each one you get right. And you lose 30 points for each one you get wrong.

1. What colors are the blood cells of the human body?

2. True or false: Whip, Stoop, Maze, Broncho, and Japanese are all types of sculpture.

3. What is the most popular hobby in the world?

4. Fish cannot drown. True or false?

5. What sign of the zodiac is known as the Twins?

Figure up your wins and losses and then turn to page 149.

Figure up your wins and losses and then turn to page 149.

Answers: 1. Red and white. **2.** False. They are all forms of the game tag. **3.** Stamp collecting. **4.** False. Fish can drown if there's not enough oxygen in the water they're swimming in. If they can't get to another area, they'll die from lack of oxygen. Many fish do drown swimming in polluted water. **5.** Gemini.

The Fierce Foursome

These four questions are so fierce they should be forbidden. Each one is worth 40 points if you get it right. But if you should miss, you lose 25 points per wrong answer.

How many are you willing to face up to? You can decide to try all four—or less. Either way, you must start with the first question and take them in order. Quick—decide how many! Ready? Now go to the questions.

1. How many signs of the zodiac are there?
2. Turtles are hatched from eggs. True or false?
3. What comic book superhero is the Man of Steel?
4. What was the name of the ranch on *Bonanza*?

Total up your new score and go to page 118.

Answers: 1. 12. 2. True. 3. Superman. 4. The Ponderosa.

Careful—Tricky Trivia Ahead

Here are five tricky trivia questions. You can try five, four, three—or even just one. But watch out! Whatever number you decide on, you have to take the questions *in order* from the top. You'll get 15 points for each correct answer, and (here's the tricky part) you lose 20 points for each one you get wrong. First decide how many questions, and then see if you can answer them.

1. True or false: Bats are blind.
2. Who was the teddy bear named for?
3. Which milk is more popular throughout the world, cow's milk or goat's milk?
4. True or false: At birth, a colt's legs are as long as those of an adult horse.
5. What color are lemons when they are fresh-picked?

Add up your score. Then move on to page 39.

Add up your score. Then move on to page 39.

Answers: 1. False. Bats do not have good vision and rely heavily on their radar to "see," but they're not blind. **2.** President Theodore "Teddy" Roosevelt. He once refused to shoot a bear during a hunting expedition. The story became famous, and the first teddy bears were named for him. **3.** Goat's milk. **4. False.** A colt does have long, gangly legs, but they're not as long as they'll be when it grows up. **5.** Green.

It's a Question!
It's a Chance!
IT'S SUPERTRACKER!

And it's a chance in a lifetime, Trackers, to pick up some big points with a Killer Question!!! We'll give you 75 points if you get it right. But we'll take away 50 points if you get it wrong. If you want to take us up on it, get right over to *page 66*.

But if you aren't feeling up to it, stay here and answer both of these questions. Give yourself 10 points for each correct answer.

1. Who wrote *Little Women* and *Little Men*?
2. What is the name of Porky Pig's girl friend?

Tally your score and go to page 50.

Answers: 1. Louisa May Alcott. 2. Petunia Pig.

Do You Measure Up?

Here is a fitting challenge for you. How many of these 20-point questions can you answer without missing one? As soon as you get a wrong answer—and you must take the questions in order, starting at the top—your turn is over. No more points for you on this page!

1. How many points is a touchback worth in American professional football?

2. How many feet are there in a mile?

3. How long is a new pencil? (a) 7½ inches (b) 12 inches (c) 5 inches

4. How often do we have a leap year?

5. How many yards are there on a Canadian football field?

Total your score. Then move to page 145.

Answers: 1. None. After a touchback, the ball goes out to the 20-yard line. **2.** 5,280. **3.** (a) 7½ inches. **4.** Every four years. **5.** 110.

Rough, Tough Trivia

These trivia questions are tough! How tough are they? They're so tough that we're giving you 65 points for each one you get right. And we're taking away 35 points for each one you get wrong. How many of these questions are you tough enough to take a shot at? Decide first how many you'll tackle—but you have to start with the first one and take them in order.

1. How many points is a double ringer worth in horseshoes?
2. Which bird is the fastest runner?
3. According to a famous book by Roald Dahl, in whose factory do the Oompa-Loompas work?
4. What do the letters KITT stand for on *Knight Rider*?
5. What was the first brand name for bubble gum (a) Double Bubble (b) Chewy Truey (c) Blibber Blubber

Add up your score. Then move to page 178.

Add up your score. Then move to page 178.

Answers: 1. Six. 2. The ostrich. 3. Willy Wonka's chocolate factory. 4. Knight Industries Two Thousand. 5. (c) Blibber Blubber.

Around the World in Four Questions

These four questions will take a world of knowledge for you to answer correctly. Give yourself 40 points for each one you get right, but take away 25 points for each one you get wrong.

1. In what country was the balloon invented? (a) China (b) Germany (c) Japan
2. How many islands make up Hawaii? (a) 3 (b) 20 (c) 41
3. Which country is shaped like a boot?
4. Which country has the most cats?

Add up your points. Then move to page 111.

Then move to page 111.

Answers: 1. (a) China. 2. (b) 20, but only 8 are inhabited. 3. Italy. 4. The United States.

The Name Game

To answer these questions, you have to name names. Each question is worth 30 points. You must take them in order and try to answer all of them—just keep going till you miss one or have answered them all. But *as soon as* you miss, you must stop right there—you can earn no more points on this page.

1. What is the name of Peter Pan's pirate enemy?

2. What is the name of Rocky Balboa's wife?

3. What is the name of Tarzan's son?

4. What is rock star Prince's last name?

5. Who painted the painting we call the *Mona Lisa*?

6. What is the name of the doll who is Barbie's boyfriend?

Add up your points. If you got all six questions right, give yourself an extra 50 points as a bonus. Then go to page 158.

Answers: 1. Captain Hook. 2. Adrienne. 3. Boy 4. Nelson. 5. Leonardo da Vinci. 6. Ken.

SUDDEN DEATH!

You must get both of these questions right to stay in the game!

1. In what activity will you find someone doing an arabesque?
2. According to TV's *The Odd Couple*, what did Felix Unger do for a living?

If you got both questions right, give yourself 40 points and then move to page 165.

If you got either one wrong, you're out! Better luck next time you play.

Who Dunnit?

For each of these questions, you must play detective and tell us who dunnit! Give yourself 20 points for each correct answer. Take away 10 points each time you miss a question.

1. Who said, "Give me liberty or give me death"?
2. Who saved Captain John Smith's life?
3. Which Peanuts character is a firm believer in the Great Pumpkin?
4. Who was the first basketball player to score 100 points in a single basketball game?
5. Who played the cowboy Roy Rogers in the movies?

Total up your points. Then keep on going to page 30.

Then keep on going to page 30.

Answers: 1. Patrick Henry 2. Pocahontas 3. Linus. 4. Will Chamberlain 5. Roy Rogers.

TRIVIA TRIP!

Attention, All Players

Trivia Trackers

Are you ready for a greater challenge? Here's your chance! You can move on over to the Trivia Master game on *page 89*.

If you want to play it safe on the Tracker course, go to *page 69*.

Trivia Masters

Brain getting a little tired? Why not try some Tracker questions for a while? You can join the Tracker game on *page 69*.

If you want to keep on mastering the Masters, move to *page 89*.

Just Playing Around

Are you game for these? Then play ball! Give yourself 30 points for each correct answer. Subtract 10 points for each wrong one.

1. What game uses aggies and cat's-eyes?
2. In which sport would you hear about a TKO?
3. Where is the Baseball Hall of Fame?

When you've added up your points, move to page 106.

Answers: 1. Marbles. 2. Boxing (TKO stands for "technical knockout"). 3. Cooperstown, NY.

DOUBLE OR NOTHING!

These questions are worth 25 points each if you answer them correctly, and if you get them wrong, you won't lose anything. But maybe you'd like to live a little. . . .

You could decide to try for a double score and earn 50 points for each right answer. But if you come up with wrong answers, you'll lose 50 points for each one.

What to do? Decide! Then go to the questions.

1. True or false: Identical twins have the same fingerprints.
2. Where do Archie Andrews and Jughead Jones go to school?

Tally your new score and go to page 171.

Tally your new score and go to page 171.

Answers: 1. False. No two people have the same fingerprints. **2.** Riverdale High.

SUDDEN DEATH!

You must get both of these questions right to stay in the game!

1. Who carved Pinocchio?
2. What do you call a bee's nest?

If you missed one, you're out. Better luck next time you play!

If you got both questions right, give yourself 20 points and move to page 82.

Body and Mind Blowers

Check out these questions. They all have something to do with your body. And they can really blow your mind! You get 10 points for each one you get right. But watch out! You lose 10 points for each one you get wrong.

1. What are the cerebrum, cerebellum, and medulla oblongata all parts of?

2. True or false: Your ears and nose stop growing at age five.

3. True or false: Blond beards grow faster than dark beards.

4. Are acrobats double-jointed?

5. How many hairs are there in an eyebrow? (a) 5,000 (b) 50 (c) 500

Total your score. Then move to page 31.

Answers: 1. The brain. 2. False. Your nose and ears continue to grow all of your life. 3. True. 4. No. There's no such thing as being double-jointed. Some people are just more flexible than others. 5. 500.

Who Dunnit?

For each of these questions, tell us who dunnit! You get 25 points for each correct answer. But you lose 15 points for each wrong one.

1. What famous composer was completely deaf when he wrote his ninth symphony? (a) Schubert (b) Mahler (c) Beethoven

2. One of the young women starring in TV's *The Facts of Life* was not an actress when she got her part. She was discovered by Charlotte Rae at a boarding school, where Ms. Rae was doing research for the show. Which one of the girls was it?

3. Who wrote *The Cat in the Hat*?

4. Who is pictured on the $1,000 bill? (a) Supreme Court Justice Salmon Chase (b) Thomas Jefferson (c) John Adams

5. Who threw water on the Wicked Witch of the West and caused her to melt away?

Add up your points.

If you got three or more questions right, move to page 176.

If you got two or less right, move to page 28.

Answers: 1. (c) Beethoven. 2. Mindy Cohen, who plays Natalie. 3. Dr. Seuss. 4. (a) Justice Chase. 5. Dorothy in *The Wizard of Oz.*

BONUS BREAK!

Here's an opportunity to break loose and get some big points. All you have to do is decide to answer one of our Bonus Questions. A right answer is worth 150 points, but you'll lose 100 points if you get it wrong. Are you feeling smart enough to try it? Think of a number between 1 and 10. That's the number of the question you must answer on *page 181.*

If you aren't feeling especially brilliant today, stay right here. These questions are worth 45 points each, and you lose only 25 points for each wrong answer.

1. True or false: Ivory sometimes comes from the teeth of a hippopotamus.

2. What is the largest animal that has ever lived?

3. Which of these mammals has the highest temperature? (a) cats (b) humans (c) goats

4. Some cats are born without tails. True or false?

Figure up your new total score. Then move to page 57. Page 57 is a Killer Question.

Answers: 1. True. 2. No, it's not the dinosaur—it's the blue whale. A baby blue whale is larger than a city bus. 3. (c) goats. 4. True.

It's a Question!
It's a Chance!
IT'S SUPERMASTER!

It's the chance of a lifetime, Trivia Masters—the chance to grab some big points by answering a mean Killer Question!!! If you get it right you gain 100 points; but if you get it wrong you lose 70. If that sounds good to you, grab your chance on *page 88*.

If you're not feeling lucky just now, stay right here and answer these two questions. They're worth 20 points each if you get them right.

1. One of Linda Ronstadt's early backup bands left her to form their own group. That group became one of the biggest bands ever. Which one was it? (a) The Eagles (b) Alabama (c) Quiet Riot

2. What was the name of King Arthur's magic sword?

Total your score. Then move to page 12.

Answers: 1. (a) The Eagles. **2.** Excalibur.

It's a Question!
It's a Chance!
IT'S SUPERMASTER!

This is a great chance for all you Masters to really build up your points. How? By answering a Killer Question!!! Get it right and you win 75 points. Get it wrong and you lose 50 points. Want to give it a shot? Go to *page 105*.

If you want to play it safe, stay here and answer these questions. You get 30 points for each right answer, and you lose 15 points for each wrong one.

1. Who was Anne Sullivan?
2. What is H_2O?
3. True or false: The Earl of Sandwich invented the sandwich.
4. Who is the human who makes Kermit the Frog talk?

Add up your points, then move to page 125.

Answers: 1. Helen Keller's teacher. **2.** Water. **3.** False. The ancient Egyptians ate sandwiches (but they weren't called sandwiches till the earl came up with the same idea, sometime in the 1700s). **4.** Jim Henson (who also created all the Muppets).

SUDDEN DEATH!

You must get both of these questions right or you can't stay in the game!

1. If you want to cool down on a hot summer day, which will work better—a glass of iced tea or a mug of hot tea?
2. How many sides are there on a stop sign?

If you got either one wrong, you're out (we warned you)! Better luck next time you play.

If you got both questions right, give yourself 40 points. Then move to page 70.

Who's Who?

A rose by any other name would smell as sweet. But a person by any other name will not earn you the 45 points you can get for each correct answer on this page. (And a wrong answer won't get you a bad name—or cost you any points!)

1. Who played Sandy in the movie *Grease*?
2. Who invented the telephone?
3. Which member of the British rock group the Police is not British?
4. Who is Tatum O'Neal's father?
5. Who wrote "Rip Van Winkle"?

Total up your points and go to page 39.

Answers: 1. Olivia Newton-John. 2. Alexander Graham Bell. 3. Stewart Copeland. He was born in the United States, grew up in the Middle East, and met Andy Summers and Sting while working in London. 4. Ryan O'Neal. 5. Washington Irving.

BONUS BREAK!

Here's a good chance to break loose and go for a Bonus Question. It'll be worth 125 points—but you'll lose 100 points if you get it wrong! Want to go for it? Think of a number between 1 and 10. That's the number of the question you'll have to answer on *page 185*.

If you don't want to risk it, stay here and answer these five questions. They're worth only 40 points each, but then you lose only 25 points if you get a wrong answer.

1. What does Menudo mean?
2. What is the name of the country of small people in *Gulliver's Travels*?
3. Which U.S. president was once a peanut farmer?
4. What number was Herbie the Lovebug?
5. Who are B.O. Plenty and Sparkle Plenty?

Add up your points. Then make tracks to page 164.

Answers: 1. The name of this group is a Spanish word that means "small change." 2. Lilliput. 3. Jimmy Carter. 4. Number 53. 5. They're characters in the "Dick Tracy" comic strip.

To Tell the Truth

True or false? The questions on this page are worth 30 points. True! Wrong answers cost you nothing. False! They cost you 25 points each.

1. True or false: Meteorology is the study of birds.

2. You are one quarter of an inch taller when you wake up than you were when you went to sleep. True or false?

3. True or false: The motto on the very first U.S. coin was "Mind Your Business."

4. True or false: We get most of our salt from sand.

5. It is illegal to hunt camels in Arizona. True or false?

Add up your points.

If you got three or more correct, move to page 13.

If you got two or less correct, move to page 15.

Answers: 1. False. Meteorology is the study of weather. 2. True. During the day gravity and your body weight compress the spine. At night it stretches out as you sleep, so that you are actually taller in the morning. 3. True. 4. False. We get it from sea water. 5. True.

DOUBLE OR NOTHING!

Here are two questions. You have to answer both of them. You can get 40 points for each one you get right, and you don't lose any points for a wrong answer.

But maybe you'd like to try a little gambling . . . ? You can get 80 points for each right answer if you decide to double. But each wrong answer will cost you 80 points.

What's your choice? Decide first. Then go on to the questions.

1. On *The A-Team*, Mr. T's character is called B.A. What do the letters stand for?
2. Do Garfield's stripes run vertically or horizontally?

Add up your points, then move to page 80.

Add up your points, then move to page 80.

Answers: 1. Bad Attitude **2.** Horizontally.

SUDDEN DEATH!

You must get both of these questions correct to stay in the game!

1. What is the most frequently used letter in the English language?
2. What is the name of Winnie-the-Pooh's donkey friend?

Did you get one question wrong? You're out. Better luck next time you play the game!

Did you get both questions right? Give yourself 20 points and move to page 141!

Answers: 1. The letter "e" is used most frequently in English. 2. Eeyore.

Cartoon Quickies

Here are four cartoon questions. Try to answer all four—and you must take them in order. As soon as you miss one, your turn is over—you can earn no more points on this page. Each right answer is worth an amazingly animated 35 points.

1. What is the name of Mickey Mouse's dog?

2. Whose girl friend is Sweet Polly Purebred?

3. What cat is always chasing Tweety?

4. Who is Pinocchio's insect friend in Walt Disney's *Pinocchio*?

Add up your points. (Of course, if you missed the first question you don't get any at all!) Now move to page 172.

Now move to page 172.

Answers: 1. Pluto. 2. Underdog's. 3. Sylvester. 4. Jiminy Cricket.

SUDDEN DEATH!

You must answer both of these questions correctly to stay in the game.

1. Where is the red light on a traffic light—on the top or on the bottom?
2. How many senators are there in the U.S. Senate?

If you missed one question, you're out. And better luck next time you play the game!

If you got both questions right, give yourself 30 points. Then go to page 133.

It's a Question!
It's a Chance!
IT'S SUPERTRACKER!

It's a chance in a lifetime for all you Trackers to earn some really big points with a really tough Killer Question!!! A correct answer will add 75 points to your score. But a wrong answer will take 50 points away. Quick—if you want to play the game, make your move to *page 76.*

If you'd rather play it cool, stay right here and answer the four questions below. They're worth 35 points each if you get them right, and you lose only 20 points for each one you get wrong.

1. What do you call the mythical creature that is half fish and half woman?

2. In what country is the Blarney Stone?

3. Who lives at 1600 Pennsylvania Avenue?

4. What actor did the voice of Darth Vader in *Star Wars*?

Add or subtract your points and go to page 48.

Answers: 1. A mermaid. 2. Ireland. 3. The President of the United States. That's the address of the White House! 4. James Earl Jones.

It's a Question!
It's a Chance!
IT'S SUPERMASTER!

We are giving you a once-in-a-lifetime chance, Masters, to really rack up those points by trying to answer a tough Killer Question!!! You'll find it on *page 127*. Get it right—you get 100 points. Blow it—and you lose 50 points.

If you aren't feeling lucky, stay here and answer these questions. You get 30 points per right answer, and you lose only 15 points for each wrong answer.

1. What do you call a baby swan?
2. What is the name of Roy Rogers' wife?
3. Will you find snow in the tropics?
4. A pigeon can find its way home from more than 300 miles away. True or false?

Add up your points and move on to page 125.

Answers: 1. A cygnet. 2. Dale Evans. 3. Yes, if you climb high enough. There are many snow-capped mountains in the tropics. 4. True. Some have found their way home from 1,500 miles away.

DOUBLE OR NOTHING!

These questions are worth 40 points each, and there's no loss of points if you get them wrong. But maybe you're game for a little gambling.

You can earn 80 points for each right answer—if you want to double. The gamble is that each wrong one will cost you 80 points.

What will you do? Decide—quick! Then go to the questions.

1. In what town will you find the corner of Chocolate and Cocoa avenues?
2. What do the letters FBI stand for?

Figure up your new score, then move to page 150.

The Big Five

Here are five fun questions. Take them in order, and try to answer them all. But if you miss one, you must stop immediately—you can't answer any more questions on this page. Give yourself 15 points for each right answer.

1. What is Barbie's sister's name?
2. Which can go longer without water, a camel or a rat?
3. What 1950s rock star sang "Jailhouse Rock," "Love Me Tender," "Teddy Bear," and "Heartbreak Hotel"?
4. What do you call a graham-cracker-chocolate-melted-marshmallow sandwich?
5. What is the national bird of the United States?

Add up your points.
Did you miss a question on this page? Go to page 141.
Did you get them all right? Go to page 17.

Answers: 1. Skipper. 2. A rat. 3. Elvis Presley. 4. A s'more. 5. The bald eagle.

True-or-False Tricky Trivia

All these true-or-false questions are tougher than they look, so be careful! You get 15 points for each right answer.

1. It is illegal to look gloomy in Pocatello, ID. True or false?
2. You can find a sphinx in New York City. True or false?
3. Goldie Hawn is the actress's real name. True or false?
4. The first postage stamp ever issued is England's Penny Black stamp. True or false?
5. Skyscrapers sway in the wind. True or false?

Add up your points. Then move to page 154.

TV Toughies

Here are some tough TV questions—but don't turn the page! Try to answer all of these questions, taking them *in order*. You get 35 points for each right answer, but as soon as you get a wrong answer, your turn is over on this page—you have to move on!

1. How many minutes of a 60-minute television show are taken up by commercials?

2. On *I Love Lucy*, what was Lucy Ricardo's maiden name?

3. Who are Sarek and Amanda?

4. What is the profession of the character played by Bill Cosby on *The Bill Cosby Show*?

5. What is the address of the house on Sesame Street where Susan, Gordon, and Olivia live?

6. Name all of Jock Ewing's sons.

Add up the points for your right answers. (Of course, if you missed the first question you get no points at all.) Then move to page 155.

Then move to page 155.

Answers: 1. 15. **2.** McGillicuddy. **3.** Mr. Spock's parents. Sarek, his father, was a Vulcan; Amanda, his mother, was an Earthwoman. **4.** He's a doctor (an obstetrician). **5.** They live at 123 Sesame Street. **6.** J.R., Bobby, Gary, and Ray.

SUDDEN DEATH!

You must answer both questions correctly to stay in the game.

1. What is another name for the first 10 amendments to the Constitution?

2. In what country was bowling invented? (a) Greece (b) Egypt (c) Italy

If you answered both questions correctly, give yourself 40 points. Then move to page 52.

If you missed either one, you're out of the game—better luck next time!

Answers: 1. The Bill of Rights. 2. (b) Egypt. The first known bowling pins and bowling ball were found in the tomb of an Egyptian child who was buried in about 5200 B.C.

Welcome to the United States of Confusion

These four questions are all about the United States. They are worth 20 points each! But you must subtract 10 points for each one you miss.

1. Which state is known as the Land of 10,000 Lakes?

2. Florida is known as the Sunshine State. One other state has that same nickname. Which one of these is it? (a) South Dakota (b) California (c) Texas

3. What state is known as the Land of Enchantment? (a) New York (b) Alaska (c) New Mexico

4. Jimmy Carter was the first president from the state of Georgia. True or false?

Total your score and move to page 31.

Total your score and move to page 31.

Answers: 1. Minnesota (there are actually more than 11,000 lakes there). **2.** (a) South Dakota. **3.** (c) New Mexico. **4.** True.

It's a Question!
It's a Chance!
IT'S SUPERTRACKER!

Here's a once-in-a-lifetime chance, Trackers. You'll give your score a big boost if you can answer a really tough Killer Question!!! It's worth 75 points if you get it right, but you lose 50 if you get it wrong. Do you want to go for it? Then go to *page 76*.

Or would you rather not risk it? Stay here then and answer these four questions. They give you 15 points for each right answer, and you lose only 10 points for a wrong answer.

1. True or false: All mosquitoes bite.
2. What vegetable do you make dill pickles from?
3. At what time are more babies born than any other? (a) 4:00 A.M. (b) noon (c) 2:00 P.M.
4. Which has the highest concentration of salt? (a) North Sea (b) Pacific Ocean (c) Dead Sea

Add up or subtract your points. Then move to page 132.

Answers: 1. False. Only the females bite. 2. Cucumbers. 3. (a) 4:00 A.M. 4. (c) Dead Sea.

BONUS BREAK!

You can grab this chance to break away and take on the challenge of a Bonus Question. Get it right and you'll earn 150 points. But get it wrong and you lose 100 points. If you want to risk it, pick a number between 1 and 10. That's the number of the question you'll answer on *page 182*.

If you don't want to risk it, stay right here with these questions. You get 25 points for each right answer; you lose 20 points for each wrong answer.

1. Who is the editor of *The Daily Planet*?
2. What is the name of the dog that watches the three Darling children in *Peter Pan*?
3. How many months have 31 days?
4. Can chimpanzees swim?
5. Americans eat enough ice cream in one year to fill the Grand Canyon. True or false?

Add or subtract your points. Then go on to page 179.

Answers: 1. Perry White—Clark Kent's boss. 2. Nana. 3. Seven. 4. No. 5. True.

You Name It

These questions are worth 40 points each, but as soon as you miss one, your turn on this page is over! And you have to take the questions in order.

1. What is the only mammal that can fly?
2. Whose secretary is Miss Moneypenny?
3. Arachibutyrophobia is the fear of having peanut butter stick to the roof of your mouth. True or false?
4. What time is 1200 hours on a 24-hour clock?
5. What character in Greek mythology had one eye in the middle of his forehead?
6. In which country do women wear saris?

Add up the points for your right answers. Then move to page 178.

Add up the points for your right answers. Then move to page 178.

Answers: 1. The bat. 2. M—James Bond's boss. 3. True. 4. Noon. 5. The Cyclops. 6. India.

DOUBLE OR NOTHING!

Here are two questions. You must try to answer both of them. You get 40 points for each right answer. You lose no points if you get them wrong.

However, want to try a little gambling...? If you decide to try for double points, you'll get 80 points for each right answer. But if you get a wrong answer, you lose 80 points.

What will you do? First decide. Then go on to the questions.

1. What was the name of the first drummer to play with the Beatles?
2. What were the names of the famous outlaw James brothers?

Add or deduct your points and move to page 45.

Answers: 1. Pete Best. 2. Frank and Jesse.

THE END OF THE TRACKS!

You have come to the end of this round of *Trivia Trackdown*. Total up the final scores. Declare a winner.

Now catch your breath, find another *It's Your Move!* page, and begin your next *Trivia Trackdown* game.

TRIVIA TRIP!

Attention, All Players

Trivia Trackers

Are you ready for a greater challenge? Here's your chance to move on over to the Trivia Master game on *page 77.*

If you want to stay on the Tracker track, move to *page 87.*

Trivia Masters

Brain getting a little tired? Then why not try some Tracker questions for a while? If you want to join the Tracker game, move to *page 87.*

If you want to keep on mastering the Masters, move to *page 77.*

It's a Question!
It's a Chance!
IT'S SUPERTRACKER!

If you want it, you've got it, Trackers—a chance to rack up some big points by trying a Killer Question!!! Remember, the points are high, but so is the risk. You gain 75 points if you get it right—or you lose 50 if you get it wrong. Do you want to take the chance? Hunt the question down on *page 14.*

If you aren't feeling so lucky just now, stay here and answer these four questions. They're worth 20 points each for a correct answer, and each wrong answer costs you 10 points.

1. Which can run faster, a man or a hippopotamus?
2. What planet is *Star Trek*'s Mr. Spock from?
3. Fill in the missing word: "Oh, beautiful for spacious skies/For amber waves of _____."
4. In soccer, what's a "header"?

Add up your points. Then move to page 94.

Answers: 1. The hippo. 2. Vulcan. 3. "grain." 4. As the name implies, a header is a ball you hit with your head!

Each of these questions can be answered by telling who dunnit! Take the questions in order, and *as soon as* you get a wrong answer, your turn is over on this page. Give yourself 30 points for each right answer.

1. Who wrote *Are You There, God? It's Me, Margaret*?

2. According to the fairy tale, who could spin straw into gold?

3. Who holds the record for most career home runs in major-league baseball?

4. On *Sesame Street*, who is the host of the game show "Family Food"?

5. Who was Pinocchio's conscience?

Add up your points and then move to page 35.

Add up your points and then move to page 35.

Answers: 1. Judy Blume. 2. Rumpelstiltskin. 3. Henry (Hank) Aaron. 4. Guy Smiley 5. Jiminy Cricket.

Those Amazing Animals

These animal questions are beastly. But you earn 35 points for each correct answer. You lose 25 points for each wrong answer.

How many of these questions will you try to answer? You've got to start at the top and take them in order, whatever you decide. Make up your mind and then tackle the question.

1. What do you call a group of wolves?
2. What insect can eat a baseball bat?
3. What is the only bird that can fly backward?
4. Which fish has its own "fishing rod" to catch other fish? (a) the angler (b) the catfish (c) the shark
5. What animal has the biggest eyes? (a) the giant squid (b) the gorilla (c) the whale

Add up your points, then move to page 56.

Add up your points, then move to page 56.

Answers: 1. A pack. **2.** A termite. **3.** The humming-bird. **4.** (a) the angler. **5.** (a) the giant squid.

DOUBLE OR NOTHING!

Here are two questions. Each right answer is worth 40 points to you, and you don't lose anything if you come up with wrong answers, unless you want to gamble a little on double or nothing . . .

If you choose to double, you get 80 points for each right answer, and you lose 80 points for each wrong answer.

Do you want to take the risk? Decide first. Then go to the questions.

1. True or false: The Dow Jones average refers to a measurement of rainfall.

2. What is basketball star Dr. J's real name?

Add or subtract your points. Then turn to page 177.

Add or subtract your points. Then turn to page 177.

Answers: 1. False. The Dow Jones average measures gains and losses in the stock market. 2. Julius Erving.

DOUBLE OR NOTHING!

Each of these questions is worth 40 points to you if you answer it correctly. There's no risk in a wrong answer—unless you'd like to take a risk?

If you decide to gamble, each question you answer correctly is worth double—80 points. But a wrong answer will cost you 80 points.

What will you do? Make up your mind! Now go to the questions.

1. Which one of these characters did Mel Blanc *not* do the voice for? (a) Bugs Bunny (b) Daffy Duck (c) Fred Flintstone (d) Elmer Fudd

2. Name the five senses.

Add up your points. Then move to page 20.

Add up your points. Then move to page 20.

Answers: 1. (c) Fred Flintstone. **2.** Taste, touch, hearing, smell, and sight.

Historical Horrors

Let's take a trip back in time. How many of these horribly hard trivia questions can you get right? Add 35 points to your score for each correct answer. Subtract 25 points for each wrong one.

1. Whose signature is the largest on the Declaration of Independence?

2. Who was the first president to have a phone on his desk? (a) Abraham Lincoln (b) Herbert Hoover (c) Harry S Truman

3. Lincoln opened his Gettysburg Address by saying, "Four score and seven years ago . . ." How many years are four score and seven?

4. Which president signed a proclamation creating Thanksgiving Day as a national holiday?

5. Who's buried in Grant's Tomb?

Figure your new point score. Then move to page 167.

Figure your new point score. Then move to page 167.

Answers: 1. John Hancock's. **2.** (b) Herbert Hoover. **3.** 87. **4.** Abraham Lincoln. **5.** Ulysses S. Grant.

The Toughest Trivia in Town

These questions are *really* tough. They're so tough, in fact, that you get 40 points for each one you get right. You also lose 40 points for each one you get wrong!

If you're not tough enough to stand up to all of them, you don't have to. Decide how many you'll try for, then go to the questions. (Start at the top and take them in order, please!)

1. Who is the love of Charlie Brown's life?

2. What was the first U.S. coin ever minted? (a) penny (b) nickel (c) silver dollar

3. What is Beezus and Ramona's last name?

4. What is the Alamo? (a) a ship that sank (b) a bridge that was blown up (c) a fort where a battle was fought

Add up your points. Then move to page 170.

Add up your points. Then move to page 170.

Answers: 1. The little red-haired girl. 2. (a) penny 3. Quimby 4. (c) a fort where a battle was fought.

Ferocious Foursome

Here are four ferocious questions. Each one is worth 40 points to you if you get it right. Get it wrong and you lose 30 points.

We're not mean enough to insist you try to answer them all. But we are mean enough to insist that you start at the top and take the questions in order. How many do you want to try? Decide first, then go to the questions.

1. True or false: The peacock is part of the chicken family.
2. What state was the first to grant women the vote? (a) New York (b) Wyoming (c) California
3. Who was the first American president to visit Communist China?
4. What is the name of Snoopy's brother who lives in the desert?

Add up your points and move to page 39.

Answers: 1. True. 2. (b) Wyoming. 3. Richard Nixon. 4. Spike.

BONUS QUESTIONS

1. What one bone makes up one quarter of your height?

2. How long do most lightbulbs last? (a) 1,000 hours (b) 100 hours (c) 5,000 hours

3. What is the secret identity of a character named Prince Adam?

4. *Swan Lake* is a famous opera. True or false?

5. What state is most closely associated with Bruce Springsteen?

6. What does it mean when the police "mirandize" a suspect?

7. What is a sonnet? (a) a kind of hat (b) a kind of flower (c) a kind of poem

8. In baseball, where does the shortstop usually stand?

9. Who were the first farmers in colonial America—the men or the women?

10. What famous actress was the inspiration for the character of Tinkerbell in Walt Disney's version of *Peter Pan*?

Add up your points. Then move to page 70.

Answers: 1. The femur, or thigh bone. **2.** (a) 1,000 hours. **3.** He-Man. **4.** False. It's a famous ballet. **5.** New Jersey. **6.** They read the suspect his rights. **7.** (c) a kind of poem. **8.** Between second and third base. **9.** The women. The men were occupied with hunting and fishing. **10.** Marilyn Monroe.

BONUS QUESTIONS

1. What mythical creature has a human head, a lion's body, a serpent's tail, and a bird's wings?

2. Which is the only major sport that was completely originated in the U.S.A? (a) baseball (b) football (c) basketball

3. What does "pizza" means in Italian?

4. How many different sports were there in the first Olympics?

5. Which has more bones—a German shepherd or a fox terrier?

6. A tarantula can live without food for up to two years. True or false?

7. Who was the only U.S. president to be elected unanimously?

8. In the book *The Rats of NIMH*, NIMH stands for National Institute for Mental Health. True or false?

9. Unicorns existed hundreds of years ago. True or false?

10. *Superfudge* is the sequel to what book?

Add up your points. Then move to page 45.

Add up your points. Then move to page 45.

Answers: 1. The sphinx. 2. (c) basketball. 3. Pie. 4. One—a foot race. 5. They have the same number of bones—all dogs do. 6. True. 7. George Washington. 8. True. The rats had been lab animals there. 9. False. Unicorns are mythical beasts. 10. *Tales of a Fourth Grade Nothing.*

182

BONUS QUESTIONS

1. Whose picture appears on the $100 bill?
2. Which two Bee Gees are twins?
3. What must happen for a pitcher to pitch a perfect game?
4. Whose heart beats faster—a man's or a woman's?
5. Sugar is used in building a bridge. True or false?
6. Who plays catcher on Charlie Brown's baseball team?
7. Which is the only dog that has a black tongue? (a) chow (b) collie (c) poodle
8. Which of these gemstones is named for a Greek word meaning "unconquerable"? (a) diamond (b) emerald (c) ruby
9. What is the common name for the constellation Ursa Minor?
10. How many players from one football team are allowed on the field at one time?

Add up your points. Then move to page 99.

Answers: 1. Benjamin Franklin's. **2.** Robin and Maurice. **3.** No batter on the other team can reach first base. **4.** A woman's. **5.** True. Sugar is often mixed with the mortar. **6.** Schroeder. **7.** (a) chow. **8.** (a) diamond. **9.** Ursa Minor actually means Little Bear, but the constellation is most commonly called the Little Dipper. **10.** 11.

BONUS QUESTIONS

1. What modern winter sport is based on the old British sports of shinny and hurling?

2. Whose boots does Mr. T always wear?

3. Who played R2-D2 in *Star Wars*? (a) Anthony Daniels (b) Ray Bolger (c) Kenny Baker

4. Which president served only one month in office? (a) William Henry Harrison (b) James Garfield (c) Andrew Jackson

5. Who are Knothead and Splinter?

6. What are these sentences called? Madam I'm Adam. Able was I ere I saw Elba.

7. What do Miss Piggy and Yoda have in common? (a) Both were created by Bill Baird. (b) Both of their voices are performed by Frank Oz. (c) Both are cartoon characters.

8. What is Barney, Betty, and Bam Bam's last name?

9. What does UNICEF stand for?

10. Where will you find Fonzie's leather jacket, the Hope Diamond, and the original teddy bear all in one place?

Add up your score. Then move to page 133.

Answers: 1. Ice hockey. **2.** His father's. **3.** (c) Kenny Baker. **4.** (a) William Henry Harrison. **5.** Woody Woodpecker's nephews. **6.** They are palindromes (sentences that read the same forward and backward). **7.** (b) Both of their voices are performed by Frank Oz. **8.** Rubble. **9.** United Nations International Children's Emergency Fund. **10.** At the Smithsonian Institution in Washington, DC.

BONUS QUESTIONS

1. Which two members of Van Halen are brothers?

2. What are cumulus, nimbus, and stratus?

3. On your television set, what do the letters UHF stand for?

4. According to the book *Heidi*, with whom did Heidi live?

5. In what sport is love bad?

6. What sport was Pelé famous for?

7. Whose original name was Leslie Lynch King? (a) Leslie Ann Warren's (b) President Gerald Ford's (c) Cyndi Lauper's

8. When Snoopy pretends to be a World War I flying ace, what type of plane does he think he is flying?

9. What is Dustin Hoffman's real name?

10. Who was the first American woman to go into space?

Add up your points. Then move to page 160.

Answers: 1. Edward and Alex Van Halen. 2. Clouds. 3. Ultra-high frequency. 4. Her grandfather (and his goat). 5. In tennis, love means zero. 6. Soccer. 7. (b) President Gerald Ford was originally named for his natural father, Leslie King. When his parents divorced and his mother remarried, the baby was adopted by his mother's second husband and renamed Gerald R. Ford, Jr. 8. A Sopwith Camel. 9. Dustin Hoffman. 10. Sally K. Ride.

BONUS QUESTIONS

1. According to the legend, what happens if the groundhog sees its shadow on Groundhog Day?

2. Which distance is greater, from Honolulu to New York or from Honolulu to Tokyo?

3. Where will you find more than one quarter of Earth's forests? (a) Brazil (b) China (c) Siberia

4. What is the name of the Ewing ranch on *Dallas*?

5. Which state is the Centennial State?

6. In *The Outsiders*, what's the name of the gang member played by Matt Dillon?

7. The shoelace wasn't invented until 1790. Until then, how did people fasten their shoes? (a) with Velcro (b) with buckles (c) They didn't—they wore laceless boots.

8. Is there more land to the north or to the south of the equator?

9. According to the nursery rhyme, what are little boys made of?

10. Whose maiden name was Mary Cathleen Collins? (a) Madonna's (b) Bo Derek's (c) Diana Ross's

Add up your score. Then move to page 164.

Answers: 1. There will be six more weeks of winter. 2. The distance from Honolulu to New York is greater. 3. (c) Siberia. 4. South Fork. 5. Colorado. 6. Dallas Winston. 7. (b) with buckles. 8. To the north. 9. Snakes and snails and puppy dogs' tails. 10. (b) Bo Derek's.

BONUS QUESTIONS

1. What living things do we get rubber from?

2. William G. Morgan of Holyoke, MA, invented a game in 1895 that required a ball and a net. What was it? (a) volleyball (b) tennis (c) soccer

3. Which of the Marx Brothers never spoke a word in any of their stage shows or films?

4. Who played the Scarecrow in the film *The Wiz*?

5. On the TV show *Knight Rider*, what make of car is KITT?

6. Are the Thompson Twins really twins?

7. What make of car was Herbie the Lovebug?

8. Where will you find Big Ben?

9. Whose motto is "All for one and one for all"?

10. According to the famous poem, when Casey was at bat what did he do?

Add up your points and move to page 87.

Add up your points and move to page 87.

Answers: 1. Trees. 2. (a) volleyball. 3. Harpo. 4. Michael Jackson. 5. A Pontiac Trans Am. 6. No. They are really three close friends from England named Alannah Currie, Tom Bailey, and Joe Leeway. 7. A Volkswagen Beetle. 8. In London, England. 9. The Three Musketeers'. 10. He struck out!

TRIVIA TRACKDOWN SCORESHEET

Carefully tear out this scoresheet—or copy
it onto a separate sheet of paper. Each
player (or team) gets one scoresheet.

MOVES	POINTS GAINED OR LOST	RUNNING POINT TOTAL	NEXT PAGE FOR PLAY
1			
2			
3			
4			
5			
6			
7			
8			
9			
10			
11			
12			
13			
14			

MOVES	POINTS GAINED OR LOST	RUNNING POINT TOTAL	NEXT PAGE FOR PLAY
15			
16			
17			
18			
19			
20			
21			
22			
23			
24			
25			
26			
27			
28			

TRIVIA TRACKDOWN SCORESHEET

Carefully tear out this scoresheet—or copy it onto a separate sheet of paper. Each player (or team) gets one scoresheet.

MOVES	POINTS GAINED OR LOST	RUNNING POINT TOTAL	NEXT PAGE FOR PLAY
1			
2			
3			
4			
5			
6			
7			
8			
9			
10			
11			
12			
13			
14			

MOVES	POINTS GAINED OR LOST	RUNNING POINT TOTAL	NEXT PAGE FOR PLAY
15			
16			
17			
18			
19			
20			
21			
22			
23			
24			
25			
26			
27			
28			

TRIVIA TRACKDOWN SCORESHEET

Carefully tear out this scoresheet—or copy it onto a separate sheet of paper. Each player (or team) gets one scoresheet.

MOVES	POINTS GAINED OR LOST	RUNNING POINT TOTAL	NEXT PAGE FOR PLAY
1			
2			
3			
4			
5			
6			
7			
8			
9			
10			
11			
12			
13			
14			

MOVES	POINTS GAINED OR LOST	RUNNING POINT TOTAL	NEXT PAGE FOR PLAY
15			
16			
17			
18			
19			
20			
21			
22			
23			
24			
25			
26			
27			
28			

OUT OF THE MISTWALL
EMERGES THE CREATURE
OF DEATH

This was some unnatural fiend, a perverted form of lion with grey vestigial wings and a mockery of a human face. And eyes as deep as a well, as a bottomless pit . . . Bith shook her head. A sphinx, the monster with eyes that could hypnotize small animals and weak beings. And men.

"Cal, Endril, Thor!" she shouted. "Wake up!" The men were all three face up and rigid as statues. She cast a blast spell, but soon the creature returned, driven by hunger. It hopped across boulders as lightly as dandelion fluff. Its mouth was bared in a lion's grimace that showed sharp lion's teeth. Bith could smell it even now, a stink of ammonia and rotten meat. The sphinx topped the nearest boulder and loomed over her, blacking out the sky. Bith cowered and waited for death . . .

RuneSword

Volume One
OUTCASTS

Clayton Emery

ACE BOOKS, NEW YORK

This book is an Ace original edition,
and has never been previously published.

RUNESWORD: OUTCASTS

An Ace Book/published by arrangement with
Bill Fawcett & Associates, Inc.

PRINTING HISTORY
Ace edition/July 1990

ISBN: 0-441-73694-7

Ace Books are published by The Berkley Publishing Group,
200 Madison Avenue, New York, New York 10016.
The name ''ACE'' and the ''A'' logo are trademarks
belonging to Charter Communications, Inc.

PRINTED IN THE UNITED STATES OF AMERICA

10 9 8 7 6 5 4 3 2 1

Dedicated to my sister, sometimes Elizabeth.
Rant, rant, rant.

OUTCASTS

CHAPTER
1

Elizebith ran and fell and scrambled up and ran and fell again.
The fresh-fallen leaves and tilted slope were treacherous under the slick soles of her boots. Naked branches of bramble
and scrub oak clutched at her, tearing and cutting, pricking
her a thousand times about the face and hands and neck. The
girl slipped once more on a leafy rock and fell, banging her
knee. She knelt, clutching her leg and crying silently. Letting
the tears flow helped the pain—in her knee, anyway. Her
heartache was something else.

Bith was tall and dark, slim and soft, with flowing brown-
black hair and eyes that were almost luminous. She wore a
dark outfit of shirt and pants with a deep blue cloak over all.
Around her middle was a wide yellow belt that matched her
fine-tooled boots. The belt's grinning devil-face buckle and
dozen small pouches marked her as a magic user.

The girl tried to quiet her breathing enough to hear the
pursuit. Far down the ravine could be heard the cursing of
men as they thrashed through the dark underbrush. Bith didn't
know how many there were, but there were enough to comb
the ravine easily without missing her. She looked up at the
fading light. The days were short now. Scaly branches made

1

a spider's web that laced the overcast twilight. The brush was so thick it was like looking up through a latticework basket. Even where she crouched there were branches reaching for her soft skin. She hadn't known how thick the brush grew up this ravine. She should have found out, she berated herself, she should have *learned* her own neck of the woods! It was stupid to not know what lay at the head of this ravine. Did it open into meadow, or more forest, or drop down again to more brush? She should have found out before now, now when she was fleeing and learning the hard way. The lesson for today. Live and learn, she thought bitterly. Learn or die. Somewhere below her a man barked an oath. Her heart fluttered. He was close. She pinched her knee into numbness and crept uphill through the brambles.

In truth, she hadn't lived in her tiny ramshackle cottage long enough to learn where much of anything was. Living alone meant so much to do. Fetch water, tend the fire, check the snares before the foxes got to them, gather roots. This was why men had wives and the wealthy had servants. It was an all-day affair just to keep fed and warm. There was no time for exploring. Or reading or studying or having any fun. It had been a long time since Elizebith had done anything fun.

And here she had to minister to the wants and needs of the peasants who sought out the ''witch.'' More wants than needs, but who was she to talk? The reason she was so clumsy at fetching and carrying and cooking is that she'd never done it for herself until recently. If only she'd known how happy she was when she *was* happy! She had been such a little girl. A spoiled little girl. Never wanting for anything. She would give anything now, even her soul, just to be able to sit quietly and not run, run, run.

Yes, the peasants had come. They wanted a cure for a toothache. A love potion. A physic to flush a baby from the womb. A curse for a prosperous neighbor. Elizebith did what she could. A toothache received the inner bark of the slippery elm. But it was only a temporary cure. A love potion was camphor oil applied to the hair of the loved one, accompanied by ''good thoughts.'' It was a nostrum. The physic to be rid of a baby was mineral oil. The poison killed the woman as well if she took it improperly. The curse could be anything as long as it was vile: hate added the rest. But she had known she couldn't keep it up for long. People hated witches. (It was a mark of the peasants' ignorance that they couldn't tell witches from magicians.) They hated what a witch could do, even as they asked her. They welshed on payment unless you took it beforehand. And they waited until the last minute, and that had been Bith's undoing. While a couple had not hesitated to make the long journey to her hut to save a cow, they always waited until a daughter was at death's door before lifting a finger. This time it had been too late. Bith had tried, but the child had died within hours. The grieving parents had blamed the witch. She should have *known*. Her mother had warned her time and again that helping people always brought punishment. But she hadn't expected it to happen so soon. Here she was, fleeing for her life.

Bith rose and pressed through the brush, uphill. It was very quiet up here, and there was no wind. Was the ravine closing in? The slopes at either hand were not just grass and leaves, but crumbly ledge. The sides were steep and not thirty feet apart. Maybe she'd pass through this cut soon, then she could run on the flat. Though she couldn't run much farther—she was almost spent. A lifetime of sailing a cockleshell on a lake and reading romances had not prepared her for a real outdoor life. She put her hand against one rocky slope for balance. It remained quiet. Had she lost them? She couldn't see very well. The sky was faintly luminous but this ravine was black as the inside of a bucket. Suddenly she bumped her nose into another rock wall. An outcropping? She groped with her hands. No, a turn in the wall. Then her heart sank.

This was the head of the ravine. A rocky wall all around, a stone box. A dead end. The slopes had to be twenty feet high on three sides. The only way open was downhill.

Bith jumped at the stone cage around her and found no purchase. Her fingers were too weak. And she couldn't see anyway. What to do? Jump like a mountain lion? Fly away? She almost laughed. Her mind was playing tricks on her. Nothing useful came to mind. Nothing. The slim girl fell to the ground and sucked air in great wracking sobs.

She was trapped. Her captors might as well be running up a tunnel at her. Except they weren't captors. They would kill her when they caught her, probably tear her to pieces. They wouldn't even drag her back to the village to burn. Was that better? She doubled over, fear and fatigue overwhelming her. She hugged herself and sobbed.

A horned owl brushed overhead with a *hoo*, startling her. Had she been asleep? Was that possible? Bith wiped her face with filthy hands and took a deep breath. She felt strangely better. She was all cried out. Did that mean she was ready to die? On the contrary, she was beginning to feel angry. Angry at these stupid, ignorant people who hunted her for no reason. The peasant girl had died this morning, true, but not from Bith's lack of care. She simmered with fury until her ears grew warm. She'd get them if she could, with the blackest magic she could conjure. But where were they?

She cocked an ear down the ravine and listened. All was quiet. Crickets chirped far off, the last before the snow. Somewhere a badger hissed. The air was full of the smell of leaf mold and crushed teaberries and red sumac. Where was everyone? Bith rose softly and felt along the stone slope. No sound. Then she heard them. A thrashing of brush. The guttural growl of men after blood. And a new sound.

Ha-rooooo! Hark, hark! Ha-roooooo!

Dogs! They'd brought up dogs! She was surely done for now. Never mind. There was one thing both men and dogs feared. And she'd teach them to fear a sorceress, too.

She found a small overhang of rock and bumped her head getting under it. She felt in a pouch with delicate fingers and plucked out a fuzzy lump that crackled under her fingertips. With the other hand she touched the bole of an oak tree perhaps a handspan thick.

And she waited . . .

As the darkness grew deeper and the sound of pursuit louder, Bith, daughter of Morea, thought of her old home and what it had meant. Her old home was a musty castle wreathed in mist. Lake water had stretched away behind the castle, and the front looked out over a hard expense of scrabble and low, tough bushes. Brimstone bubbled from fissures along the shoreline. Water leaked into all the lower rooms of her mother's castle. A rusty iron gate with iron spikes guarded the door. Every battlement had the cracked skull of an enemy mounted on it. That evil place had been her home for sixteen years. How strange that she had been content there. Would she rather be there right now? She couldn't say. How strange the way her mind worked, the mind of a spellcaster. No wonder mortals didn't understand them. They didn't understand themselves.

Hark, hark! Rowf! The bark of the dog exploded almost under her feet. Bith saw a white branch whip aside, low down, at the height of a dog's shoulder. A growl sounded off to her left. There were two dogs. They stopped. Having found her, stood still and sounded.

Ha-rooo! Rarf, rarf! Rark rurk, rark! In between calls the beasts snapped and snarled at her, foam splashing from their jaws. They kept her in place and notified their undeserving masters. The noise was ear-splitting in the narrow defile. Bith's hands were busy, as were her lips. She chanted, low and intense.

Shouting oaths the crowd of men burst into the ravine. "There she is!" "Hold her fast!" "Don't let her get away!" Someone called for a flint to spark a torch.

I'll give them a torch, Bith thought. She finished her chant and with her thumb crushed the dried firefly against the young oak tree.

FWAASHHHH! Instantly the tree was ablaze as if it had been steeping in a hot wind for an entire summer. The dogs howled in fright. The men swore and shielded their eyes with their forearms. And Bith, who had kept her own eyes tightly closed, bolted towards them.

Hot sparks and ash floated all around them as she ducked between the cowering dogs and into the crowd of men. She got between two by scooching low. She had her knife out and she poked at another to get him out of the way. He shrieked as if he'd been bitten by a dragon and tumbled backward, though Bith's tiny knife had barely nicked him. The man fell against his neighbor and both went down thrashing. Bith tried to jump clear. *How many of the bastards were there, anyway? It wasn't fair to send so many after one girl!* Men swiped at her and kicked out. A tangle of feet caught her and she fell.

Cries of "Got her now!" and "Hang onto her!" burst on her ears. One man had her by the wrist. She stabbed with her short knife but it tangled in the folds of her cloak. She bit the dirty hand instead. It tasted of pig fat and woodsmoke. The man let go, but brought his other fist down on her head with a crash. Lights flashed before her eyes. Before she could tumble to either side someone kicked her in the ribs. A laugh stung her. Bith struggled and fought but was powerless. Three men flopped onto her and mashed her face into the leaf mold of the forest floor. She might not be hacked or stoned or burned to death. She might smother. The panic came back, so bright it burned her brain even as the tree burned the night sky.

Far away she heard a man scream. It was not a laugh or a shout, but a scream like a trapped rabbit's. Then it was cut short. But another man took it up. Suddenly the weight on her back was gone. A dog howled and she struggled to free her face. *What* was happening?

In the flare of the burning tree Elizebeth saw a giant figure raise a whimpering dog high overhead. The giant had the dog's back legs in one hand and its neck in the other, and as Bith watched, it ripped the heavy animal apart as if it were a sheet of paper. Men howled—there was howling all around her—as the black figure hurled the bloody pieces at them. The chunks pinwheeled blood that rained on the villagers' backs as they ran away. They pushed each another in their mad scramble down the brushy slope. The figure gobbled and croaked madly, berating and mocking them. Then it stood still as a statue until the men's noise had faded.

Then it slowly turned towards Bith.

The figure was huge, tall and wide. His shape was indistinct under a shaggy bearskin and floppy hat. The creature advanced over the rocky brushy terrain with sure steps that pressed deeply into the ground. It came directly at her. He can see in the dark, Bith thought. Despite the wild dying light and the smoke and roughness of the ground it could see her as if it were daylight.

"How you?" the figure growled in the common tongue. "All right? No hurt?" Its grunt was painful to hear and must be more painful to make. It reached out for her—

"I'm all right," she stammered. "Please don't touch me."

The figure withdrew its great paw. Slowly it turned and squatted and wiped its hands on the crushed grass. Then it moved away.

Bith stood up and had to clutch at a tree trunk. She was dizzy with shock and the aftermath of panic. Her knees gave out and she sank down, grateful for even that small respite. The oak was all but incinerated. There was only a burning stump left, just knee-high. Bith didn't know many spells, but the ones she knew she knew well.

Bith looked up. Would she be able to slip away from this—thing—when the light was gone? Should she, now that he had rescued her?

The hulk kicked out with a foot and knocked over the burning tree. Then it half-dragged, half-carried a large dead tree to the stump and crumbled wood onto the makeshift fire. Bith knew that the tree was dead, but the cracking sounds told her the creature was very strong. Strong enough to rip a dog apart, or a magician. Stronger than any man could be.

The figure squatted again and blew at the fire. Bith saw his face for the first time. A wide, flat nose in a wide face, small eyes, thick brow. A hint of fangs behind the thick lips? She knew now what this was. She had seen paintings in books in her mother's castle.

"You're a troll."

"Hathor."

"No, you're a troll. I know."

"Me too. Me Hathor. Troll. Good one."

Sure, thought Bith, *and I'm a kind witch*. She stood slowly and edged away from the fire, towards the downhill slope of the ravine.

"Don't go," said the troll. "Eat."

"Eat?" Bith's stomach betrayed her. It rumbled at the thought of food. "Eat what?"

The troll gestured with a thick finger. "Dog."

Bith shuddered. "No. I couldn't." Her stomach squeaked so that it hurt. "Well, maybe a little."

The troll moved away from the fire. The blaze was glowing merrily now, the only light for miles, probably. It made the dark inside this ravine that much more intense. Bith's legs trembled. If she didn't sit down she'd fall. Might as well be by the fire, she reasoned. She straightened her pants and shirt, drew her cloak around her and sat. Then she moved again to plump her back against the fallen tree. It felt wonderful to stop moving.

The troll came back to the fire with the torn torso of the

dog. He had an axe in the other hand. Bith watched warily as he laid the carcass over the log not far from her head.

"Liver?" the troll asked. "Haunch? Brains?"

"Liver."

"Good." The axe came down with a whack that split the carcass. Two more whacks freed a good hunk of—something—which the troll tossed on the fire. Bith watched the flesh sear and blacken. Maybe she wasn't hungry. But she bravely fished up a stick and sharpened the end and speared the meat. She propped it up on a rock at the edge of the fire and held the end down with her boot.

More cracking and crushing noises sounded closely, then a sucking noise. He must be licking his fingers, she thought. Another hunk of meat landed on the fire with a squishy hiss.

The troll whomped the axe into the stump. Bith noticed it was not a war axe but a felling axe. A war axe was wide and thin-bladed, chased with fierce insignia, light with a short handle so a man could wield it all day. This was a simple pole axe for cutting trees. Was that good? The troll sat by the fire opposite her. He took off his floppy hat and set it beside him.

Bith studied him. The troll was surprisingly human. But she knew trolls were a type of human that had taken to caves. Or never left them. This one's features were just too—swollen. His lips were thick and protruded slightly. His eyes were small and close-set and recessed. His teeth were large; so were his ears. He had no beard, but a sort of scruffy mutton-chops. His hair was curiously soft and fine and curly golden-red. A strawberry-blond troll, she thought. He wore only a peasant's smock tied around his blocky body, but over it he wore a thick cape of brown—bearskin? His fingers were thick and coarse, with dark nails, but were nimble enough as he poked the fire. His hands had red hair on their backs, too. His feet were bare and the soles thick enough to walk on coals. He smelt, too. Not an unpleasant odor, but alien: musty and cavish.

"You pretty," he said suddenly, and Bith jumped. *Probably tasty too*, she thought. But he said nothing more, and her pulse settled back down.

Strange he should say she was pretty. It had been a long time since she had seen herself. At sixteen Bith was still developing, in all the wrong places first, naturally. She knew she looked like her mother, and men thought her mother lovely, so she might be. But she was tall and thin and gawky, she thought. Coltish and clumsy. Her face was acceptable. She had long straight hair of a color between brown and black. Her skin was pale as milk from living in the north country, sprinkled with freckles the way the northern reaches could be sprinkled with cornflowers in spring. Bith knew her most arresting feature was her eyes. She was the only human she'd ever met—besides her mother—who had silver eyes.

"What name?" the gruff voice asked.

"Name? Elizebith, daughter of—Elizebith. Bith."

"Bith," the troll tried the name. "Easy."

"You are Hathor?"

"Hathor. Thor. Hath." He followed these names with a string of others she couldn't understand. He finished, "Hathor."

"Hathor. Good." Wonderful, she thought. One night of this and she'd talk like a troll forever. "Why did you save my life?"

"Voice."

" 'Voice,' did you say?"

"Voice."

"What voice?"

He put a grimy clawed fingernail—or were they just naturally black?—to his temple. "In head. Tell me come here, res-cue you. Did."

"What did the voice tell you?"

"Told me. Come here, save you." He speared a chunk of burnt meat from the fire and took a bite, coals, ashes, and all. "Never hear voice in skull before."

Bith tended her own meat. She sliced off a strip and ate it, suddenly ravenous from the smell. She had never eaten dog before. It tasted sweet. When she could, she asked, "Did it have a sort of imperious tone, like a king's voice? Like this? 'Go, my child, hie ye hence and ye shall be rewarded.' Did it sound like that?"

Hathor nodded vigorously. "Yes, that voice. Just like that. Good."

Bith pondered that a moment, her mouth forming an unconscious pout. She too had heard a voice lately, mostly in her dreams or when she was distracted. It had told her to wait or to be content or to anticipate danger or a dozen other things. She had largely ignored it. A few short months ago Bith had been dragged from her mother's castle by some incredibly stupid men who thought she was Morea's hostage. Once they had learned she was Morea's *daughter* they'd deserted her, abandoned her in open country, alone and unarmed, without supplies. Even before then, Bith had been haunted by ghosts, had her dreams ridden through and trampled on, but since her kidnapping, night and nightmares were synonymous to Bith. It came with spellcasting. She had ignored this new imperious voice along with the screeching ones and the giggling ones.

"You send voice?"

Bith shook her head. "Me? No. I heard it too, is all."

"Who is?"

"I have no idea. Someone who wants something for nothing, I suppose. Isn't that always the way?"

Hathor bit into his meat and said nothing. He swallowed noisily and asked, "Where bow?"

"Bow?"

He mimicked an archer and then pointed at her. Elizebith had no bow. She had only the clothes she stood in, her magic pouches, and an eating knife. "I have no bow."

Hathor grunted. He got up from the fire and walked into the dark. He returned in a moment and handed her a shaft.

It was an arrow. A short one with long fletching: blue and red-streaked feathers she'd never seen before. The wood was smooth, almost like glass. The head was of some clean steel, longer and sharper than any razor. It felt no heavier than a dandelion. She held it up to Hathor. "It's not mine."

"Not?" he scratched his chin. "Not mine either."

"Well, wait," Bith asked. "Where did you get it?"

The troll rose and moved off into the dark. Outside the ring of firelight he bent over something. He lifted the bulky object and pointed to it. "In him." Bith gulped. The thing was a corpse, the body of a villager with a rusty dagger in his hand. "Stuck here." Hathor indicated his throat. Bith shuddered again.

With ridiculous ease Hathor hefted the body and *threw* it

up the side of the ravine and over the top. "Wolves get it," he said. "Not get us."

Bith looked at the sheer wall. "How strong are you, anyway?"

Hathor grinned for the first time. Yes, those were fangs in his upper jaw. "Strong."

Bith slumped back to the ground with the shaft still in her hand. She looked at the arrow and tried to guess where it came from. Who it came from. But her brain wouldn't budge. It was falling asleep, and so was she.

"Sleep," Hathor told her. "I watch."

Sure, Bith thought. The dog was dinner and I'm breakfast. She dragged her cloak around, lay her hand on the ground, and lay her head on her arm. With the fire in front and her back to the large log and its reflected heat she was very cozy. This was a pleasant place to be: better than burning or smothering or being hung. She'd rest just a moment, then sneak away when the troll dozed off.

The last thing she saw as her eyes closed was the ugly troll peering at the beautiful arrow. A strange sight after a strange day. . . .

CHAPTER
2

Bith wandered the halls of the castle looking for her mother.

Up and down the stone passages she went. She had to climb, for the floor slanted crazily. It was very dark inside. Though there was light at the end of the halls, the girl couldn't reach it. Spiders as large as dogs passed by. An orc skull turned to watch her go, its empty eyes lit with green. A door sprang open and a pack of bloody dogs howled. They chased her until her lungs burned. The daughter of Morea ran for the end of the hall but couldn't get there. A rushing noise rose and rose, and water poured down the halls after her. A door changed into an axe blade ten feet across. It swept into the sky over her, edge down, and dropped. . . .

Bith screamed as the monster with the axe loomed over her, ready to strike. She screamed again and covered her eyes.

When nothing happened she uncovered her face. The thing was still standing there, axe poised, a puzzled frown on its ugly face. Then she remembered.

She remembered the growly sound of pursuit close behind, the rasping of her breath, the cold feel of the rocks as she was trapped, the crackling of the ignited tree, the thud of boots into her back, the thrill of rescue from a stranger. She sat up with a shudder and mopped rain, or cold sweat, off her face. An early morning shower fell around her and pattered gently on the fallen leaves.

The troll continued to look at her. He looked even uglier in the grey misty morning than he had by firelight. His skin was pale but knotty and lumpy underneath. Bith wondered how soon she could get away from him. He growled at her. "All right?"

Oh, that's right, she recalled. He worries about me. And saved my life. Because that voice commanded him to. "Yes, I'm fine." In fact she was. Her body was wracked with bruises and stiff muscles, but it was delicious to be alive.

It was a misty, wet autumn morning. Birds grizzled to one another about the weather and ignored Hathor's whacking. He chopped another armful of wood and poked up the fire. Raindrops hissed. The troll spitted some white objects like large slugs on a stick. Bith realized they were oyster mushrooms that grew on beech trees this time of year. He hadn't just thrown them on the fire. He must have learned to spit things from me, she thought.

"Isn't there any more meat?" she asked.

"Sure," he replied. "Lots." He fetched some and spitted that.

"Aren't you having any?"

The troll shook his ponderous head. "No. Don't eat meat."

"You don't eat meat?" Trolls, she knew, were often cannibals. She was still surprised to have woken alive. "What was that you ate last night?"

The troll grinned that toothy grin. "Can't waste."

"Did you watch all night?"

Hathor pointed to his lumpy head. "Eyes sleep. Ears watch."

"Oh."

The two of them were quiet during their meal, her dog meat and his mushrooms, which he shared. Finally Bith wandered off to neaten up. She wiped her hands and face with water from bushes, combed burrs from her hair. She came back to the fire and patted her belt. Everything she owned she wore right here. She didn't even have a walking stick. There were a few things in her hut far down the ravine, some books, a

candle, a cache of white money, but she couldn't go back
there. The brave villagers might be waiting for her return.
She would have to make her way up out of the ravine and
through the woods to the road. She wrapped some cooked
meat in leaves and stood up.

The troll stood up too. He kicked the fire apart and dumped
sodden leaves on it. He cinched up his bearskin cloak and
clapped on his floppy hat, which hid his face fairly well. Then
he stood with the axe hanging in his hand, as ragged as a
gorsebush, as still as a statue.

"Well," she announced in a matter of fact voice, "I'll
guess I'll be off."

"Where we go?"

Bith bit her lower lip. She had been afraid of this. *"I,"*
she said slowly, "am going somewhere else. *I—*"

"Where?"

"I—I don't know. North, for now, I guess. Away from that
wretched village. There's a town to the north, a day's hike, I
know. And *I* have to get going—"

The troll shrugged. "Let's go."

Bith sighed. She'd have to sneak off later. Wouldn't it look
lovely, she thought, her walking down the road with this mon-
strosity trailing after her. Though she had to admit no one
would bother her. No, more likely they'd run screaming. She
raised her hands and dropped them. "All right. Let's go."

With Hathor's help she clambered up and out the ravine.
The forest floor here was flat, the tree boles large. She could
see a long way. White deer tails flickered off to her left and
were gone. Something grey slunk off to her right. She noticed
the body of the man killed last night. The wolves or wild
dogs had been working on it. Ribs stuck up at towards the
sky. Scavengers ate the guts first. But then, so had she with
the dog.

The body reminded her. She turned and found Hathor
standing silently at her elbow. "Can you give me a little more
room?" He moved off a few more steps. "Thank you. Did
you bring that arrow?"

Hathor produced it from under his cloak. The thing fairly
shone in the morning sun. It was very short for a war arrow,
not much longer than her forearm. The metal of the head was
more like silver than steel. Bith handed it back to the troll

without a word. She looked all around, but the forest was now empty. She sighed and started walking north by a little east.

They found the road. It was just a pair of ruts wide enough for a cart and horse. It twisted back and forth, around the trees. The road was as deserted as the forest had been. They settled into a steady arm-swinging tramp that ate up the miles.

The rain stopped and the sun came out. The smell of leaf mold was replaced by the scent of grass. Bith was well-exercised by midday and sore by the afternoon, but Hathor moved along as easily as a boulder down a hill. Neither of them said a word all the day long. They drank their fill at a stream and ate their meat and mushrooms and walked and walked. The only people they passed were a young boy on the road who led a cow, and a woodcutter. Neither gave the disguised Hathor more than a curious glance. It was Bith, tall and slim and raven-haired, who attracted their attention. Maybe her "hound" would work out. It was nice not to be alone, even if her company wasn't quite human. She was surprised to find she didn't fear him at all now. Maybe it was because he wasn't human.

Eventually they came upon fields and then a village as the short day drew to a close. From their perspective on the outskirts it looked to have some two dozen small houses and a marketplace, which meant there had to be at least one inn with a tavern. That was the place to go, Bith thought, to find loose talk and loose change. And food. But she wouldn't be able to get any dumb farmer to share his meal without him expecting something in return: she wouldn't know how to ask, anyway. Bith had led a sheltered life, but she knew enough about men to avoid them. She had no money, nothing to sell or barter. Except perhaps her belt buckle, but that was the only thing left from home. She'd not part with it. She would have no time to work up spells, and didn't think it wise anyway this close to that last village, not after her experiences with the people there. Unless she was willing to sell herself—she wasn't—it was sleeping in the woods again. And eating mast. Or . . .

"Come on, Thor. Let's take a walk. Pretend we're passing through."

Hathor grunted something and Bith had to ask for an explanation. "Horses not like me. Smell bad."

Bith stood with hands on hips looking at the town. It was no good to stand here, for they were attracting looks of their own. A town this small wouldn't see many magicians. Or trolls.

"That can't be helped. Let's walk."

They strode through the center of town, turning heads and making children point and dogs bark. They soon reached the center. Bith took a quick look around the sleepy marketplace. There was an inn, The Blue-Bellied Boar, with a stable behind. Horses tied before it whickered when they caught Hathor's scent, but the two kept moving. In no time they were past and in the forest again. Bith stopped and ordered Hathor to find a place to camp.

"We sleep night?"

"We nap for a while. Then when it's truly dark and the town's abed, and men are in their cups, we'll sneak back and raid the kitchen."

"Steal?"

Bith flushed. "Well, yes, I'm afraid so." Guilt and fresh anger sharpened her tongue. "I have no other way of getting food, and it was filthy peasants like this who attacked my hut! They will have made off with any money I had! We'll just take something back!"

The troll shrugged. "What you say."

Bith sniffed and followed the troll as he entered the woods. They found a place to snuggle among the brown leaves. They made no fire and curled up to sleep.

Bith awoke with a start. It was pitch black all around. Something had moved and startled her. Then she realized it was Hathor. She would have to get used to waking in strange places, she thought. For someone who, until a few months ago, had awakened every morning in the same bed in the same tower chamber where she was born, it was not easy to accept the night and its noises. The girl pulled her cloak close and thought about home.

Hathor loomed in the dark like a dead tree trunk. "We go?"

Bith sighed and rose. "We go."

They stumbled to the road—or rather, Bith stumbled while

Hathor stepped easily—and found its white stripe in the tunnel of trees. Bith realized she had no idea which direction they'd come from. She'd have to learn to orient herself better or get lost often. Hathor understood her confusion and pointed a gnarled finger. "Right," Bith said, "I knew that." Carefully and quietly they picked their way toward town.

The moon was up. The town was washed white, especially so after the black tunnel of the road. As soon as they got to the edge of town a dog picked up their scent and began to bark. That woke other dogs who took up the call. Bith and Hathor retreated. They waited until the first dog had been kicked quiet. "It might be you," the girl said. "I'll see if I can get on ahead. Wait here but come running if I call."

"Got it."

Whether she was quiet enough or scentless enough she didn't know, but she got as far as the inn without being detected. Through an unshuttered side window she could see a small light and hear men's voices in conversation—late risers talking away the night. The rest of the village was silent and black. Elizebith slunk along the side wall and peered around the back. By moonlight she could see the back stoop of the inn, the woodshed, the privy and stable and smith's hut. Every surface was splintery silver under the moonlight. Small doors held the stalls closed in the stable. She heard a horse's hoof strike hollowly as it lashed out in a dream. She could smell manure, both horse and human, and sweet hay and stale water. Lightly she picked her way to the back door. The packed earth around the steps was sticky with mud. That was a good sign, she thought, for it meant this was probably the kitchen door. She put her nose to the crack under the door and sniffed. The smell of ham and salt and cooking fat and spices made her mouth water. No dog barked, no cat swiped at her nose. Gently she took the door handle in hand and pressed the thumblatch. It gave but the door did not. Barred, she thought, to keep out thieves. Like me.

She eased out her knife and tried to work it into the crack along the latch, to try and pry the bar up, but the frame was built to prevent that. All right then, you bastards, she thought, try this.

Bith fished in one of her pouches and extracted a pigeon feather. The door itself was made of planks with some small space between, and she stuffed the feather in between the planks where she guessed the bar was. She worked it in farther with her knife point. Then she set both hands against the door, cupped as if holding the bar. She whispered,

> *"Up and up, float ye high*
> Mimic the birds, make the sky.
> Light you be, ye can *fly*,
> Up and up, *float* ye high."

She chanted this three, then four times while holding onto the invisible bar, until she thought it had failed. She thought of the food she'd miss and how hungry she'd be, and she gritted her teeth. Suddenly the imaginary weight left her hands and she knew it was up. She floated the bar in her mind up and out a hair. Then she halted the spell.

The bar fell with a clatter that made her jump. *Fool,* she berated herself, *idiot. You should have floated it to earth!* She waited breathlessly—her chest hurt from all this breath-holding—but no one came to investigate. Perhaps the door from the kitchen into the front room was also closed. Silently and with shaking hands she eased down the thumblatch and pushed the door open.

The smells from the room washed over her, redoubling her hunger, as she put her head inside. It was black. There was no one inside. Lightly she hopped into the room and felt around for any kind of foodstuff. Her hands touched a plate of cold greasy meat and she recoiled. Better were the blood sausages and hams and cheeses hanging over the fireplace. She grabbed five objects and then realized she couldn't carry it all. Such a glorious problem! She groped around and found an apron. She spread that and filled it with smoked meats and cheese, then searched for more. Some turnips and dried onions and a bottle of something went onto the pile until she reckoned she'd overstayed her welcome. She plucked up the four corners of the apron and swung the bundle over her back. With a wary eye on the front room door she skipped to the back door and hopped out and down the steps.

And crashed full into some fool coming in. The corners of the heavy apron slipped from her fingers. The plunder thumped and bounced all over the steps.

"Uhh!"

"Mides and Mithra!" Bith burst out.

The blockade grunted while backing up. "What are you doing? Hey, who are you?"

"Get out of my way or I'll *kill* you!" Bith snapped. She started to squat to retrieve the food but then stopped, undecided whether she should pull her knife, snatch food, or just run. She settled for drawing with one hand and scrabbling with the other.

"What's going on?" It was a boy's voice, though he was as tall as a man. "How did you get inside?"

"I *will* kill you!" Bith repeated. "You've ruined *everything*!"

Inside the kitchen the front-room door creaked open and then slammed against a table. "What's going on? Hey, stop, there! Thief, thief!"

Bith had a sausage or something in her right hand. With it she batted at the boy in her way. She tried to press past him but a hammy hand clamped onto her shoulder. "You imp! Stay—" He howled as Bith's tiny knife slashed the back of his hand. That hand disappeared but another grabbed her by the back of her loose hair. The long locks were almost ripped out of her skull as she was yanked backward. She tripped and fell, landing on her rump. The proprietor, for it could only be he taking such an interest, steadily dragged her backwards to keep her off-balance. Within a minute there were three large men around her and she was still on the floor.

"Look what I caught, Bert! Lookee here! A minx after the larder!"

"*Heeeeey,*" said another man. "That's the witch from Blackrock! The one we chased up that ravine! Ain't it, Rogie?"

Bith looked up at their frowning, beer-blowsy faces. She could expect no sympathy. She was a common thief in this town and a killer witch in another. The proprietor, in an apron and thick mustache, still had her by the hair in a position she couldn't twist out of. In the doorway she saw the one who'd foiled her escape. It was a brown-faced boy in faded wool with straw in his hair. A stupid stableboy.

"Yeah, that *is* her!" said the third man. He gave Bith a

swift kick in the leg. "She killed Carew when she called up that monster!"

Bith yelled, "I didn't kill anyone! An arrow did! And you were out to kill me for no reason!"

"You shut up," Bert told her. "We'll burn you now fair and square, with the whole village out to watch."

A shudder passed through Bith as if they'd doused her with water. A day hadn't passed and she was right back where she'd been. Only this time she couldn't rely on help. Oh, yes, she could, she remembered. She raised her voice and screamed, *"Thor! Help me, Thor! Quickly!"*

The last man kicked her again, but he swore as he did. "That must be her monster!"

"Well, bar the door, you oaf! It can't break that down!" The boy was gone. The two men stepped over Bith to slam the door into place. Drunk and sleepy, they got in each other's way and stumbled over the fallen bar. They almost had the door closed when a sword blade slipped in between them.

"Back up," a voice commanded. It was a boy's voice but a man's tone. Bert and Rogie staggered back away from the blade. Into the room stepped the stableboy. He still had straw in his hair and manure on his boots, but he had a boss shield and naked sword in his hands. The sword was of an old-fashioned design and pitted and the shield was scarred blank, but it made an impression on the farmers.

"Cal!" barked the proprietor. He let go of Bith's hair to wave his arms about. "What the *hell* are you doing? These are friends of mine! Put that thing down!"

The boy Cal didn't take his eyes off the men as he said, "Girl, get up and get out of here. Run!"

Bith took a moment to register herself as "Girl" and that he was helping her escape. Then she was up and streaking out the door. She paused only to snatch up a cheese and ham before she pelted around the corner. She heard him call, "Go on ahead, and I'll—*unhh*—" His words were cut off with a grunt. Bith didn't care. She ran across the village, now awake to the cacophony of barking dogs. Halfway across the marketplace she found Hathor jogging towards her.

"You get food?" he croaked.

"Shut up and *run*!"

They did. Out of the village and down the inky road into the night.

They walked swiftly for the rest of the night to get distance between themselves and the village. By midmorning Bith was too exhausted to go on and they sacked out in the woods for a nap. Later they walked some more. Bith looked over her shoulder often.

In the middle of the afternoon she glimpsed someone trailing them. She pulled Hathor into the bushes to one side, but the figure was already trotting to catch up. He wore a sword and a light pack with a shield tied atop. The sheriff? No, he would be mounted. A boy's voice called, "Hey, wait up! Wait up!"

Bith stepped into the road and blew out her cheeks in disgust. She waited with a curious Hathor. As the boy drew even Bith said acerbically, "Ho, *stableboy*. What do *you* want?"

The boy shucked his pack and set it in the road. He huffed slightly as he looked her in the eye. "Well," he puffed, "a thank you might be nice."

Bith set her hands on her hips. "Thank you for *what*? Thanks to you I spilt a week's food on the ground!"

The boy lifted his chin. He was taller than Bith, with average looks and brown hair that escaped from under his leather helmet. He wore a soldier's helm, baldric, scabbard, pack, and shield, and no piece of it matched any other piece. The baldric was brown, the scabbard black, the pack green, the shield scrubbed clean of any emblem. His clothes were plain and patched and faded, his boots worn white. His young face was showing some wear too, brown from an outdoor life with a scar on the right side. A sword tip had nicked him on the upper lip and continued onto his chin.

The boy had a soldier's insolence, too. He burst out, "*I* saved your *life*! *I* caught a meat cleaver on the back of the head—the flat side, luckily—just for you! Thanks to me you're not ashes blowing in the wind! They were serious about burning you! I could tell."

Bith shuddered involuntarily. She kneaded her hands and couldn't look at him. Uncertain what to say, she said, "Thank you, then."

The boy snorted. "That sounded like hard work! Didn't they teach you any manners where you come from?"

The sorceress's daughter turned on him hotly. "Where *I* come from *I* was in charge of a dozen slaves of my *very own*! When I *commanded* something they *did it* or suffered the *consequences*!"

The boy snorted again and looked her up and down. "You're dressed fine, all right, like a princess. But who knows but you stole the *clothes* too." He gestured at the remnants of the netted cheese and sausage that hung from her belt. Bith whipped her cloak over them. He went on, "And I don't *see* any dozen *slaves*, just one motheaten—whatever he is."

"He's a troll, and he'd gut you and eat your liver if I commanded him to."

The boy stepped back and put his hand to sword. But when he looked at the troll he smiled. The troll was grinning widely and shaking his head. "No," he growled, "no eat meat. Only flowers."

Bith looked at her traitorous companion sharply. He lost his grin but the boy laughed. "Oh, yes, I see how your slaves obey. They must have feared your highness greatly. *Quivered* at your name when you ordered them flogged."

Bith was beside herself. She snarled, "Do you know who my mother is? She is *Morea*, the most feared woman in the world! And *I* am her daughter!"

"Morea?" The name gave the boy pause. He rubbed his downy chin and looked her up and down again. He took in the magician's belt and knife and myriad pouches. Then he shook his head. "Spellcaster, maybe. But not from behind any Mistwall."

Bith breathed, *"What?"*

"I don't believe you."

"You—don't—*believe*—me? You're calling me a *liar*? I don't believe *you*! You *cad*! If we were in my native land I'd have the skin off your back for book covers! I'd—"

"But you're not," the boy retorted. "So curb your tongue and act your age, *girl*."

Bith sputtered and spit and finally got out, "You—you— *stableboy*! You stand there with dirty hands and horseshit on your shoes and you dare insult *me*! I should, should— *Ooooh!*" She turned and stalked away down the road. Hathor followed her silently, trailing just behind and to the right, like a faithful dog.

Bith had not gone twenty paces when she spun to her left and screeched, "Where do you think *you're* going?"

The boy looked bland. "This way. You don't own the roads. Or do you? Does your mother collect a toll here?"

Bith resumed walking. "I won't be seen walking with a *stableboy*!"

"No, I suppose not. A *princess* has a reputation to uphold." He was still walking not ten feet behind her. "Funny thing about this country," he mused as if to himself. "It's more full of princesses than milkmaids. Why, you can't swing a goose switch without hitting a princess some days. Yes, sir, there must be a pile of queens somewhere having babies, that every girl you meet has royal blood. Yes sir, yes sir."

Bith paraded down the road with her nose in the air. "Hathor, kill him."

The troll only chuckled, a sound like flint on steel.

"All right," Bith said to the air. "We'll leave it at this. If any *stableboys* smelling of horsesweat are still with us tonight, we'll cut their throats as they sleep and leave them to the wolves."

Behind her came two chuckles, one human, one trollish. Bith stalked along and damned all men of all races.

That night the three shared a campfire.

Cal was still with them, for Hathor didn't mind and Bith refused to acknowledge his presence. Eventually though, as the blackness settled in and closed the sky around their tiny pool of light, the silence pressed upon the girl. Cal stropped his sword with a whetstone. It was a hopeless job, for the old thing was so deeply pitted it could never shine. Bith said, "There's not much point in sharpening that thing. It's not much of a sword."

Cal stroked the blade. "No. It's nose-heavy and wont hold an edge, but it's all I have. A soldier is judged by the condition of his weapon."

"Did you steal it from your former master?"

"No. I looted it from a battlefield. I don't know if it fell from the hand of some barbarian or was left by others who didn't care for it, or whether it had lain there since an earlier battle. The field I was on had seen many battles, I'm told.''

"Did you win the battle?"

"I don't know." Cal paused in his stropping and looked at her bewildered face. "That seems a strange thing to say, but I really don't. Sometimes whole armies retire from the field and don't know."

"That's ridiculous! How can you not know if you've carried the day or not?" Bith would have criticized more sharply, but she was wrapped in this boy's blanket.

"There's nothing more confusing than a battle. The old soldiers say that. Old sailors argue that being on a ship in a storm is more confusing, but I don't see how it can be. Either you're afloat or you're not. But a battle. Have you ever seen one?"

Bith admitted she hadn't. She almost replied that she'd read of them in books, but that would sound foolish. In books the hero was never in doubt as to what had happened. And he always won. Hathor too was intrigued. He leaned forward by the fire attentively with his huge ears seeming to point forward.

The boy settled to polishing the blade with the flat edge of the stone. His voice settled into storytelling.

"You have to understand what happens in a battle. And before it. One day you're training and hoping to get your chance in a battle. Then the king sends a messenger through the land to rouse all the knights. Your master, the local knight, makes a speech as to why we hate the so-and-sos in the next country over. He summons his retainers—squires, cooks, men-at-arms—and you report to the castle. I was a squire to a knight, Sir Edric. I only had one more year to go before my vows. Anyway, now the laird makes a speech about this ghastly enemy who's coming to kill you all and how you must fight for justice and such, then you march off. And march and march and march and march, and some men slip away into the night and go home, and some others are caught and horsewhipped. And the knights argue with one another about what they know of the enemy, which is usually nothing, except that the old men know but no one listens to them, which is too bad. Some of the knights beg their lords if they can't just buy their way out of the fight and go home. You pick up mercenaries at some town, filthy long-haired bastards who'll steal anything not nailed down, and cut your throat if you don't sleep light. You get to the big town, and the king is there, and he makes a speech, same one you've heard already. Some believe it. Off you go, marching some more. Finally, one day, a rider comes gallopin' up and tells you the enemy's in sight.

"Then everyone goes over their armor and weapons and makes sure their cinches are tight and edges sharp, and then you wait. For two, three days, sometimes. Your side sends messengers to their side and they argue about where the battle should take place and what's the maximum they'll pay for any knights they capture for ransom and a bunch of other money concerns. Then they announce that *tomorrow* will be the battle—the big day. Unless it rains, which means the ground'll be muddy and the horses will get bogged down and maybe hurt, which knights hate like fury. They don't care if they lose a hundred peasant footmen, but having to kill one warhorse is a crime. So the next morning everyone gets up while it's still dewy, and you wait some more. Sometimes all day and into the next and everyone wonders what happened. You can't eat 'cause your stomach's in a knot, you can't sleep 'cause you're worried. So you just sort of stumble around and pick fights with your friends and fidget with your weapons. I've seen men pick their arrows clean to pieces fidgeting."

Bith interrupted him. "How many battles have you been in?"

Cal grinned. In the firelight the disjointed scar on his lip and chin gleamed. Someone had come close to splitting his face. "Two. The first was lucky for it was hardly a battle at all. We came out of the woods onto this plain and the enemy spotted us. We had them outnumbered three to one, so they just turned and fled into the woods. We peppered 'em with a few arrows and that was all. Still, you should have heard the men tell the campfollowers what a great battle it was and how brave they were. My second battle, well, I'll get to that.

"Finally someone blows a trumpet and you crowd forward. The lord up there on his high horse makes a fine speech full of flowery words while a sergeant screams cuss words in your face, and you form up. I was just a plain squire with an old horse and my master's spare sword. It's funny, but for all the fear you get caught up in the fever. The words and the pounding on shields and the screaming gets to you and pretty soon you're screaming along with the rest and all you want to do is get some enemy on the end of your weapon and tear his guts out.

"This was some battle, too. Lots of men and horses on both sides. Like you'd hear about from a bard, though there's never been a bard on any battlefield that I've seen. We came onto this rise and looked onto the opposite rise and there were the enemy, and we all guessed right away we were pretty evenly matched. So there'd be a fight, and a big one. Then up goes the cry and we thunder forward like a giant wave, down this hill and *crash* into the other fellows.

"Mars and Mercury, what a *mess*! Men are screaming fit to burst their lungs and slashing at everything in sight. They'd chop an enemy or their best friend or their own leg if it got in the way. It wasn't half a minute everyone was so mixed up and turned around you couldn't tell friend from foe. Not that it makes much difference.

"Now you have to understand that this army is made up of individual lords, most of whom hate each other's guts. Each lord has his own knights, and each knight has *his* own squire and *his* own peasants. So in a battle you stay close—as close as possible—to your knight, and him to his lord. And what with all these knights charging right and left and every which way, and men trying to follow them, you're doing some travelling, slashing every foot of the way. And then some lord will get cold feet and just turn and run. Or his horse will get cut down and he goes down and the peasants stick him full of steel till he looks like a hedgehog. Then suddenly his knights don't have a leader anymore, or any reason to be there except for capturing something valuable. The mercenaries aren't going to get paid, so they just chop anyone they think's got money in his purse. Or if the lord runs away, his men follow, and there's a great hole in your flank. Or two lords will forget the enemy and decide to settle a blood feud right there on the battlefield.

"Anyway, there's this surging and fighting and smashing and after three minutes you're hoarse and thirsty and tired and all you want to do is sit down and rest, but you can't, of course. People get killed all around you, or disappear. So you can't really tell if you're winning or not. No one can. I always figured, and so did a bunch of old soldiers with scars to prove they'd been there, that if you were still breathing after a battle, you had won and that was that.

"And as if it weren't confusing enough, *magic* makes this mess a hundred times worse! Some damned hand-waver will be up on the hilltop—*way out* of arrow range—wiggling his fingers and blowing smoke from some stinking pot—and suddenly there are spells all over the place. The sneaky kind. Like a horde of knights will suddenly be bearing down on you and you duck and cover your head, only to have them sweep over you like fog. And you realize they weren't making any noise. Or three giant men come running at you, and they all look alike as brothers, and are even raising their axe the same way. My master told me how he was once charged like that, and he rode straight for the middle giant and impaled him on a lance, and the other two ghost pictures, they were—curled up and died too. Magic, *pah*! And glory too."

Cal shoved his helmet back to wipe his brow. He had goose bumps from the memories he conjured. His voice had turned dark and broody, as if an owl in the night had suddenly begun to tell its sad story.

"My master knew a thing or two, but not this time. The battle went back and forth for two hours or more, with all of us with our arms hanging by our sides almost, when suddenly our lord was seen being carried off towards the woods. I don't know what exactly happened—I didn't see it—but my master up and blows his horn and yells 'Follow me!' We did, though we couldn't see why. It was dark then and the battle was winding down. Off we went into the woods, but we didn't find nothing. It was just some illusion he saw, he reckoned.

"When we got back to the battle, it was over. We had lost, our side said, and it was *our* fault because my master ran away! My master got into an argument with another lord that'd always hated him. They got off their horses to swing swords but the other bastard refused, said my master had disgraced himself. Ooh, was he mad! Other noble knights who were fighting for the glory of the gods were squabbling like vultures over dead men's goods. We got driven off the field without a chance to collect any loot at all. And there was something wrong with my master. I don't know what. But I think he believed he was a coward somehow. And I wasn't too proud of myself either. It's a damned fool who goes off to war.

"Believe me," he finished, "this guff you hear about battles being glorious and romantic is just that—guff. They're nothing more than a chance for some fat lord to get out of his castle and kill a few of his hungry mouths and maybe pick up some land or some loot in the process. Ach!"

Bith breathed, "But what happened to you?"

"Hunh? Oh, nothing. We camped that night and set a guard, but the guards ran off. When I awoke everyone was gone. Everyone, just like that. Stole my horse, too.

"Oh, was I mad! There I was, no food, no weapons, no master, no friends. I snuck back to the battlefield and picked up this stuff—" he gestured vaguely to his sword and shield and harness—"stuff no one else wanted. I scrubbed the emblem off the shield with a rock and went into business for myself."

The troll asked, "What you mean, business?"

Cal blew out his cheeks. Hunched over by the fire, he looked very thin and young. "Well, after years as a page I had worked my way up to squire, and in one more year I would have made knight. Then in one day I was demoted clear back to foot soldier. A soldier of fortune, with no fortune in sight.

"Anyway, I hear they're mustering some sort of army to the east, on the coast somewhere. Maybe they can use one more hand."

Bith yawned despite her interest in his words. "That's all you know, that someone is mustering an army somewhere, and you might join? What kind of a life is that?"

Caltus Talienson pursed his lips. "That's a soldier's life. The part you don't hear about in stories. Good night."

With that the former squire sheathed his sword and arranged it by his right side. He put the shield on his left. He propped his head on his helmet and laid a moth-eaten sweater over his chest as a blanket. In three slow breaths he was asleep.

Bith looked at Hathor, who looked back as docile as a sheep.

"Sleep. I watch," the troll said.

''You'll get some sleep too?''

Hathor shrugged an awkward shrug. Bith pillowed her head on her arm and pulled the blanket to her chin. She fell asleep with the rush and cry of battle in her ears. Men screamed and swore and died. They cursed one another and the gods. Horses dashed past her and arrows whizzed above. Cal swung a sword and looked confused. . . .

Finally the night was quiet.

At midnight a stranger was sitting by their fire.

CHAPTER
3

Cal's first thought was "Vampire!"

Something woke him up. He'd opened his eyes expecting to see either a pretty (though snotty) girl or a lumpy (but friendly) troll. What he saw was a nightmare.

The boy snatched his sword from its scabbard and rolled far to one side, coming to his feet, clumsy but upright. Bith jerked awake and muzzily raised her hands in a dramatic sorcering pose. Hathor trotted up from somewhere off in the woods. He shouted something in trollish and lifted his felling axe high.

The stranger at the fire lifted pale eyes and looked complacently from one to another to another. After a long look round he asked, "Yes?"

Cal let out his breath in a gasp. "Who are you? What are you doing here?"

"Sitting," replied the pale man, "by the fire."

Cal waved his free arm to take in the forest. "That's not what I meant! I mean—" he panted—"I mean, what are you doing here? Besides the damned fire, I mean. Oh, hell!" The boy had to stop talking to get his breath back.

It was the dead of night. No dew had formed. The stranger

sat and stared at the invisible flame over the coals. Cal studied the shadowed face. Although the boy had never seen one,
he was pretty sure this wasn't a vampire: it wasn't sinister
enough. But it surely wasn't a proper man.

The being was tall, taller than most men Cal had met. He
had pale, almost translucent skin, paler than a fish's belly.
His thin beard was so white it was almost not there at all.
His eyes were green like a cat's. He wore clothes very plain
but exceedingly fine-woven of a leaf green. On his head was
a soft hat with a sprig of holly, and over his shoulders he
wore a cloak of some very light material. Cal could see the
tail of something (not his tail, surely) sticking out behind and
lying on the ground. It looked to be a sword scabbard, but
was far too narrow. On the other side showed a quiver for
short arrows. A short, curved, foreign-looking bow lay across
the man's lap. What was he? Cal wondered. A jongleur? A
magician? A doctor? A prophet?

Elizebith had been studying the stranger too. Now she burst
out. "You're the one who shot the arrow!"

The pale man nodded slowly.

"You're an elf!" Bith berated herself for not realizing it
sooner. She'd seen pictures of elves in books. She had even
seen one in the flesh once. A dead one.

"Ulf?" grunted Hathor.

"Elf," Cal corrected. Which was as bad as a vampire. The
young soldier pointed his sword. He said, "Whatever you
are, sir elf, you be gone. Now. The road is that way."

The elf continued to stare at the fire.

"Didn't you hear me? Up with you, and out! We'll not
have your kind here!'

Bith said, "Cal!"

The man turned green eyes upon him and said, "You've
not heard the voice."

"Voice? What voice?"

Bith piped up. "We've heard it, sir elf! Hathor and I! This
troll."

"My name is Endril."

Cal waved a hand to shush people, though no one was
talking. "What's this about a voice?"

Bith told him how the voice had contacted both her and
Hathor. The elf nodded, "I too. As you guessed, t'was I who

shot the arrow and kept that villain from stabbing yon troll in the back.'' He addressed the troll in a string of words that gobbled and gulped. The troll replied in kind with a smile.

Cal was waving again. ''Be damned to all that! What's—''

Bith said, ''But why, if you shot that arrow, didn't you join us in the ravine?''

''Why you not help us?'' the troll ended. ''And how you get past me to fire?''

Endril replied, ''At the time, you were too far removed.''

''We were trapped in a box! Where were you?''

''I was atop a hill opposite.''

''Hill? I didn't see any hill.''

''It was—some distance away.''

Bith bit her lower lip. If he was speaking true, this elf had shot an arrow from the top of a faraway hill, in the dark, and killed a man. She didn't know if she believed it or not.

Cal stepped in front of Bith, blocking her view of the elf. ''Bith, wake up. He's hexing you.''

''Get out of the way, stupid!''

''We can't have him here. Elves are evil! They curse crops and poison wells! They steal children, they drink blood, they do all kinds of horrible things!''

Bith shook her head until her hair flew. ''You don't know anything. Elves are the fair folk who were here before men! They live in castles and the forest and they compose beautiful songs—they *invented* songs. They do . . . nice things.''

The soldier pointed his sword at the elf again. ''And which is it?''

The elf closed his eyes momentarily. ''At any one time, any thing is true.''

''That's your answer,'' the boy snorted. ''Nothing. Elf, last warning. Get you gone.''

When he didn't move, or even blink, Cal suddenly screamed a battle cry and swung his sword two-handed.

In fact, Cal didn't intend to harm him. He only hoped to jolt the elf out of his seat, to get him up and running. Usually one close swipe of a blade was enough to make civilians run. So his charge was more bluster than bloodlust.

But the elf was gone.

''Cal, behind you!'' Bith's voice called.

He spun. There was a blur of green against the backdrop

of brown forest, then—nothing. Thinking the elf had ducked behind him—already anticipating a cold dagger in the back— Cal whipped around on his heel and slashed viciously without looking. Something *clinked*. His sword arm stopped in mid-air. The rest of him kept going. He tripped over his feet and fell sprawling. His sword disappeared, plucked from his hand like a feather from a bird's wing.

Standing over him was the elf. His face was blank and unaccusing. He held Cal's sword *by the blade* in his left hand. His right was empty. With no expression at all he offered the sword back to the boy, hilt first.

Wondering, Cal took it. It was only then he noticed the elf was wearing a glove, a metal gauntlet, on his left hand. The white figure (who really was very tall) stepped back to the fire, all without word or sound. When Cal looked again the gauntlet was gone.

The boy stayed sitting on the ground, though he held onto his sword. "How did you do that?"

The elf's only answer was to wave a breezy hand. They were long thin hands with blue veins. Hands strong enough to stop a sword thrust? That couldn't be right. And how could a metal thin enough to make a glove still stop a blade? It had to be magic. Elf black magic.

Hathor looked at the two humans who stared at the elf. To the troll they all looked the same. He asked the crowd, "You want mushrooms?"

Endril said, "Enough. I seek answers. Have you aught clue as to *his* origin?"

Bith shook her head.

Hathor asked, "What he say?"

Cal asked, "*Whose* origin?"

Endril nodded as if he'd received an answer. Without speaking he sat crosslegged by the fire. The elf spread his hands onto the ground beside him, threw his head back, and closed his eyes.

Caltus Talienson walked close to the fire and peered at him. The elf sat still as a rock. His mouth was open slightly and his face blank. Bith stood near Cal and stared also. The lower lip clamped in her teeth betrayed her nervousness. Hathor scratched his lumpy head and sat down. He dozed.

After a long time Endril opened his eyes and glided to his

feet. His every move was fluid and graceful, like a cat's. Cal wondered if maybe elves were related to cats. That would explain a lot. The elf said, "Nothing there." He turned with his hand to his chin, studying the glade they camped in.

Endril squatted and stoked up the fire, arranging the embers in some pattern, then fed on small sticks to prick up the blaze. Soon its warm yellow light was reflected on the faces of the four travelers.

Endril stooped low to peer into the fire as if it were a crystal ball. He drew forth a small pouch from beneath his cape and sprinkled a pinch of some powder on the fire. It gave a green glow for only a second.

The elf shook his head. He harrumphed.

Now he walked around the glade, studying the trees. He circled and touched each one, murmuring to himself in his own language. It sounded as if he were singing under his breath.

"*What* is he *doing*?" Cal asked the two.

Hathor woke up with a grunt. Bith shrugged.

The elf's voice came from the dark. "Boy, bring light!"

The boy sniffed at being called a boy, but his curiosity got the best of him. Cal took a burning brand and swung it lightly to whip up the flame. Bith and Hathor walked on his heels.

Endril stood back in the forest about fifty feet. He had one fine hand on the bark of a thin tree. "This one would die soon anyway, and take its neighbor." He gestured upwards. Cal and the others looked. This slim tree was a leaner. High up it had cracked, probably from lightning, and now it was cocked over so it rubbed against a healthier neighbor. A woodcutter would take it in an instant. But Endril set his forehead against the bark and prayed for a moment. (Bith and Cal wondered to whom.) Then the elf took out a long knife. It had a shining white blade and a handle wrapped with silver wire. (Cal wondered how much other stuff the elf carried under that cloak.) He made a square cut in the soft bark of the tree and then pried it loose. Silver wood was exposed, and the elf signalled the light close. He peered at it closely and frowned. "Not a druid god. What then?"

"Beats me," Cal replied. "What are you looking for?" Bith poked him in the arm.

Endril didn't reply. Back at the fire he pondered some more

as the humans and troll pondered him. He turned their way and stared right through them. Suddenly he said to Cal, "Will your helm hold water?"

"What?"

"Give it here." Without waiting he took it off Cal's head. The helmet was made of bands of iron lined with leather. Endril walked off into the dark, this time alone.

"What's he want with *that*?" Cal asked.

"Thirsty?" Hathor asked.

Bith was biting her lip again. "I *think* . . . he's trying to contact our—contact."

"*What* contact?"

"The one with the voice."

"*What voice?*"

Bith said icily, "The one in our heads."

Cal retorted, "*I* haven't heard any voice."

"Maybe he only talks to intelligent beings."

"Hey!"

Endril came back into the firelight carrying Cal's helmet. It was full of water. The elf set it carefully by the fire. He studied the water's surface and startled his companions when he said, *"There."*

More startling was the faint squeak that replied, "Yes, good work." It sounded like a child talking at the bottom of a well. Cal and Bith and Hathor crowded close. Peering into the dark water they perceived—a face!

It was a man's face, stern and frowning, for all that it was young. The brows were knitted, the eyes slanted and slitted, the nose sharp cut, the mouth thin-lipped. There was a hint of beard, though it was hard to tell. The face filled the bowl like a man's reflection seen in a bucket. But there was no man above. Only an elf and three astounded compatriots.

"List me," the voice said. "We have much to instruct you, our servants."

"I'm no man's servant," Cal blurted out. "Who is this clown?"

Endril told him. "It's a god."

Hathor asked, "That a god?"

"A little titchy one, maybe," Bith answered him. The tiny man might have been some drowned soul frozen under ice. "Who are you? What do you want from us?"

"You will address us as Magnificent Lord, Exalted Master, and Ruler of the Twelve Spheres!" the god tried to thunder, but his voice was so tiny and tinny he sounded like a kitten. Cal and Hathor laughed outright. Bith giggled. Only Endril remained silent.

"I've a better idea," Cal replied. "Why don't we tip over this bowl?"

"Into fire," Hathor added. They laughed again.

The god's face twisted and he spit out in a sparrow's chirp, "Insult us, whelps? Die, then!"

Cal's laugh stopped as if he'd stopped an arrow. With jerky motions he scrabbled up from the ground so quickly he clonked heads with Bith and Hathor. With a howl he jumped clear and ripped his sword from the sheath. As the pitted blade caught the firelight Bith saw the god's face on the blade!

"Die! Die! Die!" Cal shrieked. He lunged.

Hathor shot out a rough arm that knocked Bith over on her back, unfortunately too close to the fire. Her sleeve fell onto hot embers and burst into flame. Hathor himself dropped to the ground so that Cal's thrust carried him over the troll's back. Straddled, Hathor stood up and dumped Cal on the ground, but as the boy landed he slashed out and caught Hathor on the back of the leg just below the hamstring. Hathor roared and jumped and would have fallen back onto the upthrust blade, except for the forgotten Endril.

The elf's boot caught Hathor square in the rump. The troll shot forward as if launched from a ballista to crash on top of Bith. She had been frantically flapping her sleeve to put out the flame but had only fanned it hotter. Bith now got a face full of smelly stale troll as the wind was knocked out of her.

Cal, meanwhile, had swung with new fury on Endril. The elf only spread his feet and arms wide and waited. He'd donned his metal glove again. He sidestepped the clumsy charge and then deftly tripped the boy. Cal plowed headlong onto the forest loam. Endril stepped on his sword arm, bent and wrenched the weapon loose, then threw it far out into the dark woods. He stood with both feet on Cal's arms.

It grew quiet. Cal lay on the soil and panted like a dog. Then he blew dirt out of his mouth and rasped, "What happened?"

"You mocked a god," Endril told him.

"I did? Oh, that's right. I did. But what happened then?"

Endril told him. Bith shook off Hathor's help and sat up. She batted at her sleeve and clothing and inspected her wrists. "Where's that idiot god gotten to?"

Endril stepped to the fire and peered into the helmet full of water. "Still here."

The dish rocked. "Mock us, will you? We'll kill you all! We'll send you to the darkest pits of hell! Below that even, where your bowels will be impregnated with serpents, your eyes ripped out with hooks, and your lungs drowned in brimstone fire!"

Endril squatted, looked into the bowl and addressed it while the others crept close and did not laugh. "Before you do that, oh Magnificent Lord, Exalted Master, and Ruler of the Twelve Spheres, pray tell this measly servant thy name that I may sing thy praises to all the ears of men and mortals."

There was a pause, then the tiny lipless mouth spoke. "We have many names, but men know us most often as Vili."

"Ah," said Endril. "Many tales have I heard of Vili, the most noble, most high, most feared, most wise of the gods of the north. Verily, I grow faint in the majesty of thy presence." With his hands behind him Endril waved his companions back. Then he started to creep backwards himself. "Excuse this frail one, oh lord and master, I must pause for breath ere I swoon."

Endril joined the three at the edge of the firelight. He signalled them even farther back among the black, looming trees. There he told them, "So we have it. Our mysterious shade is Vili, a god of the north."

"Who's Vili?" Cal asked. "I never heard of him."

Bith said, "I have. I've read about him. He's brother to Odin, king of northern gods, which makes him kin to Loki and Thor."

"Thor?" asked Hathor.

Endril nodded, but with a cant to his head. "Those tales may be true or not. He may or may not be Vili."

"What?" Cal asked.

Bith answered. "I know what he means. Gods lie. There are all kinds of stories about the tricks they play or the disguises they wear. To fool each other or to gull men. Loki especially is known as the trickster, and he's Vili's cousin

This fellow could be anyone. We have to be careful we don't fall into a trap.''

Endril nodded. ''One cannot be too careful when dealing with gods. They are more like children than adults, with dangerous and arcane powers. Some are fools, some liars. But all of them welcome flattery. Put honey on your tongue when addressing them and you'll be rewarded. Some of the time.''

''How do you know all this?'' Cal demanded.

''T'is common knowledge.''

''What are we to do?'' Bith asked.

''Wait a minute,'' Cal said. ''How did you know to put out that bowl of water?''

''I didn't. I provided several opportunities for this god of whatever to manifest himself. I opened my body to receive him as a host. I built up the fire to perhaps glimpse a fire fiend. I stripped a tree to see a druid god. It was water that did the trick. Cool water.''

''Hunh?''

Endril explained as if to a slow child. ''This god is a northern god—a cold elemental—and so needed a cool surface on which to manifest himself. The water was cool and so he appeared there. Your steel sword served as well.''

''Why didn't he just show up in person, like a ghost or something?''

''Watch your tongue!'' Bith spit out.

Edril answered. ''Yes, please do. We've enough—otherworlders visiting us now. For your question, I suspect this godling needs a medium through which to manifest himself because he *cannot* do so 'in person.' He must be too weak to enter this plane. Thus so far we have only heard his voice.''

Cal harrumphed. ''The less we have to do with gods the better. Especially weak ones.''

''Weak ones seek weak vessels.''

''Hey!'' Cal blurted. Bith laughed.

''I mean,'' Endril continued, ''this god seeks our help. Gods always want something, usually something they can't have. Like children and men.''

''That's men, all right,'' Bith muttered.

''...d gods crave worshippers to sing their praises. Or
...wants something from this plane, something he
...self.''

"He won't get much with threats," Cal said. "Why should we help him?"

"Why indeed? Let us talk. Try to discern if he is indeed Vili. Then we can see what he wants."

"Why not?" Bith sighed. But her tone was too casual. She was curious.

"I don't like this," Cal murmured.

"Then leave," the girl told him. "We didn't invite you here anyway."

"Oh? In that case I'm staying."

Hathor laughed and shook his head.

The four again crouched over the helm full of water. They had moved it away from the fire so it would not grow warm and rigged a torch on a pole so they could see. The god's face rippled like the path of a fish's tail.

Endril did the talking. Gently and subtly, with many honeyed words, he asked Vili about his ancestry, his homeland, his ideals, his reasons for summoning them. "That we might know how to serve you, master, best."

Vili replied, though it took some time. His tiny voice droned on and on, and the petulance in it became clearer and clearer. The godling claimed to be the younger brother of Odin, and anyone with siblings could read the jealousy there. He was ignored by his brother Odin, eclipsed by his nephew Thor, picked on by his half-cousin Loki. Only the kind Balder would speak to him or take him seriously. The elder gods had the tribes of the far north firmly in their grasp and they protected their influence ferociously. It was Balder who had suggested that Vili move farther south to "build a following."

To this end, Vili had left the land of ice and pine and rock and spume. He'd found a new land of low mountains and green hills and thick forest. And a long rolling wall of colored mist.

In this new land Vili found potential for followers. He hoped to attract worthy men, men of great wisdom and strength and heart. Men, he had heard, liked geegaws—sacred objects, venerated relics, fine tools. So Vili had dwarves construct him a set of *runeswords*.

"*Runeswords?*" The word tolled like a bell in Cal's mind and mouth.

"Hush!" snapped the three.

These swords were forged in the bodies of mountains and tempered in the god's own blood. With them in hand his priests would "gather worshippers, assemble armies, conduct war, and conquer kingdoms!" Like his brother Odin, Vili would forge unbreakable bonds with the earth and make himself *supreme*!

Or so he thought . . .

"What went wrong?" Bith asked.

"Nothing went wrong!" snapped the tiny god in the bowl. "Our plan was good! It was worthy! But the men squabbled among themselves, and then the Dark Lord came. . . ." Vili's plan fell apart. The swords—Vili wished now he'd never commissioned them—were scattered over the earth. "The nearest one is to the northwest. A thrice-cursed wizard drains its power—*our power*—for his own petty ends, to protect his kingdom from the Dark Army that encroaches."

"That doesn't sound so petty," Cal opined.

"Dark—Army?" asked Hathor.

"*Shhh!!!*" Bith hissed.

The tiny voice finished, "And so it comes to you."

"What?" asked all four together.

"Capture the sword!" hissed the voice. "Cast down the wizard and kill him as an example to those who would oppose our will!"

"Why should we?" Cal asked, and this time no one shushed him.

"Do this thing for us," proclaimed the squeaky voice, "and we shall reward you with gifts such as no mortal has ever yet beheld!"

"Like what?"

The face in the bowl was silent. Cal thought he detected a pout on the thin lips.

"Well?" the boy repeated.

"Gold! Jewels! Spell books! Fabulous magic swords and ncient crowns of kings and potions and fabric from far lands!

less—"

" Cal put in. "Big ugly ones with clubs."

d Bith. "Evil spells to drive a person mad or stop their hearts. Homunculi and incubi

"Trolls," Hathor put in. His three companions looked at him.

"Cowards!" crowed the god. "You are afraid! Wastrels! Feeble ones! Pusillanimous—"

Cal flicked the edge of the helmet with his finger. Unbound, his brown hair fell into his eyes and he had to brush it back. "We're all that and more, but we're not stupid. None here would embark on a doomed quest at the behest of a god so feeble he can't even hex a chicken."

"Beware," Endril murmured. He hadn't spoken for some time. "He hexed you."

Cal started and touched the pommel of his sword. Endril clamped a hand over his. The elf's hand was warm but hard as a ring of iron. Cal tried to shake it off but couldn't. "I'm all right!" Endril let go.

"I drink god water?" Hathor asked.

Endril held up a white hand. "No. We've listened enough, though. Let us talk. Or better, see. Can you, oh Vili, show us some picture of our destination?"

"The sword?" came a squeak.

"The treasure," replied Cal.

"And the magic," added Bith.

The face screwed itself up as if in disgust. Then it faded away.

"He gone?" Hathor asked.

Cal peered close. "Looks like. No, wait. *Look!*"

A room came into view, a tiny picture in the round bowl. Everyone bumped heads to catch a glimpse. The room revolved slowly. Bith gasped as a workbench crowded with books and retorts and crocks and skulls and stuffed birds came into view. Hathor grunted at the jeweled armor and splendid battleaxe seen on one wall. And Cal gasped loudest of all when he beheld a sword hanging in mid-air: a sword etched with runes along its length.

Then suddenly the sour face of their god confronted them.

"Well?" he demanded.

The four mortals were silent. They tried to look at one another surreptitiously, to gauge each other's reaction. Finally Bith broke the silence. "How much help do we get?"

Negotiations went on for some time. The mortal party fired questions and answers at the beleaguered god and he answered as much as he knew (or would tell them). He could scout ahead for them, spy around corners and amongst the enemy (whom he would not name), warn them of trouble. Maybe possess a soul or two as needed, enhance their abilities, speak to them in their minds, direct them back together if they should separate. He made many more promises they weren't sure he could keep. But in the end they consented, in a way.

"We'll take a look," Bith said.

"From a distance," Cal agreed.

"Nothing sure," Hathor added.

"The journey costs nothing," confirmed Endril.

"Then get on with it," commanded Vili, and faded.

Endril tilted the bowl, then dumped it out. "I think his power is spent for now."

Cal got up from his knees and stretched wide. "*Unhh!* That was interesting, but I have a feeling there's a *whole lot* he didn't tell us. Hunh. I've never talked with a god before, though I've called out a few of their names when I was fighting."

"Beware lest your prayers be answered," Endril supplied.

"When do we start for the northland?" Bith asked.

"Tomorrow," replied Endril.

"Good," Hathor echoed. "Sleep now."

"Not yet," said Endril. "We must make a pact."

"Pact? What kind of pact?"

"Can't that wait until we're on the road?"

"What a pack?"

"A bond. A pact of honor," the elf explained. "And no, it cannot wait. We've been brought together and we need to seal our friendship. Rise and attend me, you all."

Wondering, glancing at one another sidelong, Cal and Bith and Hathor shuffled forward and tentatively advanced their hands.

Endril shook his white head. "Not here. Here." He stood at one side of the fire and extended one hand over it. The flame had died to embers that threw a lot of heat. But he stood there as still as a tree with a branch extended. Cal joined him and put his brown scarred hand on the elf's. The fire began to slowly bake it. The troll stuck in his hairy knotty hand, and finally Bith's slim short-fingered one was added to the triangle.

Endril nodded. "An elf takes an oath not lightly, and I hope humans and their kin do likewise. Let us pledge. That we shall share peril and plunder and plague together. That we shall defend one another unto death. That we shall work together and never at cross purposes. That we shall succor one another and expect succor.

"As the winds have four homes and the seasons four turnings, as the world has four directions and this fire four sides, let us have four hearts. A brotherhood of four.

"So be it!" Endril finished.

The other three echoed him. "So be it!"

They dropped their hot hands. With the dying down of the fire had come the pressing of the night. A minor breeze rattled through the camp. Bith shivered and drew her cloak close about her. Cal said, "I'll stoke the fire for you."

Hathor said, "I get wood."

"And I will stand watch," added Endril.

Bith asked, "What do I do?"

"Sleep."

The girl was too tired to argue. She settled against a fallen tree dragged up by Hathor and laid down. "This has been a long day," she yawned.

Having dumped an armful of wood, Hathor laid down to sleep in the dirt like a dog. Endril wandered off while Cal stacked the fire.

Hathor picked his head up and looked at the starry sky. "Not four directions. Six."

"What's that?" Cal asked him.

"World has four directions. North, south, east, west—up, down."

"Go to sleep, Hathor." The troll dropped his head back down and slept.

"Besides," Cal mused, "we're five, including our little god friend."

Bith answered sleepily, "Gods don't count. You can't depend on them."

Cal chuckled. "A brotherhood of outcasts. Some bunch."

"Go to sleep, Cal."

He did.

A shimmering sword etched with runes flashed in his dreams.

• • •

Three days walking found them far to the west. They went directly west because Endril had said they might as well face what they were fighting as soon as possible.

They climbed through increasingly hilly country. The forest thinned out as the land rose. The trees stayed in the bottoms of gulleys that soon became valleys and promised to become gorges. The grass was replaced in some places by rock. The four were often the tallest things around save for curiously conical stone spires. Cal asked Endril if they were fashioned by hand, but the answers he got were so vague as to be useless.

They passed through three hamlets. Two of them were deserted. In the third only their money was welcome. The residents—gruff and scruffy men and women—would say that "strangers and stranger ones" had passed by and caused "some trouble." More than that they would not tell. The villagers sold them trail food and waterskins at an exorbitant price. They learned this tiny village was almost the end of civilization, that beyond there was but one valley of people left, a valley with a castle and a village around it.

And the party learned from these downtrodden and scurrilous people that they had become true outcasts, for the villagers did not try to hide their contempt and fear of the elf and troll, and even of the human magic user.

With money lent by Cal, Bith had bought herself a blanket, a teapot, a mirror, and some other camp gear. She tucked her supplies into the blanket and tied it across her back. She and Cal wondered at Endril and Hathor, who carried only their weapons. Comfort was nothing to them. Hathor ate anything he could chew and he slept in the mud or the rain. Endril found food for them—game birds and animals, roots and grasses—but ate little himself. And the elf never slept, it seemed. He would only sit crosslegged and rest his eyes. He sang lilting yet monotonous airs in a strange language that started and stopped in no particular way. The pale figure wandered off at times and returned later without a sound or explanation. Their companions' inhuman fortitude began to grate on Cal and Bith as the days passed.

They tramped across heathered moors and autumn-yellow plains. Mile after mile, on and on.

Endril found the newness of the land enthralling. True, he had walked these same miles before, many times in his long life, but each time he passed through there was something new to see. A robin had found a new place to build a nest in the top of a sundered tree. Conies had split their former colony in two, occupying two hilltops now. Lavender had worked its way up from the south to grace the side of a mountain stream. The light through the grass had a different translucency as the land settled. It was all beautiful, he found, all one with itself. But it could not compare in any way with his homeland, and often his heart was downcast. It was then he would dream his dreamless memories and sing of home.

Bith wished she'd worked more as a youngster, so her body would be tougher now. She had to struggle to keep up with the elf's swinging gait, the troll's roll, and the soldier's stolid marching. Blisters grew and burst on her feet inside their fancy yellow boots, burst and leaked and chafed anew. At nights she could barely sleep for their aching, just as the hard ground mashed her soft curves and left her stiff in the morning. She thought this an empty land, grass and rock and nothing else, empty of life and laughter and intrigue, and she often wished she were some place exciting, or even home in her mother's castle. Her mother was pure evil. The girl knew that now, and nothing could make her go back to that dark structure. But this outdoor wandering life was alien to her too; she didn't belong here, and the land seemed to know it and oppose her at every step.

Hathor strolled and walked and plucked up food and thought about things or didn't. Everything was colorful and noisy and interesting. He liked the red in the rocks underfoot, the blue in a bird's wing, the yellow and green of the grass stalks. He watched the clouds drift together to form a thousand different shapes, then drift apart to form a thousand more. He liked the sounds the wind carried, the click of beetle and the scurry of ants, the hoot of a sleeping ground owl. He liked the new tastes of the roots and plants he found, a hundred different sensations on his tongue. He enjoyed it all and was glad he'd left behind his dank moist caves and his cruel people.

Between Endril's singing, Bith's silent misery, and Hathor's complacence, Cal began to feel very alone despite the company. This land was not very different from his homeland, and sometimes the breeze carried scents that triggered memories of childhood. Yet that homeland was lost forever, and he came from a race of people that accepted their fate without complaining. So it had been with his father and so with his mother. The stony silence was comfortable in its own hard way, for it reminded Cal of the times in which he'd marched and sung with stout soldiers to face a common foe. In these harsh reaches he could breathe clear air deep into his lungs. His head was free of the cobwebs of the forest. So the silence was not so bad.

It was one bright morning they sighted their first goal. Endril, in the lead, reached the top of a slope and announced, "There it is."

Bith, then Hathor, then Cal in the rear, joined him on the flinty crest. They drew a sharp breath at the strange sight. On this cloudless day in this cloudless clime, far to the west, they beheld the common enemy of all the speaking races.

The thing was a line of cloud, or fog: a storm cloud come to ground. The bank was tall, very tall, reaching almost to where normal clouds would fly. The clouds that formed this bank were not still. They roiled and boiled and fluttered and rippled up and down its sheer face. Color flitted through the cloud like a dirty rainbow—grey where it touched the ground, a tinge of purple here, a jot of red there, green where the sun hit it along the top, with orange streaks. But none of the colors were beautiful. They were the colors of bruises on skin, of mold on vegetables, of dried blood or vomit, of sun-bleached bones and things long dead.

But the most curious feature of the cloud was its straightness. True, the wall of cloud billowed out here or receded there, but its front edge was as cleanly cut as if with a knife. The tremendous wall ran from north by east to south by west, and it stretched from horizon to horizon and obviously beyond. It was all the eye could see in looking west, a giant sea wave poised to come crashing down on all civilization.

Cal said aloud to no one in particular, "So that's it, eh?"

"Aye," replied Endril. "The Mistwall."

CHAPTER
4

"It's beautiful," said Bith.

"No, it's not," Cal snapped. "It's a curse on all mankind!"

Bith shook herself as if in a trance. "I—I suppose you're right. It's full of color, but there's something wrong with it. . . ."

The four stared at the long wall of bilious cloud without moving or speaking.

It was Endril who broke the silence. "I remember when it was far to the west. Very far. I remember when it didn't exist at all." The elf's gaze was fixed in space, but not upon Mistwall.

Cal found the regular swirling of the mists arresting and hypnotic, like watching water pass under a bridge. If a man stared too long he could slip quietly over the edge. . . . Cal shook himself. He turned his back and rubbed his eyes. A few more minutes of this and the whole party would march off into its depths. "Maybe we should get away from it. Out of sight."

No one answered. His three companions just stood and stared. The soldier reached back—without looking at the distant Mistwall—and grabbed Elizebith by the arm. Roughly he jerked her down below the brow of the slope.

"What? Let go of me, you—ruffian!"

Hathor looked up at Bith's cry and jumped down beside the girl. He growled at Cal to let the girl go. Cal did, but he asked her, "Feel better?"

Bith looked around and put her hand to her throat. "Well, yes. I do. Thank you, I guess."

"It's going to be a jolly journey with that thing always at our left hand."

"Maybe we'll get used to it."

"Never."

Endril alighted beside them without a sound. "Shall we resume our trek?"

The three of human stock stared at him. Cal asked, "Doesn't that wall *do* anything to you?"

Endril shook his head. "It saddens me. I suppose it's our fault it's here."

"The wall? How do you reckon it's your fault?"

Endril didn't answer. He set off down the slope, swinging his short bow as if it were a willow switch.

"Hey, wait up!" Cal called. He took Bith's hand and helped her along. They slid down the scree to the shaley bottom of a slope. They set off north along a goat trail, out of sight of the Mistwall.

Cal caught up with Endril. "Slow down, you! What did you mean, it's your fault?"

Endril almost shrugged. "Is omission or commission the greater crime? At the first coming of the Dark Lord we elves did nothing. We discussed it at length, but dismissed it as yet another manifestation of man's ignorance and urge for self-destruction. Too late did we learn it was more, something that may eat up the land permanently. We never thought you capable of that. We were wrong."

"You could have stopped the Dark Lord, yet you didn't do anything? That's horrible!"

Endril watched the sky to the north. "We did nothing. Perhaps we couldn't have stopped it. We didn't try. That is the worst crime of all."

Bith and Cal both trotted to keep up with the elf. Hathor strolled along far behind, in no hurry to catch up. Endril slowed his stride somewhat. The girl asked, "What do you know of the Dark Lord? Is he human?"

"I don't know."

"Why not?"

Endril gave her a look that in a human would have been irritation. "Why anything? He—or she, or it—is what he, she, or it *is*. I know only that it is not elven. What more need I know?"

Cal spit out an oath and stopped in his tracks. Bith stood beside him. In a moment the elf had passed over a hill. Hathor walked up chewing on a piece of sapling he'd cut. Cal asked Bith, "What do *you* know about the Dark Lord?"

"I? Nothing. Nor—well, nor my mother, either. She's wondered for years about him, or it. Asked every—traveller—that came to our castle. But no one knew. Not even his priests have a clue."

Cal's tone was snide. "Oh, yes, your castle again."

Bith put her nose in the air. "And who are *you* to be doubting me? You forget the state of your person—and your boots."

"Horseshit," Hathor supplied.

Cal barked, "That's enough out of you, troll. And you too, *princess*. If you're so high and mighty, where is this castle of yours?"

"My castle—my home—is beyond that veil."

"What? Really?"

Now was Bith's turn to be snide. "Oh. *Now* you choose to believe me."

Caught, Cal was suddenly flustered. "Well, yes. I guess so. But how can you have a home beyond the veil? Only evil beings dwell there."

"And now you say I'm evil. I can't say I care for your conversation."

Cal waved his hands uselessly. "Look, I don't know what to believe. All I've ever heard is—"

"I'll tell you this," the girl's voice was direct. "I *am* a princess, because I *am* Morea's daughter, and Morea *is* the most powerful woman in the world. And the most evil. And if you stopped to think for even half a moment, you might wonder this: *Why* is her only child, heir to her throne and all her power and all her wealth and all her gramarye, out here?—

wandering in the wilderness, no home, no shelter, alone and penniless, with only the clothing on her back? Why?''

Then Cal was alone, for the girl had turned and stalked away, up the slope where the elf had gone. Hathor followed her.

Cal contemplated their receding backs and the sigh of the silent plain. Damn! but he was tired of bringing up the rear and listening to the quiet! And having *sensitive* people bark at every word he spoke! Soldiers were entitled to grumble and to question: it was one of their few joys. And he had his pride. . . . But so did the others. The poor always had the most pride—it was all they could afford. Maybe they were all on edge in these eerie wastes. The empty wind whistled around his ears and he shuddered. Cal's pride wasn't worth a crooked copper out here. He jogged to catch up.

"Hey! Bith, Hathor, wait up! Let's not fight! Hey!''

He walked as best he could alongside the girl, but as she had the center of the narrow trail through rock and heather, he had to stumble along on the side or walk behind her. He talked fast.

"Look, I'm sorry if I doubted you. Or said that you were evil. That wall makes me edgy. And sad.''

"Sad? Ha!''

"No, really, it does. Because I come from the Lost Lands, too. In a way.'' He saw a glimmer of interest in Bith's eyes. He kept talking as their party stepped out across the heathered plain. The Mistwall had come back into sight, filling the western sky. They didn't look at it.

"My father, Talien Berefordson, had a small fief in the west, at the northern tip of an island. I don't remember it very well. I was just a baby when the wall first appeared— I'd never even seen it before today. I remember my mother saying it was the queerest cloud structure, not like a storm coming on, but like it was alive. One day my people realized that it wasn't just a cloud bank, for the fisherfolk who sailed into it seldom came back. Some who did came back mad. Some complained of nightmares, awful ones, so vile they killed themselves, sometimes after killing others. My father could see it was poison, but he didn't know what to do.

"Then one day—my mother told me all this, mind—an army of monsters came out of the mist. There were orcs and giants and other kinds of misshapen things. No offense, Hathor. My father, who never listened to the council of anyone in his entire life, finally decided to set out with his army to drive them away. *That* I remember, little though I was. I remember my father had a pennant, a green one with a red eagle with a fish in its jaws, a sea eagle. The strongest man in the army carried it in a boot on his saddle, and it fluttered in the breeze. The army rode off one day when it was dark at noon.

"They didn't come back. Not one man out of a hundred. Not a single horse. We could only assume they were all dead."

His voice was running out like the end of a rainstorm. His pace slowed, as did his audience's: one girl and one troll. Cal talked on, but more to himself than to anyone else.

"When they didn't come back after many days, and the wall had drawn closer, my mother bundled me up and we fled, with only one servant and a horse. We never had much. We travelled east. My mother died. The servant was old—Hamish, his name was—and he put me in the service of Lord Edric. You know what happened after that."

Cal had stopped walking altogether. The unceasing wind plucked at his garments and sent the loose threads of ragged ends streaming. His brown bangs blew into his eyes and wisps fluttered about his ears. "Then Hamish died. I'd nothing left of my father's estate, or my mother's either, all gone behind that evil wall of mist. Nothing but the memory of a big man bearing a pennant. A red eagle carrying off a fish. I've thought of painting it on my shield, but there's no one can vouch for me."

Hathor stopped chewing and threw away his stick. "Sad," he said. He seemed to be remembering something himself.

Bith put a soft white hand on Cal's brown one. "I'm—sorry to hear all that, Cal. It is sad. It really is. That's something like what happened to me. I lived in a castle that was always in the mists. Sometimes I wonder if I could travel back inside and go home. But I don't think I can. . . ." She stopped and rubbed her nose. "Ooh, this wind is tiresome. Could we—should we find a place to camp for the night?"

The three stood together as the shadow of the wall overtook them. Lying along the west, it eclipsed the sun and created a false twilight before the real dusk. The wind took on a new life and edge, with a smell of corruption. "Yes, let's," Cal said. "But not within sight of that wall."

"You know, we can't go on like this."

"Like what?"

"Wandering around without any plan or sense," Cal replied.

"We've a plan," Bith said. "We're bound for the north, now. And Endril's the only one of us who wanders, and he always comes back."

The four of them were hunkered around a campfire. They had found a hollow among some low hummocks. The land around was clad in tough grey weeds and tall grass that hissed in the eternal wind. But down here only the holly sprig in Endril's hat was riffled. It took a lot of cutting with Hathor's axe to get stems for firewood, but they had enough for the night. The elf had returned with a rock goat they roasted on a spit.

With his new contrition, Cal was weighing his words so not to offend. He waved his sharpening stone as he talked, trying to recall how his father had made suggestions. "It's not just Endril's wandering, it's our whole manner of travelling. We've been lucky, but we're going to get in trouble sooner or later. Especially now that we're in dangerous country. More dangerous. Look at the way we hit the bushes."

Even in the firelight they could see Bith blush. "What I do in the *bushes* is none of *your business*!"

"No, no, not you personally. We all have to hit the bushes. But we need to have some sort of plan for—hitting the bushes or going for water or taking point or whatever. I mean," Cal couldn't look at Bith for blushing himself, "with a bunch of soldiers, if a guy has to, uh, hit the bushes, he just goes a short way off where everyone can see him. Not that they look, but he stays close enough that no enemy can pick him off. You wouldn't believe how many men get killed with their pants down. But we're *always* getting out of sight of one another. If anyone starts tracking us we'd get picked off in a day."

Endril asked calmly, "What would you have us do?"

"I don't know! Something, some plan. And we should have a leader."

"Who?" Bith asked. "You?"

"No, not me necessarily. But someone should be in charge. Not for everyday stuff, but in case we have to make a decision quickly. That's when a leader counts."

"We've done all right so far," Bith commented. "I don't think we need to turn ourselves into *soldiers*. From what I've seen of *soldiers*, that would be a step down—for a lizard-man."

Cal said nothing. He stropped his sword blade viciously.

Bith drew a blanket around her shoulders. For a time the only sound was the sough of the wind through their hollow and the crackle of the fire. "It is a strange life we lead, though. The Mistwall has displaced Cal and me, we find. What about you, Hathor?"

Hathor was cutting the goat hide into strips and braiding it with the end looped over his big black-nailed toe. He looked up, surprise in his beady eyes. "Hunh? Me?"

"Yes, you. Why do you wander?"

"Oh," his croak had an embarrassed sound. "Not like my home. It not a nice place."

"Why not?"

"Oh, trolls not nice people. Kill anyone who not a troll and eat them. Not much food in caves. Mushrooms, white fish with no eyes, nothing else. Bats no good, no meat on 'em. So trolls come out at night, catch deer or bear, possum, people. People slow, easy to catch. But very salty and tough." The troll had not noticed his companions' faces, or he would have stopped talking. But he was warming to his subject. "We not stay out in the daytime because sun hurt our eyes. No can see good. And elders say sun burn us, make us blind, kill us. We stay in dark.

"But one night, me got lost in woods. Stuck out when sun come up. Thought me would die in sun. But no. See lots of pretty colors. Green grass. Flowers all over, white ones, yellow ones, even blue ones. Birds in trees, and little red flowers even on trees! Liked it, didn't go back. Learned to eat other things. No meat. Hair turn red."

Cal stopped in mid-strop. "What?"

Hathor pointed to his flat head. He'd removed his hat, as

he always did at night. The humans realized now it was as a sun shade that he wore it. "Stop eat meat—not much, anyway—hair turn red. No troll ever have red hair before."

Cal asked, "Is that true, Endril?"

"I never saw one with red hair before."

Bith said, "It's probably the sun that changed your hair from brown to red, Thor. Not the lack of meat."

The troll pulled at his lip with a craggy finger. Then he grunted and continued his braiding.

Bith said, "And you, Endril. What brings you to the land of men?"

Endril sat without saying anything for some time. Hathor slid the goat off the spit onto a flat stone and used his axe to quarter it. He handed the sections out. Each ate with a knife and his or her fingers. The silence stretched out, and finally the elf filled it. His voice matched the night breeze in the way it lifted and fell. It was sonorous and other-worldly.

"The lands of men and the lands of elves overlap," he began. "Some of each are common, some not. Before, a long time ago, elfhome ranged wider and farther. Magic, or perhaps something else, has leeched some of it away. Now elfhome recedes like the tide, as the ocean once receded from the land herself. This spot we occupy was once under water. You can often split a rock and find a seashell inside."

Cal gave a grunt that sounded negative, but he said nothing. Bith and Hathor chewed on strips of goat and listened raptly.

"The land, the ocean, the wind, the sun, all run in cycles, waxing and waning, growing and shrinking. Nothing ever goes away, it only bides its time. In times past the land gave rise to the speaking races. First elves. Then came men and others. Something is lost as each new race arises. Elves are most a product of the land."

Cal asked, "More than men?"

"Yes. Humans do not live with the land, they live on it."

"What's the difference?"

"The difference is in how the races treat Mother Earth. Humans take from the land and give nothing back but their bodies when they expire. Elves give back *as* they take. They give more, and improve the land."

Cal pointed with his greasy dagger. "Wait a minute, what

do you mean, 'improve the land'? Humans do that. If a passel of humans travel to a valley that's empty, that has nothing in it but grass, and they build houses and plow the soil and bring forth a crop, if they thin the forest so you can move through it and divert a stream to create a pond full of fish and do like things like that, how can you say they haven't improved it? There was nothing there before and there's suddenly plenty!''

"If you say so, man. But that you can think a valley full of grass is 'empty' speaks volumes.''

"I don't understand.''

"No, you do not.''

Cal and Endril glared at each other for a while, then Bith put an end to it. "Be that as it may . . . ummm . . . Endril, I have a question. I have heard that the lands of the elves— improved as they are—are ever so much more beautiful than the lands of men. Is that not true?''

The elf replied, "It is.''

Cal snorted.

"And I have furthermore heard that elves love their land more than their very lives. That they suffer homesickness and loneliness in the extreme, more so than any humans can even understand. Isn't that true?''

The elf's reply this time was quieter. "Yes. It is.''

"Then why do you choose to travel the lands of men?''

Endril didn't reply, and Bith repeated the question, but gently. Finally the pale figure spoke. "I—have no choice.''

"Why not?''

Endril's face was as solemn as they'd ever seen it. "I—am no longer welcome in the lands of the elves.''

It was Bith's turn to say nothing. Cal asked, without rancor, "Why? What did you do?''

The elf sat, saying nothing, looking at nothing, for the longest time. Then he rose and walked away into the blackness.

Cal stood up. "Hey, come back! Hey—'' He trotted out of the firelight, but there was nothing to see.

The boy sat back down. He stirred the fire with a crooked stick and then tossed it in. "Great. He's gone.''

"What do *you* care?''

The soldier glared at the magic user. "He's *off* again! Wandering all over hell and gone, leaving us in the lurch to get our throats cut! And what did *I* do anyway? You're the one started asking him questions!''

"Some questions you shouldn't ask."

Cal raised both hands to the sky. "Oh, excuse *me*, your royal *highness*! I'm sorry if I want to know something about the people I break bread with, and stand watches with, and turn my back to! I'm *sorry* if I want to know whether I can count on someone in a fight, or whether they'll disappear like a wisp of smoke!''

"You think the magic users will run out on you too, eh?"

"I didn't say that!"

Bith slammed herself back against a grassy hummock. She folded her blanket just so and snuggled down inside, then arranged her cloak about her shoulders. "I'm *done* talking. Good *night*!''

"What about setting a guard?"

"You like it so much, *you* stand guard!"

Hathor had already lain down and pulled his hat back on. Cal did a poor job of banking the fire and then flopped down himself. He spread his blanket loosely over himself. He positioned his sword alongside his right leg and his shield at the left. He said to the air, "Fine, fine. Good night yourself, all of you. I hope you wake up alive.''

"Cal!"

The regal voice shouted in Cal's ear even as a drumming trilled along his spine. Soldier's instinct shot him into the air.

Something was charging at him from the dark. His mind registered simply *Not one of ours* and he swung the sword while putting up his shield.

A club clomped against his wooded shield even as his blade bit into the attacker's side. Cal could tell by the feel that the edge had cut into muscle before fetching up against bone. The depth of the cut and the sag of his opponent's body told him it was a mortal wound. He shoved the body away—it would act as a partial shield on his left—even as he put back his right foot to spin to that side.

Sure enough, another assailant was coming up fast behind—a coward who had held back just long enough to let his companion rush in and draw attack. Cal completed his turn, hooked his shield around. Since he was already moving in that direction, he used the momentum of the swing. Back-handed, he threw power to his shoulder and tensed his fore-arm, cracked his wrist at the last moment, and connected with something soft. He dragged his shield back across for protection, but he'd done enough damage to stop his oppo-nent. The creature (he sensed it wasn't a man) was down before him in the dark. Cal looped his arm over his head and added another stroke to his invisible enemy. The tip of the sword split a spine and his foe crumpled.

Cal stomped his feet to get his balance and sucked cold night air to wake himself up. So far he'd done no thinking—every action had been pure training. And even as he awoke, his instinct was running down a list. What to do next? Get his back to a wall, or promontory, or the fire, or any unpass-able obstacle, preferably one that would stop missiles. There was nothing solid here, so it had to be the fire. But only temporarily, for it would light him up while his enemy held the darkness. What next? Gauge the number of enemy as best he could. A pattering in the earth under his feet said they were all around. Not too many, maybe four. He'd killed two, and that made sense. Six was a common number for a patrol. There were sounds above the gurgling of the dying. Some-thing was growling in an almost human tone, but something else was snuffling. Dogs? Impossible to tell how many. Four live enemies then, two or more dogs. Bad odds, though the fire at his back helped. What to do? Run to a safer position, maybe keep going. But—first check the state of his compan-ions. His eyes had taken in nothing but one slim shape as he'd moved in battle. Endril was still gone then, and now Hathor was missing too. Damn them! He'd *told* them—never mind. Work with what you have.

"Bith!" he hissed. "Wake up! We're under attack!"

"Hunh?" A sleepy murmur sounded from the ground. He'd been up and killed two somethings and she hadn't even woken! "Wha—?"

"Bith, damn you, wake—*Crom*!"

Cal jumped forward. Two dark shapes had materialized from the grass over the girl. Cal couldn't see them well, only their shapes as they blocked the stars just above the horizon. But it was enough. He took one, two, three short solid hops—for the worst thing you could do in a fight was to fall down—

and screamed and swung. He prayed that Bith would keep
her head down. *"Hyaaaaa!!!!!"*

A monster shrieked as Cal's swing chopped into its arm.
He'd meant to only nick the beast and let his sword travel on
to also sting the other. Incapacitating two foes was better than
killing one outright and leaving the other whole. But it was
hard to judge the distance in almost total darkness. He smelt
the copper tang of blood as the thing retreated. The other
ducked and latched onto Bith with impossibly long arms. It
tugged at the girl, who came fully awake for the first time.
Cal hopped in, way too close—close enough to get fingers
stuck in his face—but the beast was centered on the girl and
not paying attention. These whatevers were poorly trained,
the soldier was relieved to see. He crashed his blade onto a
bare back. He heard skin split and ribs crack and then the
thing was down. Two foes dead, two wounded. Where were
the others, and the dogs? Could he and Bith get away quick
enough?

"Bith! *Get—ahh*!"

Bith had been dreaming of home again. She'd heard the
screams of prisoners in the dungeons, the cries of ravens outside her window. Then something was looming over her,
stepping on her. Wide awake (or so she thought) Bith rolled
over in a tangle of blanket and cloak.

And collided with Cal's leg. Off balance, the boy fell square
on top of her. Bith *oof*ed and Cal tumbled clear.

"What are you *doing*?" the girl demanded.

"Shut up! We're under attack!"

"Attack?"

"This way!" Cal snatched her billowed sleeve and pulled
her close to him. "Stay at my back and keep quiet!"

"Where are Hath—"

"Shut *up*!"

Bith shut up. She hooked her hand in the back of Cal's belt
and stumbled along in the dark after him. She discovered that
the grassy hummocks that has seemed so smooth and uniform
in the daylight were suddenly full of chuck holes, rocks, roots,
and ridges. She tripped again and again until she learned to
put her feet flat. She thumped into Cal's back a half dozen
times as he shuffled and stopped, ducked forward and
crouched, backed up and crabbed along sideways.

"Where are we *going*?" she finally had to whisper.

"There's a—where is it?—pocket with some trees—somewhere here. I found it earlier when I walked around. We should be able to—is that it? Yeah!—get under the leaves—*Watch it!*"

Bith heard only the rapid patter of feet and a low growl. Then Cal grunted and slammed full into her. A hideous snarling split the darkness where Cal had stood. The boy rasped, "*Leggo my—hand*, you *lousy*—Bith, use a sleep spell!"

"I don't know one!" the girl wailed.

"*Don't?*—well, what *do* you—*get a-way!*"

Bith didn't know what to do. Cal had to be wrestling with a dog, but she couldn't see a thing. That was it! Light would help! With clumsy fingers she dug in her pouches and produced a dried firefly. Chanting as quick as she could without mangling the spell, she flicked the tiny carcass into the grass a dozen feet away.

Fire broke out and quickly licked among the dry grass. Within seconds there was light enough to read a book as a patch of grass blazed in the night. Bith shielded her eyes from it and looked for Cal.

The boy was in trouble. A wolf almost as tall as Cal had him by the sword hand. It was a fierce-looking beast, long and gaunt and ribby with shaggy patches of grey-white fur. Its head was wide and flat and the black eyes shone like lamps. Fortunately, Cal had on his leather gauntlets. But the wolf's jaw was locked on his sword arm and could not be shaken off.

Cal turned from the light with a curse. "*No!* We're blind enough!—" He gave up talking and tried to slam the wolf with his shield. He tried to kick its belly or back legs, tried to wrest his arm loose to get in a blow with his sword. But the animal was as clever as it was sturdy. It danced on its back feet to keep out of range even as it dragged its victim forward and off-balance, all the time snarling quietly with its muzzle locked shut.

Bith fingered all her pouches as she tried to think of another spell that could stop the wolf. Then something hit her from behind and she went sprawling. Claws skittered along her sides as teeth snapped on her hood. The girl gasped. If she hadn't had her thick hood up, the teeth would have met in the back of her head. Then she went flat on her face under the full weight of the body. She bleated, *"Cal! Help me!"*

Cal sucked wind and smacked twice at the wolf's head with the iron edge of his shield.. The blows rapped on the tough skull with no effect. He switched tactics, shucked his shield from his left arm, and fished for the dagger on his belt. But the wolf twisted its powerful neck and knocked him over sideways. His sword thrashed against the grass. *"Bith! Get away!"* he shouted. The wolf thumped both huge front feet onto his chest. By the light of the burning grass he saw two rows of yellow teeth draw back to rip out his throat.

The jaws suddenly snapped shut. The wolf's nose dropped like a rock to bang Cal's nose, then the full weight of the beast thudded onto him. It was dead weight. Something had killed the wolf.

The boy shoved away the smelly carcass and rolled onto all fours. He hunted for his sword as he looked for the answer.

Tall and dark against the grass fire, Endril the elf stood poised over Bith and her attacker. From white hair to long grey cloak to thin bony arms, his soft outline was like a ghost's. At the end of his arm was a slim black blade that had transfixed Bith's wolf as he had dispatched Cal's. He whipped the almost-invisible blade out of the dying wolf's body. With his boot he shoved the carcass clear of the girl's body. He caught her by the upper arm and lifted her. She thanked him shakily.

Cal recovered his shield and sword, pulled his baldric round straight and approached Endril from an angle where he could be seen. *"You!* Where have *you*—"

The elf shot a hand in the air. He canted his head into the wind. "Hist! T'is Hathor!"

"What about him?" Cal asked, but Endril was off, loping across the prarie with long strides. Cal swore and ran after him. Bith trailed along.

Topping a hummock brought them back to their campsite. The fire had died down to coals, but there was enough light to see Hathor fighting for his life.

The troll had tossed away his hat and bearskin cloak. In the red firelight he looked much like his enemies. These were a pair of dog-like men wielding clubs. They were just over

five feet tall and stooped. Short bristly hair stood up all over
their bodies, growing in a mane that travelled from their
crowns down their spines. Their shoulders and arms were
wide and powerful, their legs bent curiously like a dog's.
They wore no clothing other than their native spots. Most
disturbing was their faces. They had receding brows and
pointed ears, and elongated snouts with dark noses like a
hound's. Their teeth were yellow and long, curled in snarls
uglier than the wolves' had been.

The two worked as a pair. One waved his gnarled club in
Hathor's face as the other circled. Animal-like, they were
quick to jump back whenever the troll swung his long felling
axe. At each swing the foremost beast would dance back while
his partner got in a solid rap. Even as the three breasted the
ridge they heard a painful *crunch* that made Hathor stagger.
The two yipped and raised their clubs for the final blows.

A clear singing call arrested their arms and made them
turn. Endril leapt down the slope with his sword swishing in
the night sky. The creature behind Hathor bleated and turned
to run. The elf overtook him and ran the blade through his
back. Cal charged breathlessly for the other assailant, but
Hathor's axe made a noisy *thwack!* that folded the beast over
like a sapling. In a frenzy the troll set both feet wide and
slammed the axe again and again into the lifeless body.

The crunching, chopping, smashing sounds made Bith ill.
"Thor!" she shrilled. "Stop, Thor! *Please, stop!"*

Hathor slammed his axe down a final time and stopped.
Spent, he held onto the handle and panted like a bellows.

Cal trotted back up the slope and scanned what he could
see of the horizon. Only the wind moved. A cool night breeze
dried the sweat on his brow and chilled his damp clothes.
When Cal was satisfied all was clear, he rejoined the party
by their ravaged campsite.

Hathor had snatched up a scrap of filthy clothing that he
used to wipe his axe clean. Cal wiped his blade on the grass,
then stropped it with his stone to bring back the edge. All
the while he kept casting about, turning around in the dark.
Endril studied the faces of their dead enemies. Only now did
Bith realize there were more than two dead bodies on the
ground. Where she had been sleeping were two more. She

joined Endril and grimaced at the ugly masks of death. She'd seen these things before.

"Well," Cal panted, "What *are* they?"

The first sneak thieves, the ones Cal had killed, were like deformed men, skinny and shrivelled, but with knotty arms and legs. Their faces were mostly massive bony brow ridges and heavy jaw. Their teeth were snarled and fanged. Their skin was a dirty grey, and they wore only scraps of leather armor that must once have belonged to men. Clubs studded with obsidian lay near their bodies.

Endril pointed with his invisible blade to the first attackers. "These be orcs, common ones. Hardy, stupid, vicious. Not terribly strong or able, their strength lies in numbers, and the way their commanders drive them. There are other types of orcs, taller and stronger, wiser, crueller."

He stepped to the others and pointed out the snouts. Lines of black trickled away from the monsters: fleas and mites deserting a cooling body. "These be gnolls, hyena men. They are only half sane but with a wolf's cunning."

Bith shuddered. "And were those wolves that attacked me and Cal over the hill?"

Endril frowned, his face long and vampiric in the half-light. "Too large for wolves. They must have warg blood. Bred by the dark lords, most likely."

Hathor had finished cleaning his weapon. He stooped now for his cloak and floppy hat. "Should move camp," he growled. "More come, maybe."

"Yes, that would be best," Endril agreed. "These may be an isolated raiding party, or the vanguard of a larger group. The sooner the better—"

"Nothing's going to be better for quite some time!" came a bark from the edge of the firelight. It was Cal. "We'll just walk square into some other disaster. We might as well get ourselves killed here as anywhere!"

His three companions stared at him.

"Don't give me those looks! The lot of you are responsible for this! We're lucky, damned lucky, to be standing here at all."

Hathor said, "We fight—"

"Cut it!" the boy interrupted. "Any more fighting like this and we'll die, singly and painfully! Look what happened!

Bith fast asleep, and me—I admit that. No idea where Endril is or even if he's coming back! Hathor who knows where when the fighting starts, and then having to fend for himself back here because Bith and I are fleeing to a stronger position! A fine lot of babes in the woods we are!" Cal rubbed at a raw claw mark on the side of his face. In doing so he found his right glove was mangled along with the hand beneath. He stripped off the ruined glove and threw it on the ground.

The wind sighed. Ashes swirled in the fire pit. Endril said, "Let us move camp before we speak again." He, of course, had nothing to pack, nor did Hathor. Bith rolled up her blanket and camp gear. Cal savagely jammed his blanket into his light pack and slung it over his shoulder. He tramped off to the north.

The others trailed along, Bith stumbling like Cal in the dark. Endril and Hathor moved as easily as if it were full day. After Bith had jolted herself a dozen times, her fatigue and exasperation gave vent to her innermost thoughts.

"You don't need to protect me just because I'm a woman, you know!" she said to no one in particular.

Cal turned around and walked backwards. "What?"

"You always protect me because I'm a woman, I said!"

Cal snorted. "Girl is more like it. And it's not true. We protect you because you're a mage and defenseless. You've got nothing but empty hands and belt full of geegaws to keep off the beasties when they come at you. And, you know, it *would* be right handy to know exactly what spells you *do* know. When those wolves were ready to bite our faces off I asked you for a sleep spell, and *then* I learned you don't have one. I thought *every* magic user knew *that* spell!"

"Shows what you know about spelling!"

"I won't get much older to learn anything at this rate. What spells *do* you know?"

Bith did not answer as they trudged along.

Cal turned back to the trail and his voice carried over his shoulder. "See? Secrets. Wonderful. I don't know nothing about spelling, or much else except swinging a sword. But I'll tell you, when I travelled with soldiers and knights at least I knew what we *didn't* know. We didn't have any secrets that counted. But with mages and elves and trolls it's a surprise every minute. Too bad you almost have to get *killed* to learn something. Never mind, I can see I'm wasting my breath."

The party did not go far, only a mile or so. Endril said they could not really hide if there were more orcs around, for they could sniff out their trail. But they found a flattish dish rimmed with brush that would be shelter from the wind yet leave them free to flee in any direction if necessary. They didn't bother with another fire. Wrung out from their exertions and lack of sleep, the humans and troll fell to the ground and fumbled to make themselves comfortable. Endril squatted in their center and gazed around the horizon.

Cal had grumbled quietly every step of the way. Now he raised his voice and asked tiredly, "Who's got first watch? Or are we to trust in the fates again?"

"I will watch," Endril replied. "T'was I who was remiss in leaving the party."

Cal grunted.

Hathor mumbled, "Sun come up, we practice fighting. Together. Be good fun."

Bith said sleepily, "Haven't we done enough fighting with each other today?"

"Sleep," Endril told her.

Cal propped himself up on one elbow. "You know, Bith, the reason we protect you is because you're one of us. Like it or not."

Bith yawned. "S'nice—to have—friends."

And practice they did over the next few days. At breakfast and dinner, before turning in or while walking. They also talked. They worked out some simple battle orders and formations, they discussed which spells Bith might use to support their actions. They formed wedges with Hathor the axeman in the middle, Cal and Endril flanking him, and Bith acting as backup. They worked out watches and schedules and smoothed rough edges. They still maintained their secrets and privacy, but at least they knew where and when to expect each other.

Endril still wandered afield, but he told them when he would return—usually. And it was while wandering one day that he made a discovery.

CHAPTER
5

"Hoy!" came a distant shout. They turned and looked up the trail, which wound its way into a broken land of head-high rocks and fissures. Endril stood in the middle distance, a black scarecrow shape against the white sky. He waved his bow and called something they couldn't hear in the wind.

"Wonder what he's found now?" Cal said.

"Probably some exotic mushroom," Bith replied.

"I like mushrooms," Hathor added.

Bith smiled. "Come on. Let's see what it is."

Endril led them into the rocks, down ravines that dipped and climbed, to stop at the bottom of a gully. This was almost a pass through the hills. The walls were fragmented and craggy, in some places only head high, in others towering above. They were shot through with cracks and pockets and probably caves higher up. The floor was smooth in the center, trod by a thousand feet, speckled with fallen rocks.

Endril pressed his ear against a stone wall. He waved them to it. "Listen."

"To what?" asked Cal.

Bith put her ear to the crack. It was about nine inches wide.

She strained to hear and then started. "It's a voice! Calling for help!"

Cal listened. Faintly, weakly, far back, he too thought he could hear a cry for help. Or it could have been the wind.

Hathor was more sure. "Someone there, all right. I got good ears."

Cal stepped back and looked at the wall. It was more fractured here than solid. In fact, now that he studied it, the space was part of a huge rift jammed with rock. Dirt and weeds had settled into the hollows.

"How could anyone be alive in there? Is there a cave or something? They would have had to crawl in from the other side. Or come up from underground. It might be—fairies or some kin."

Hathor had his blocky head to the crack. "It Vili."

"Vili? In there?"

Cal brightened. "Hey, that reminds me! When those orcs attacked the other day, a voice shouted to wake me up. It must have been Vili."

"He's good for something, anyway," Bith observed. "But he should be able to float out of there."

Endril nodded. "It is strange. Vili hasn't much power in this plane, but he should grow stronger as we go further north. But then, the closer we come to the sword the more his power is drained. Or so I guess."

"Why doesn't he just jump out onto my sword as he has before? How much effort can that be?"

"Draw your sword," Bith suggested.

Cal did, but no face appeared. Hathor called into the crack, "Vili! Come out to sword!"

"What will you?" piped a small voice.

The adventurers bumped heads to peer at the blade. In the foggy pitted surface of the sword they could see a man's face as if under water. In the wan sunlight it looked a demon's face, like the one on Bith's belt buckle.

"What were you doing in that cave?" Bith asked the tiny god.

"Cave?" squeaked Vili. "I am in no cave, but am rather— here and there. And busy. What do you require?"

Cal waggled the blade. "*You* asked us for help. Now you're out, what do you want?"

The sword waggled itself. "Addle-pated fool! Cretin! Crack-brain! I am in no cave! Now *leave us*!" The face vanished.

The four stood for some while looking at the crack in the wall and at each other. Hathor listened. "Someone still in there."

"Someone else?" Bith asked.

Hathor shrugged.

After a time Cal said, "We're not moving, so I suppose we've decided to free him."

"I suppose," the girl agreed.

"How shall we do it?"

They talked. Cal asked Bith if she had some spell that could "suck him out of there." Bith told him no. She did float a light spell inside, but it couldn't penetrate very far. Hathor suggested they return to a tree they'd passed earlier and cut it as a lever. They dispatched him to fetch it. Cal climbed the wall and inspected the top for promising cracks. The stones were locked tight and tamped down flat. It looked as if a tor to the left had split and collapsed into a side ravine. Dwarf trees decorated the top. Cal searched for an entrance to a cave beyond, but there was nothing. Bith recalled a spell that might help and they discussed its use. Endril brewed tea and spitted a brace of ptarmigan as they waited for Hathor's return. Eventually the troll returned dragging a tree trunk that Cal doubted anyone else could lift.

As they ate the sparse meal Cal aired some thoughts. "I still wonder what kind of being can live under a pile of rocks. Have you looked at that wall and the cap? There are *trees* on top of there hundreds of years old! What kind of thing can live in a cave for hundreds of years?"

Endril stared at the sky and said nothing. Bith bit her lip. Hathor said, "Not trolls."

The elf said slowly, "Many things live long by man's standards. Elves, fairies, turtles. Demons, giants, rock lizards. You cannot judge a soul by its age."

"But what if it's not a real person? What if it's an old magic trap or a will o' the wisp or something?"

Their magic user said, "We'll never know what it is until we dig it out."

"Curiosity kills cats," the boy told her.

"But never soldiers?"

"Never. Drink and the pox kill soldiers."

Hathor spoke. "We help him because he need help."

No one could rebut that, so they finished their meal and began.

Cal used his work-worn dagger to pry a rock loose from the wall. Together the three males set the lever into the socket, wiggled it into place, and heaved. Boulders groaned and shifted. Soil clouded around them. A section of wall tumbled down and they repeated the process. And more. Grit settled onto their faces and slid down their necks. A leg-breaking rock dropped practically on Cal's foot, making him jump. With wiggling and straining and dropping the bar and not a little cursing they eventually gouged a hole six feet deep. But then they fetched up against a boulder that showed no edges. It could have been any size and it completely blocked their path.

Cal rubbed a dirty sleeve across a dirty face. "That son of a bitch better really be in there. Your turn, Bith." The men sat down to watch and sip water and get their breath back. Cal did, anyway. Endril and Hathor seemed hardly put out.

The girl crept into the hole and scooched forward to the offending rock. She seemed calm enough, but her lower lip betrayed her, clamped as it was in her teeth. The girl leant sideways to gather some light. With her small knife she scooped a hole at the lower edge of the boulder and into it placed a fresh green weed. She then trickled water from a skin down the face of the rock and onto the weed. Then the men could just hear her whisper in a queer cadence.

Bith finished with a shake of her head and scrambled back out of the hole. She stood poised, like a ferret over a rabbit hole, watching.

Cal asked, "Well? Are you—"

"*Shhhh!!!*"

Grrrruuuunnnnnnnnnn.

"What's that?"

Aeeeerrrrnnnn. Grrrnnnuuuuu.

It was the boulder. It was growing. It was swelling like a gas bubble, like a loaf of bread dough.

Cal whistled. "Whoa! That's something!"

Bith raised a hand in the air. "Yes, but—"

As the rock expanded it shoved at its neighbors. The boulder pressed outwards from the hole. Cracks ran up the face of the rock wall. Dirt under pressure geysered from the top. As if in a dream, Bith watched the course of her destruction run. The boulder showed no signs of stopping.

"LOOK OUT!"

The wall above them gave way as the whole side of the ravine split open. Bith spun and caromed into Cal. Out of the corner of her eye she saw her companions disappear. Endril was off the ground and gone like a grasshopper. Hathor leapt at the wall behind him, dug his fingers into soil and rock, and clattered up the slope like a squirrel up a tree. Cal caught the girl and almost knocked them both down. She pushed at his chest.

"RUN!"

With a *crump!* the side of the ravine fell flat on the place they had stood seconds before. The earth shook so hard that Cal fell to his knees. Bith landed on top of him. She was surprisingly heavy for so small a thing, he noticed. But she was very soft. Then the two were coughing in the gout of smoky dust that plumed up and down the ravine. Lamely the boy snatched Bith's sleeve and scrambled for air somewhere down the trail.

The two finally stopped where the weak autumn sun fell on them. Every move made dirt trickle from their clothing and start them coughing again. They sat down and gasped for breath.

"Good spell," the boy hacked.

"Thank—you."

Eventually the dust settled. Endril and Hathor and Cal and Bith reformed and gingerly picked their way down the now-blocked ravine.

They found their tiny hole had grown into a pocket clear to the sky, twenty feet high and wide and deep. The keystone had fractured into a dozen pieces from the stress of expanding and then shrinking. In the process it had shattered the whole wall and tipped it onto the ravine floor. Cal grunted and grunted again. "That's some spell, all right. Does it always work that well?"

The other males murmured assent. Bith looked embarrassed. "Never, never this well. When I've used *enlarge* before it made things twice their size, not—ten times. I—I think my powers are—more powerful here. But I don't know why."

At the back of the new pocket they could see a tiny black hole that went straight back. Cal said, "That must be where our mysterious captive—"

"Ho." Hathor had turned around to point to the opposite wall of the ravine, high up. "Look there."

The others turned. There was something poised along the wall, watching them. Its four-legged shape was silhouetted against the sky. Cal asked, "Is it a goat? Shoot it, Endr—"

The elf shouted, *"It's a—"*

The thing leapt thirty feet to hit the ravine floor with a *thump!* Bith screamed and covered her head as the thing landed right beside her.

It was a monster. Big, long, and low. Body like a lion. A tawny belly and brown back, black claws, white teeth. A brassy smell. Tiny wings and a human face.

Bith ducked and skittered past the unmoving men. She put herself behind the stolid troll and this horrendous menace that had fallen from the sky.

"Thor! Your axe! Hit it! Quick! HIT IT!"

But the troll didn't move. Neither did Cal or Endril. All three of them stood where they had turned, staring.

Bith shot a glance past the troll's wide shoulders. Bal and Bast, what *was* it? Everything in her first nightmare impression was true. A perverted form of lion with grey vestigial wings and a mockery of a human face. That face stared back at her, *stared* with wide brown eyes, deeper than any animal's. Eyes as deep as a well, as a bottomless pit . . .

Bith shook her head. Dizzy, she stumbled over a rock and fell. The shock of hitting the ground seemed to wake her. What was wrong with her? Ah! She was succumbing to a spell! This was the way she'd felt when her mother had demonstrated control spells to her daughter. But a monster that spelled? Then she knew what it was.

It was a sphinx, the monster with eyes that could hypnotize small animals and weak beings. And men, for some reason.

The men!

"Hey!" Bith shoved at the men's backs. Nothing happened. She put her hand in front of the elf's eyes and waggled

his head. He stood still as a statue. "Cal! Endril, Thor! Wake up! Oh, *please* wake up!"

The beast growled and padded towards her. Panic overwhelmed her and she ran. She hunkered down behind a boulder, and peeped over the top with tears distorting her vision.

Bith watched the lion-thing as it sniffed at the fronts of the three men—or one boy, one troll, and one elf. Damn Endril, she thought, he of all people should have been able to resist the spell! Men were so clumsy at anything cerebral! Bith watched the tufted tail twitch in anticipation of a meal. What to do? To make a spell work—any spell—she'd have to run over there and touch the monster, which would get her bitten in half. What could *she* do to badger a *sphinx*? Ignite it? Confuse it? Enlarge it? (*That* was a brilliant idea!) Oh, wait! Animals hated loud noises. Now if she could just find the right sort of rock . . .

Bith scuttled around, swearing at herself and the monster, and the men and the rocks of this canyon. Then she spotted a stone that looked promising. It was of tough stone with a dark vein of flecking in it. She looked again towards the monster. It had pushed the men over like dummies. It twitched its tail and checked Bith's movements. It licked its chops: it wanted to eat now. Bith bit her lip. She wasn't even sure the spell would work. She rolled the rock in her hands as she tried to remember her mother's words.

Whatever she said must have worked, for the rock began to glow. And glow. It grew hot in her hands and Bith almost dropped it. But that would be death. Clumsily she juggled the glowing stone, trying to look at the sphinx and yet not look. Then she yelled, "Hera and Hermes *help me*!" and threw it.

The explosion in the tight canyon was incredibly loud. Rock splinters shot everywhere. They whined around her ears and ricocheted off the walls to plink into her hair. Too late she thought to duck. But then she hadn't totally believed it would work. A blast spell was for experienced sorcerers, not novices. To do it right one should first place a hold spell on the object, *then* work the blast spell, then get clear and release the hold. What would her mother say if she saw this clumsy attempt?

But it had worked. The sphinx gave a horrid sob and leapt

high in the air (so high that men thought they flew) and landed far down the canyon. That was more than Bith could have hoped for. She whipped her cloak free of her legs and sped to Endril and the rest. The men were all three face up and rigid as statues. Violently Bith wrenched at Endril's shoulders and shook him.

"*Wake up!* Wake *up*, you sanctimonious old curmudgeon! You're going to be *eaten*!" She slapped the elf's pale face and felt his shoulders sag. An eyeball twitched, but no more. He was slipping into unconsciousness. Bith let him go and he fell back limp as a dead fish. She crawled the short distance to the recumbent Hathor and pounded on his chest. Maybe the troll was made of sterner stuff.

Another sob whooped in the canyon, not far away. The sphinx was coming back.

Down the canyon it padded, wary of another blast but driven by hunger. It hopped across boulders as lightly as dandelion fluff. Its face was horrible to see. The twisted human visage had been pulled like putty, tugged forward and round in the cheeks so it resembled the way the sun was portrayed in books. But its mouth was bared in a lion's grimace that showed a lion's sharp teeth. Bith could even smell it now: a stink of ammonia and rotten meat. She gave up on the troll and fumbled for another rock, but none were the right color. The sphinx topped the nearest boulder and loomed over her, blacking out the sky. Could she wield Cal's sword? She wondered what a lion's claws felt like when they struck.

She never found out. As the girl cowered and waited for death, something grey leapt clean over her head and into the sphinx's face. There was a snarl of surprise from the monster, then a grunt as it was rocked back. It tumbled from the rock with something like a great grey spider attached to it.

The battle that followed was shrill and violent. There was a tumult of screeching and snarling and howling and ripping that boomed up and down the ravine. The magic user's curiosity overcame her common sense and Bith latched onto a boulder to pull herself up where she could see.

Something—they thrashed so wildly Bith could barely make it out—had appeared from somewhere to attack the sphinx. The new thing was built like a man, but like no man could be. It was grey all over, naked as a snake, with short legs and two long arms. It had a bald pointed head and big mouth with sharp teeth. And it was *big*—it made the huge sphinx seem no larger than a hound dog.

The giant fought as savagely as the animal. It had clamped its teeth into the sphinx's muzzle. One long arm had the sphinx by a forepaw, and the other hand (or claw) was twisted into the monster's mane. Because its muzzle was locked in a powerful jaw, the sphinx could bite nothing. Having one forepaw trapped in the air meant it couldn't get its balance, and with the man-thing pulling down on its mane, the sphinx's head was tilted painfully.

The sphinx could still sound though, and it did in that painful half-sobbing, half-roar that set Bith's teeth on edge. It keened with pain and rage and humiliation all rolled into one, as if the thing knew it was an abomination with no ancestors, no home, no love or companionship or reason to be. The tortured wail echoed up and down the canyon as the monster felt itself being overpowered.

The grey giant kept after the beast. With its own shark's teeth drawing blood from the sphinx's torn lips, he dragged down inexorably upon the mane while shoving up on the forepaw. The sphinx thrashed madly in the air for a minute, then was flipped over on its back. It went down with a *crash!* Claws windmilled in the air and connected. A rear paw studded with talons whipped around and scored across the giant's chest. Bith shuddered and closed her eyes. The big man's back was towards her, and she thought surely he must have been disembowelled. He'd crumple over and die and the beast would live, and come after her. She started to back over the rocks when there came a scream—the sphinx's.

The giant was still alive, still in command. He held the monster's head down with his left arm, pinning it to the ground. The flailing forepaw was now locked in his teeth. Before the sphinx could rake him again, the giant raised a knotty fist high into the air and slammed it down on the cat's ribcage. Bith heard bones break. The fist sailed up and down again, and again, and each time it pulped bone like tinder. Blood spurted from the cat's nose. The fist rained again and again until the sphinx stopped moving. The giant spat out the limp forepaw and pushed away from the sphinx.

The cat, however, was not dead. Quick as a thought, as a

blur, the beast jerked upright and launched itself at the giant. It crashed into the grey man's chest and spilled him over. Slobbering blood and drool, it fastened its teeth into his face and hung on.

Bith wanted to scream. She felt as if she hadn't drawn a breath since the battle had started, and it seemed she'd been here forever. The giant had to be dead now. What would happen then?

But the giant was unkillable. The two long arms with those rock-like fists rose on either side of the sphinx as it twisted its jaws and tried to rip the giant's face off. When the two fists struck just below the ears the lion-thing was staggered. Rattled, it let go. Its eyes glazed over. The giant's short legs kicked and the creature slid off his body. The sphinx's jaws clacked as its chin banged a rock.

Immediately the giant was up and on it. He grabbed onto the fallen animal's back legs and lifted. Grappling, scrabbling for purchase, the giant folded the monster over backwards, and pressed, and shoved, and strained, until the beast's back legs were almost over its head. Bith hissed through her teeth and peeked between her fingers. She knew what was coming.

With a *snap!* the sphinx's spine broke. The beast gave one last bleat and stopped moving. The color faded from its eyes. The giant let go and the carcass dropped to the ground. The grey giant stood and watched it, unmoving. Rivers of blood trickled down the stone-like surface of his body. All the blood was from the cat.

Then he turned and noticed Bith.

The girl stared, as hypnotized by the giant as she had been by the sphinx. She didn't know whether to be thankful it had saved her life, or fearful that it had saved her for last. Still staring, Bith crept backwards and slid over the edge of the boulder.

She hurried to where her three male companions still lay like toppled trees. She took Endril's face in her hands and patted his cheeks and pried open his eyelids. "Endril! Wake up! I think we're in trouble again! Wake up! Please!"

After few moments the elf did rouse. He slowly reached up a hand and rubbed his face. Then he sat up and looked around. "What's happened?"

Bith waved both hands. "You saw a sphinx and it hexed

you. And Cal and Thor. Understand? But a—giant—or something came from—I don't know where—and killed it. But now he's just on the other side of this boulder—*oh*!''

The elf peered up at the apparition that loomed over them. Tall on the boulder, taller against the sky, the giant seemed taller than the sides of the ravine. Blood and foam and hanks of brown hair still clung to his narrow chest. As they got their first good look at him, they realized he was the strangest being that Bith or even Endril had ever seen.

The giant was over seven feet tall, but his proportions were all wrong. He had a long head, pointed on top, entirely free of hair, with long pointed features uniformly grey. His eyes, pupils and whites, were grey, even his teeth. His skin had a fine soft sheen like a river-polished stone, or a lizard's hide. His shoulders and chest and hips were narrow. His arms were longer than a man's would be, and his legs shorter and bowed, so his hands hung almost to his knees. The hands and feet were equally long, twice as long as a man's, with cat claws. The hands scratched at the long gashes made by the sphinx's black talons, gashes that showed only as fine white lines.

The being stared down at them for a time, then turned and hopped away. After a few moments the girl and elf could hear tearing, rending noises. And the champing of jaws.

''What's been happening?'' Endril asked again.

Bith told him the full story, for the elf could remember nothing after glimpsing the black eyes of the sphinx.

Endril's face was unreadable. He said, ''Why didn't you just run away?''

Bith rubbed her chest, which hurt for some reason. ''What? I—I don't know. I was thinking of too many different spells, or something.'' Her hairline hurt too, and when she rubbed it she found a bump and blood.

Endril rose. ''Or something.'' He roused the boy and the troll by pouring water from a skin onto their faces. He whispered, ''Be cautious. We are not out of the fire yet.''

Cal and Hathor finally got to their feet. Bith spilled her story yet again. At the end the elf pointed. Together the four peeked over the boulder to look at the giant.

The tall creature was just finishing the sphinx. It had cracked open the cat's skull and scooped out the brains. He'd split the belly and gulped down the internal organs, twisted off the legs and munched on the rump and thighs. As the four watched in mixed awe and horror, the giant splintered the leg bones and dug out the marrow with dagger-like fingertips. Bith and Endril grimaced in disgust, but Cal and Hathor found they were hungry.

Suddenly the giant turned and addressed the party in a surprisingly deep voice.

"You are well?"

The party shook their collective heads at the words. It was Endril who finally asked, "Good sir . . . *what*, pray, are you?"

The giant belched and rubbed his chin. He was now entirely covered in gore: dirt, blood, dried spittle, hair, grease. "I? I am a stone giant. Not so big for I'm not old. Ratcatcher is one of my names. Varnog is another. Ratatosk and Grimbod, Thunderer and Smite. Before I was trapped in yon hole I was called Mountain Back Breaker. That is the name I shall use in these days."

"Mountain Back Breaker?" said Cal.

Cal straightened his baldric and checked his sword. The giant's stony fists, swung at the ends of those whip-like arms, must be fearsome weapons. They'd be even deadlier if he chose to expose his talons. Cal thought a fighter couldn't be better equipped, born with built-in maces, daggers, and war hammers.

The giant looked all around the ravine, up at the sky and seemingly beyond. He scratched his chest idly. "Much has changed."

Bith, trying not to look at the naked giant, looked rather at the gaping hole they'd dug and broken open. *"You* were trapped behind that stone? How long were you in there? And *how* did you get in there?"

The deep voice boomed, "I was cast there by demons on a lark. We giants and demons have fought since time unknown. A pack of them thought it amusing to drop a mountain on me." He looked around again. "It's been some time."

The party didn't have much to say to that. Cal asked, "Why did you say your name was Vili when Endril here heard you?"

"I told you. I have many names. Vili is one, after the god of the north country."

"That's what I'd call a vast coincidence, for we are in Vili's—the god's—service these days. Funny you should mention that name to us, of all of them you and the gods have."

The giant only grunted. He picked a bone splinter out of his teeth. "Strange is fate. Glad I am I called my name. Trapped in there, it has been my sorrow to hear everything said by those who've passed this way for many a year. Yet always I was helpless to make myself heard. Hope of rescue has been mine a countless thousand times, yet always it came to naught. I am in your debt."

Endril replied, "And we in yours. You killed yon monster while we were helpless."

"Yes."

Cal filled the silence. "I still think it's a *big*—"

Bith cut him off. "Cal."

The soldier shut up. He reckoned the giant was lying, and he didn't like it. He didn't like anything about this character. The point on his skull reminded Cal of the sharks' fins he'd seen trailing fishing boats. Cal looked around at his companions for some help but they just watched him. He resigned himself to dealing out the harsh words. "Fine, look, uh—Backbreaker—you're free now, free to go wherever you like. We've places to go—"

"And I with you. I would see the world and its changes."

His bony hands joined were a lump of stone larger than Cal's head, and the boy stepped back. The giant's knuckles popped like rocks shattering in frost.

Cal shook his head. "No, I'm sorry. We are four and we plan to stay that way. Am I right, fellows?"

Endril said nothing. Hathor frowned. Bith bit her lower lip. "Where we're going it might be nice to have someone strong with our party—"

"That my job," Hathor interjected.

"Well, of course, yes, Thor," the girl corrected herself. "But to have *two* mighty fellows would be even better."

Endril spoke. "Do you know the reaches to the north of here?"

The giant bobbed his pointed head. "Aye. I am from the north country, the far stony hills."

Cal tried again. "I don't think it's a good idea to sign anyone else on now. We've just worked out our strategies—"

Bith countered, "Why are you in such a hurry to be rid of him? We were in no hurry to be rid of *you*!"

"Yes, you were! You weren't going to be seen with a stableboy, remember?"

"That was a long time ago."

Cal hesitated. He wasn't himself sure why he wanted to leave this giant behind. Some warrior's instinct just told him to stay clear. But here was Bith complicating things. And glaring at him. "Fine, fine. Never mind. What's one more? Let's be walking north."

The giant nodded. "Let's. I would stretch my legs."

Bith said, "Ummm . . . do you think . . . you could . . . find something to wear? It's, ummm, cold at night. . . ."

Endril had retrieved his bow and inspected the string. He said to the giant, "She would have you cover your nakedness."

The giant glanced down at his filthy body. "This? T'is not a tradition among us to wear the skins of dead things."

The elf pointed to the split hide of the sphinx. "Where we go it is. I suggest you garb yourself in yon skin. T'will ease our minds."

The giant shrugged and picked up the skin. He ripped off some loose strings, poked rents in it with his fingers, and pulled it over his body. It covered what was necessary to cover, Bith was glad to see.

"Fine," Endril said. "Does that suit you, good Bith?"

Bith nodded, her cheeks afire. She strapped her blanket roll over her shoulder and took off after Cal down the canyon.

Cal, in the lead for once, stopped and checked on his companions. Endril was nowhere to be seen. Bith strode along with her decorous sway and her head held high. Hathor stumped along behind her like a dog. Mountain Back Breaker trod along in his sphinx skin.

Cal faced forward and marched. He grizzled to himself, "*That* fellow ought to charm the locals. A *fine* kettle of fish. Soon we'll be an *army* of outcast misfits and *still* have no leader."

So saying he passed from the head of the ravine and out on the flat again. Far to his left the great wall of cloud clung to the earth like dirty wool. It was sunset and the cloud cast a shadow on the land before it. A long and dark shadow.

• • •

Six days later they were still marching over the yellow plain. They could see the land dipped ahead, all across the horizon, and they wondered where the land went.

Endril popped into sight up there, as sudden as a hare. As usual, he'd been on point. Now he waved them down with long sweeps of his hands. They hunkered into the tall grass and waited. Endril joined them, practically on his belly.

"We arrive. There be scouts about. Follow me to shelter. Keep low, off the skyline."

The party crept awkwardly through the grass, across scree, and into a rocky fissure. The fissure terminated at the edge of a bluff that overlooked a wide valley. The strung-out party reached the edge and stopped one by one. Endril first, flowing like a ghost, Cal scuffling in his broken boots, Bith with her light step, Hathor with his sturdy stamp. And bringing up the rear came Backbreaker, scrabbling as much with his arms as his short legs.

They gazed down into the valley and were silent.

The valley ran east-west. The eastern arm flowed out of sight. Green conifers and red-yellow hardwoods dotted the slopes of yellow grass. The western arm was shut off by the Mistwall, tall, silent, roiling. On the opposite side of the valley, two or three miles away, the land rose again in a gentle slope before striking mountains that ran off into infinity. The peaks were stark, inhospitable. They looked impassable. This valley, then, was where the fabled and mysterious highlands began.

Directly across from the party, caught between the fertile valley floor and the sharp mountains, was a flattened slope, or shelf. On this shelf was a castle with a small village around it.

Castle Cairngorm.

The castle perched at the farthest end of the shelf. Behind the shelf dropped off into a chasm. The castle was not big as castles go, nor were its grounds or the village expansive. But it was singularly awe-inspiring in that the stone structure literally hung upon the lip of the shelf, as delicately balanced as a butterfly on a leaf. It reminded Cal of a seagull riding placidly on the crest of a giant wave. The castle was squat, with a single tower: the tower was actually stepped *over* the chasm, or so it looked from the party's angle.

What was on the other side of this chasm they could not tell, for the Mistwall pressed close around the castle in a semicircle, as if eager to eat it up, but afraid to begin.

The front of the settlement, the landward side, was ringed by two stone walls upon which soldiers could be seen. So the place was inhabited.

And pressing as close to the front of the castle as the Mistwall did the back, covering the valley floor, was an army.

It was a varied and multicolored army, with little uniformity and no obvious discipline. The adventurers on the bluff could see pennants and cooking fires and spits and tents and lean-tos and pots and bones and garbage scattered over what had been fertile fields. There were figures of all sizes, some knee-high, some twice taller than a man. All of them moved with curious crabbing motions.

The mob looked like a sprawling nest of spiders.

Endril pointed his short bow to where a steady stream of figures issued forth, like a black train of ants, from the Mistwall itself.

"Behold," the elf pronounced, and his voice was so ominous they all felt a chill.

"The Dark Lord's Army."

CHAPTER
6

It was Endril who spoke first. "Magic."

"Eh?" The humans had been hypnotized by the sight of the awful army—there were so many of them!

"Magic," he repeated. "Yon castle, how it hangs in the air. Some powerful talisman holds it thus, else it would have tumbled into the depths long ago. 'Tis magic and not mortar at work. I should not be surprised if it's that which we seek."

"Hunh?" said Cal.

"He means," Bith translated, "it's probably Vili's sword keeping that castle up. There are very few other artifacts that could, especially in such remote regions and shabby surroundings. I wonder that I never heard of this castle's wizard. With such power, his name should be known far and wide."

Cal adjusted his baldric, loosened his sword in its scabbard, then shot it home. "I could have said that castle was our goal without knowing anything about magic."

"And how's that?" Bith asked.

"Because if a god needs us to find a sword, where else would it be but between the Mistwall and an army of orcs?"

The five travelers looked down at the valley and collectively sighed. Endril sat down and set his back against a slope.

Bith smoothed her cloak behind and perched on a rock. Cal took out a dagger to point out aspects of the army and mutter to himself. Hathor sat at the edge of the fissure and swung his big, dirty, hairy, black-toenailed feet like a child. Backbreaker scratched a hairless armpit.

After a long time—long enough for the sun to drop behind the Mistwall and so elongate its shadow far across the doomed valley—Cal spoke. "That's it, then."

"What?" Bith asked him.

"We can't do it."

"We must," replied Endril.

Cal shook his head. "There's no way."

Bith looked from one to the other. "What are you talking about?"

"This task, this trip," Cal answered. "We're done. We tell Vili to go fish up a tree. We're finished."

"We gave our bond," Endril intoned.

"We gave our bond," Cal replied with heat in his voice, "to venture north and see if we can retrieve Vili's sword. Well, we did, and here we are, and I for one say we can't do it."

Bith asked, "Are you afraid?"

Cal pointed to his chin with his dagger. "There's a stupid question. I've a scar right here to prove I'm not. I've fought in battles, two anyway, and I needn't prove anything to some girl raised on her mother's lap and fed on white bread. I'm a soldier to the bone, and I can tell you you might as well fall on your sword *here* as walk down *there*. Five people do not attack an army. It wouldn't be brave, it'd be plain stupid."

As if in echo, a howl sounded from the valley below. The noise was neither human nor animal.

It was quiet for a while, then Endril said, "To walk away would not, methinks, be as simple as you describe. Gods have long memories and hold grudges to suit. We've promised Vili to try and he will expect it of us, or find ways to make us pay. And we gave our bond."

Cal asked, "Will you lead the charge?"

"There are other ways than direct attack."

"Such as?"

"Outflank them."

"Have you no eyes? They encircle the castle."

"Not to the mountains."

"Those mountains are sheer rock! And if there are scouts over here—" Cal remembered that and lowered his voice "—there are bound to be more over there. A fly couldn't get through those lines."

The troll's gruff voice startled them. "Caves."

Cal asked, "Where?"

The troll pointed to the mountains. "In mountains."

"How can you tell?"

"Can just tell."

Cal shook his head some more. "Orcs come from caves. They'd be thickest there."

"Infiltrate the army," said the elf.

"Good luck. We're white as ghosts compared to that lot. Bith especially wouldn't get past the first flank. Not whole."

Beside him the girl shuddered, but Cal didn't try to retract his words. It was madness to proceed, and Cal was wary of the elf's powers of persuasion. He'd have them marching to the walls in a parade, singing, if he talked long enough.

Indeed, the elf turned to Bith. "Could you fly over them?"

Bith shook her head.

"We must join them, then," Endril said.

"Take prisoners." Hathor grunted.

Cal asked. "What? What good would taking prisoners do? No one would ransom them."

Hathor pointed to the three fair people, then Backbreaker. "Take you prisoners. Him, me. Tie you up. March to edge of army, ask to see leader. Walk right through. No one touch us."

"Why would no one touch us?"

"Whole army afraid of leader. Prisoners be brought to him. Anyone interfere, cut head off. We walk right to wall, jump over."

Cal waved a hand in the air. "Wait a minute, Hathor. Let me get this right. *You're* going to tie us up and lead us down there as prisoners, right through their lines, to the leader's tent? And how do *you* know about their leader?"

The troll ignored Cal's second question. "No, take you to wall."

"Not I." This from Endril.

Cal whipped his head around. "What do you mean, not

you? Who's the one carping about our bond? Who's the one keeping us here?''

Endril was placid. ''You are the one keeping yourself here, so blame not others. But no, I cannot go amidst that army. The smell of an elf would bring a thousand orcs on a rampage that no leader could stop. I'd be hacked to pieces in a trice. That part is impossible.''

Cal asked, ''But we lesser *humans* get to be trussed up like chickens? How do *you* propose to be of any use?''

''I can enter the castle by my own ways. But none can come with me. As it is, I may not arrive at all.''

Cal pointed his dagger. ''Look, I've had it up to *here* with your high-and-mighty elfness! Anything you do is fine for *you*, but not for *us*! We're just sheep to be led to the slaughter—where are you going?''

Endril stood and swung his bow in his hand. ''Hathor's is a suitable plan. I shall endeavor to meet you inside the castle walls when you arrive. If I do not arrive, then I never shall. May you walk in peace.'' He climbed the shelf and looked around. Then he crept out onto the grassy plain, into the gathering gloom.

Cal put his hand to his hilt and trotted after him. He hissed. ''Hey, you! Wait up! Who do you—where'd he go?''

Bith scurried up beside him. Together they crouched and peered into the dusk. They could still see some distance across the plain, and there was nothing to obstruct their vision. No trees, no rocks.

Cal kicked the toe of his boot. ''*Damn him!* Damn him to whatever hell he fears. What a—a *snot!*''

He turned to look at Bith and found Hathor and Backbreaker looming in the near-dark. Their outlines against the grey sky were chilling. Hathor had a coil of rope. ''Good plan, start now. We tie you up.''

Cal backed around and this time drew his sword a good four fingers from its scabbard. ''Hold on, here! I haven't agreed to a thing yet! We're still just talking—*hey!*''

Hathor lunged and with one sweep of his foot knocked Cal sprawling. The heavy-muscled body crashed onto his chest and knocked the wind from him while the nimble and broad feet pinned his arms. Cal was as helpless as a trout on the shore. Bith cried out once before Backbreaker covered her

mouth and entire face with his monstrous hands. Cal unleashed a truly spectacular string of swear words as the coarse
rope was wrapped around his torso. Hathor unhitched the
boy's baldric, and slung it and his shield over one shoulder.

Five minutes later, bound like squabs, Cal and Bith were
being frog-marched down the long slope towards the valley
and its invading army.

Hathor towed the humans along with no more trouble than
a child dragging a branch. Backbreaker stamped behind.

The first pluck at Hathor's memory came as he reached the
floor of the valley. Across the tall billowing grass came a
whiff, an odor, a scent—of home. The rope around the two
humans jerked taut as they caught the smell, but Hathor
dragged them on. Along with the rotten-egg and low-tide
smell of the Mistwall came the stink of orc dung and urine,
bad meat, unwashed bodies, dried blood, rancid hides, pus,
corruption, vomit, and the thousand other smells of several
thousand soldiers packed in one place. Hathor flared his nostrils and took a deep breath. To someone raised in a warren
of dank caves inhabited by cannibal trolls since the beginning
of time, it was like old times. Hathor discarded his man's
hat, tightened his grip on his axe, and marched.

The humans twitched at the end of their rope but Hathor
just hauled harder. The captives had two choices; walk or be
dragged. The giant Mountain Back Breaker chivvied them
along.

Exposed by firelight, the black mass of troops resolved into
detail.

The first thing they passed, at the outer fringes of the army,
was a trio of ogres. These were he-ogres, each as wide as
two men. Evidently they preferred the outskirts where they
had room to move. They wore wide bullhides clumsily
stitched and stretched across their hairy backs and legs. They
looked not at all sinister, but rather like fat greengrocers
blown out of proportion. But one with a gleaming bald head
wore two human skulls in helmets as earrings. The ogres
watched the troll and giant and their prisoners pass without
comment.

The next group was a large party of orcs, some thirty or
so, small hunched creatures with craggy faces and pointed

ears. They wore scraps of armor or nothing at all. They looked greedily at the trussed humans but fearfully at the striding troll and giant. One of them yipped like a coyote as they passed.

Hathor jerked to a halt. He turned in surprise and found Cal leaning back on the rope. The boy had planted his boots against a rock and snubbed the rope tight. Hathor quickly released his hold and Cal tumbled backwards. The troll stomped angrily and loomed over the boy. The fangs in his lower jaw champed as he shouted, "What you do? Get up or I kill you!"

Cal stayed where he was. Bith had stopped too and hunkered down behind him, trying to make herself small. Cal swore a soldier's oath and hissed, "Thor! This is madness! We'll never get out alive!"

Hathor kicked with his bare feet at Cal's boots, and it was the boy who winced. The troll raised his felling axe high aloft and shook it. "You get up *now*!" he thundered. "Or I break both legs and drag you!"

Cal's eyes shot hate at the troll. Bith's flickered to one side. Approaching them was a party of three beings. Trolls, just like Hathor.

The lead troll was as big as Hathor and even deeper in the chest. His grubby hair was the same washed-out color as his greasy fur vest and kilt. He sported a bandolier with three hatchets in it. The other trolls were smaller. One wore a wrapping of grimy cloth and carried a war club studded with obsidian. The other wore only a loincloth. A hideous pucker covered one whole side of his face. The eye on that side was white as a boiled egg. He carried a mallet.

The foremost of the trolls rumbled something to Hathor in his own tongue. It sounded to the humans like a dogfight. He appeared friendly enough towards his brethren, though the grimace on his face revealed four yellow fangs. Hathor only growled something short and turned back to his prisoners. He wrenched savagely on the rope, hard enough to bring a bleat of pain from Bith.

The one-eyed troll stepped around the leader. With a snarling laugh he started to say something to Hathor, but was cut off. Hathor roared, "I said, *go away*!" and lashed out. The back of the heavy woodsman's axe caught the troll square in the face. Cal and Bith heard a sickening crunch. Blood flew. The troll went down to writhe on the trampled grass. Hathor hauled the two humans to their feet by main strength. He set off through the army without looking back at his kin. Cal did look. The two trolls had walked away and left their compatriot twisting in the grass.

"Bast and Belial!" Bith whimpered. "Did you see what he did?"

"I saw," Cal grated.

The girl glanced over her shoulder, but the sight of the grey-skinned alien Backbreaker was unnerving. "Something's wrong with Hathor."

"Nothing's wrong with him. He's gone back to his own kind, is all."

Bith quavered, "I can't believe that."

"Believe what you want."

"What will happen to us, Cal?"

Cal stared straight ahead without seeing anything. "If we're lucky, someone will kill us right away."

Bith bit her lip and cried without tears.

Cal was glad it was full night now, for it meant less to see. Dogs scuttled up to bark at them, skinny cowardly things that fought with each other. Dead ones roasted in the fire. One pack fought over the guts of their brother. Ugly trophies and war booty were to be seen at every hand. A lady's velvet gown, torn and stained with blood, hung on a spear along with a scalp. A gilt hand mirror winked from a scabby shield. One orc tore leaves from a book to transport fire. Others sat on a green woven carpet. Cal counted with hard eyes every helmet on every hideous head, all of which had to be human—or dwarven-made, for none of the lesser speaking races could work metal. He counted over two hundred before he gave up. There were men's swords, men's shields, men's spears, and more.

The noise was equally horrid. A hooting went up ahead where two small beings knife-fought by a fire. Far away a bubbling scream went on and on, the product of torture.

Every step—dragged foot by foot—brought the two humans deeper into the Dark Army and brought them more attention. Dark twisted shapes pointed and gibbered and laughed at the two prisoners. Cal kept his eyes forward and looked at nothing. Bith kept her eyes on Cal's back.

Hathor trudged along with slit eyes. He growled or spat at anyone who even hinted at getting in his way. He tried to recognize the minions of the Dark Lord's army. They were mostly orcs in all shapes and sizes. There were a handful of giants, at least two tribes of trolls, gnolls like upright jackals, tiny twisted pink piglets, and some species of speaking races that Hathor could not identify. He saw females of various races too. Dull-eyed, they tended fires or scraped skins or carried water while the males jeered them. They were as skinny and filthy as the dogs, with less spirit. Far off, over the shorter orcs, Hathor could see patches of bronzed skin. Those were men, soldiers who had turned their hand to the Dark Lord's service. Their heads swivelled and fixed on the smallest in Hathor's party—they'd spotted a human woman at half a mile in the dark. Calling to one another, they picked up their weapons and started to push their way through.

Hathor scanned as he walked, looking for some sign of authority. He was far enough across the valley now that he had to pick up his chin to see the castle at the top of the hill. The pitch of the hill was steep, steep enough that a man would need one hand for his weapon and one hand to climb. And the slope was flinty and crumbly, supporting no weeds or trees. In the reflected light of fires he could see, some two hundred feet away, the first wall. Helmeted heads with dark faces underneath peered over it, motionless. A hundred feet behind that was the second wall, and just behind that, the blackened castle. From here Hathor could see its outlines were soft. The castle was old and crumbling. The well-lit houses around it were tiny. The two walls that protected the community had fresh stonework and no moss. There were no living invaders on the slopes. Only a goat could rest there. But there were occasional bodies prickled with arrows. Dogs pulled at them.

Hathor scanned the terrain to either side of him. Ahead, at the front edge of the army and closest to the wall (though not close enough to invite arrows) were the army's only tents, therefore those of the leaders. A half-dozen small tents formed a ring around a very large one. Flagpoles made an avenue to this tent. Pennants stirred in a night breeze. Large guards faced one another across this corridor.

A shout from their left made Hathor turn around. A cluster of soldiers—men—were coming their way. They had their heads high and their swords loose.

Bith gasped. "Quick, Hathor! We must away! They'll take me!"

Cal grunted, "He doesn't care."

The girl shuddered. "Please, Hathor! They'll kill you to get me! They'll cut you down!"

Hathor turned right abruptly, so abruptly that a cluster of orcs did not part quick enough. He crashed his axe onto the head of one and then kicked the body out of the way with his big feet. He shoved onward through the crowd in the direction of the tents, towing his prisoners behind. He heard a growl behind as Mountain Back Breaker snarled at someone.

The crowd was thicker here—and more foul—and they clustered around. The human soldiers shouted after Hathor. A fight was in the air and the bloodthirsty crowd wanted to see. Hathor broke free of the press and found himself in the only open space—the corridor of trampled grass leading to the largest tent. The soldiers were not far behind. He jerked at the rope to snub his prisoners tight. A flag hung just overhead, brushing the troll's curly hair.

"What now?" Cal spit in his face, "You collect a reward?" Bith only bit her lower lip.

The two humans' eyes widened in surprise as Hathor hissed, "Turn around. I loosen ropes. You can hold them?"

Cal frowned. Bith was quicker to recover. She whispered too. "I can put a hold spell on them. Oh, Thor, I *knew* you were still with us! But what shall we do?"

The troll nodded a fraction of an inch up the hill. "Run for wall. I don't know if we can make it, but we try. Those men close. You right, Cal, this bad idea."

Cal only grunted, but it was a relieved grunt with a hint of apology, a soldier's only acknowledgement that he had been wrong. He spun around as if he had been slapped and presented his bound hands for Hathor to "tighten." Bith did the same. Cal heard her whisper a spell and suddenly his bonds were tighter than before. But she shot him a quick, tight, smile. Cal smiled back, then frowned anew as the troll spoke.

"Hey? where Backbreaker go?"

The others looked. The giant was gone. Tall as he was, he should have stood out easily. But there was no sign.

Cal croaked, "Good riddance—"

Hathor jumped. A large orc, grey-faced, with spiky black hair sticking out all over, loomed over them. He wore shiny black armor like a turtle's shell. He carried a halberd.

"What you do here?" he growled. Hathor growled in reply. The orc pointed with a forefinger like a dagger. "What these?"

Hathor glanced around him. The crowd was thick on all sides. There was seemingly half an army between them and the bottom of the slope. They could hear the voices of the men soldiers swearing filthy oaths as they tried to push through. Hathor looked for a way out. He snarled at the orc and spit on the ground.

"Prisoners."

The orc pointed at the big tent. "They go there."

The troll hefted his axe, and tried to think. The flags flapped overhead and the humans looked up. The rope in Hathor's hand suddenly snapped taut. He looked at Cal and then looked up.

Overhead were standards: pennants and banners, each one a different color and pattern, each one representing a king or kingdom, a particular army, or a large and prestigious band of heroes. There were so many standards they could not even be set side by side, but were rather clustered like sheaves of spears. There must have been hundreds of them, each one representing a portion of the world lost to the Dark Lord and his army.

Cal stared upwards as if hypnotized, fixed on a single sheaf of pennants. To Hathor they looked much the same: a yellow streamer with a red dragon, a blue square with four crowns filled with stars, a orange and white striped flag with a black bar, a green rectangle sporting a red eagle with a fish in its beak. . . .

"My father," the boy whispered. "My father . . ."

The orc guard prodded Cal with his halberd. The boy jumped sideways but did not otherwise move. He only whis-

pered again and stared upwards. The orc raised his pike high
to split the human in half—

The shaft of his halberd *slam*med against something solid.
Twin grunts sounded. The head of Hathor's axe had stopped
the orc's halberd as solidly as a rock. The two weapons became the focus of a contest. The orc flexed his muscles and
pressed downwards: Hathor gritted his fangs and pressed up.
All this time the blade of the halberd quivered inches over
Cal's head, but the boy was oblivious. He whispered and only
Bith could hear him. "So he's really dead. He's really, really—dead. Dead . . ."

Bith tried to do what she could with her hands tied. She
shoved the boy with her shoulder. "Cal. *Cal! Wake up, Cal!
Please!*" Another shove almost sent him sprawling. "Cal,
we have to *go*!"

The boy shook his head and looked at her as if at a stranger.
He glanced back towards the sky.

Hathor huffed, "*Hyah!*" and threw off the orc's halberd.
He stared the orc down, picked up the tail of the rope, and
dragged his prisoners into the dim tent of the Dark Army's
leader.

The night air had been chilly, but it was hot inside this
tent. The interior was lit all with yellow, from a hundred
candles, from torches, from the glint of gold. The floor of
wheat had yellowed from lack of sun. There were blond rugs
and skins piled around. The light reflecting on the canvas roof
suffused the glow. After the dark night and dark things they
had seen, the inside of the tent was dazzling as a fairyland.

The inhabitants were not. The sagging canvas, itself hot
and stale, trapped an eye-smarting stink of stale sweat and
spoiled food that was worse than outside. Dark as spiders
were myriad guards and hangers-on, whispering or croaking
or arguing with one another. These were mostly the larger
burly orcs that stood outside as guards, along with some trolls
and coarse men and some olive-skinned creatures, hairless
and fish-eyed, that none of the party recognized. The first
humans Bith noticed were the concubines who lolled around
the throne. They were huge coarse women clad only in taw-
dry makeup and body tattoos and rolls of their own fat. No,
there was only one dazzling person in the tent.

The man on the throne.

He was the biggest man any of the three had ever seen. Cal, who had seen some large soldiers, reckoned his height at close to seven feet. As it was, he was taller sitting down than Cal was standing up. The man's skin was brown from the sun, a healthy glow that contrasted sharply with the dark-loving creatures who served him. His body rippled with muscle: his skin looked tighter than a snake's. But something had happened to his body, or was happening. It was somehow pushed to it limits. His chest was overlarge, bigger than a barrel, and they could hear his abnormal breathing from where they stood thirty feet away. His features might once have been handsome, but now they were—what? overdeveloped? His chin, his ears, his nose, his brow, all were enlarged. Even his teeth were big as a horse's. His hair was thick and blond, yet lifeless, like sun-baked thatch. Cal thought he had never seen a man so fit and yet so on the verge of dying in his life. The man—the leader of the Dark Lord's Army—stared at them with wide white eyes with yellow centers. He raised a hand as big as a lion's paw and waved them forward.

Hathor gently pulled on the slack rope between them. Together the three advanced across that hot, steaming space. The crowd quieted as Hathor, Bith, and Cal stopped in the middle of the tent. Their legs would carry them no further. It grew very still in the tent. The only sound was the hoarse breathing of the giant before them.

When the three didn't move and the silence drew on, the leader left his chair—a throne of gold, with more gold and jewels heaped around it. He advanced upon them without a word. They could see now he wore a breechclout of some tawny hide that still bore a tufted tail like the sphinx's. Otherwise he was naked except for jewelry. His chest was hung with pendants and chains, his arms were adorned above and below the elbows with bands of copper and gold and silver. His shaggy head with its tiny gold circlet brushed the tent in places. He towered over the three. Cal, who was tall, had to crane his head back to look at the man. His chest heaved and they could smell his breath, curiously sweet. Sweat rolled down the leader's breast and trickled off his nipples. His mouth hung open as he panted like a horse run thirty miles.

Twice the man licked his lips as he looked down at the

party. Cal felt his legs turning to water. Bith wanted to cry. Hathor wished he were back in his cave deep below ground. The man reached out a great hand and brushed the boy and troll aside. He spoke only to Bith.

"What brings *you* here?"

CHAPTER
7

No one, especially Bith, knew what to say to this golden giant and his strange question, so they said nothing.

The silence in the yellow-hued tent dragged out. The various retainers watched their master and waited. Cal and Bith and Hathor stared up at the man, as trapped and helpless and confused as flies in a web.

The leader of the Dark Army spoke. "No answer, good woman? It's unlike you. You've always had a loose tongue and a sharp wit. Or is it the other way around?"

The man's eyes were staring yet unfocused. Cal looked at Bith, Bith looked at Hathor, Hathor looked at Cal. All three swallowed. They were suddenly thirsty. Maybe it was the giant's panting that did it.

The leader put his massive hands out in the air. He waved them gently and leaned towards Bith. "Speak! How is it we find you here on the wrong end of a rope? Is your magic gone? If so, we are all in dire straits indeed!"

Bith let go her lip from her teeth and stammered, "S-sire—"

"*Sire!*" The giant barked and made her jump. "Sire! *She* calls *me* sire!" He roared with laughter and the retainers about tittered along with him, though clearly none understood the joke.

"Sire! A goodly jest, Morea! What unguessable misfortune has befallen you?" The giant leaned close and peered into Bith's tiny face. "Gog and Magog, what queer times we live in!"

Cal and Hathor were dumbfounded. What had he called Bith? Morea? But that was the name of Bith's—

The name—and the truth—had tolled like a bell in Bith's mind. Tossing her nose in the air and straightening her back, she gave a haughty shake of her head. "So," she pronounced, "you've recognized us."

The giant laughed again, a deep hearty laugh that rattled their breastbones. "No man who'd seen you would forget you. It's said all through the Mistlands—"

"Stop!"

The man stopped.

Bith shrugged her shoulders, a ripple that made her lithe body shimmer bewitchingly. She rapped a command, a ringing cry in some obscure language. Then her hands were free and entwined over her head. The ropes had fallen behind her onto the dead grass. The crowd murmured.

Bith proclaimed, "I need my false bonds no longer then. The ruse had failed."

"Yes," said the giant, though he was now as befuddled as anyone else. Cal found himself wishing for a cool day and a clean hot battle—or anything he could understand.

Bith wiggled her fingers and the giant stepped back. "Feed us," she commanded. "Bring wine."

The leader barked and servants scuttled away. He backstepped to his throne and waved Bith after him, deferentially. She came, demurely. The leader of this vast army clearly considered her an equal. He shouted for a chair and one was brought, a heavy wooden chair carved with intricate designs. Bith nodded towards the painted harlots and they were dismissed. Hathor and Cal tried to remain invisible.

Bith was served wine and fresh fruit. She ate decorously and talked with the leader (whose name Cal and Hathor still didn't know). Conversation flickered back and forth between the two like fire between dragons. It ranged through a half dozen languages that only they could follow.

The talk went something like this:

He: "I ask you again, what brings you here in these circumstances?"

She: "Circumstances change."

"The Mistwall?"

"It moves, does it not?"

"We drive it like wolves before sheep."

"Or it drives you."

"Soon we'll have all the speaking races under our thrall."

"And what is your position then?"

"Exalted leader. Supreme among men. Second only to the Dark Lord. Almost a god. And you?"

"I?"

"Yes, you. Would you stay here?"

"In this chair?"

"Don't tease. At my side."

"There's room there only for a sword."

"At night a man needs a woman."

"Morea is more than a woman."

"Queen, then."

"Empress?"

"As you wish."

As they bantered back and forth, Cal whispered to Hathor. "What the *hell* are they talking about?"

Hathor muttered without moving his lips. "Don't know."

"He keeps calling her Morea. That's her *mother*. And something about an alliance," Cal said.

"More than that," the troll replied.

Cal hissed, "Don't *you* start talking like them. We'll all go mad." He thought a moment. "We better find out his name. It's clear Bith doesn't know it."

Hathor grunted again. He took a step and caught a passing orc by the arm. He squeezed as he demanded, "What his name? Quick!"

The orc twisted as he replied. "Schlein. Him Schlein, leader all armies."

Hathor released the creature. He asked Cal, "How we tell Bith?"

"Beats me. What are they doing now, arguing?"

The conversation had become even more arcane—some of it in elven, some in the Old High Tongue and some in a weird, clacking cant. Schlein's voice had taken on an abrasive edge. The giant was fingering his beltline. Cal couldn't tell if he was straightening the tilt in his kilt or reaching for a knife. Bith's voice grew shrill as a crow's.

"I'll not be subservient to *any* man, god, or demon in *any* of the seven planes! I say you grant me a retinue *now*, access to a laboratory *now*, and such materials as I need, *now* and when I have had time to gather my intelligence and energies, *then* and *only* then shall I speak more of marriage or otherwise!"

Schlein's tone hovered somewhere between placating and commanding. "You misinterpret my advances, mistress. I need to know better your—skills, so we can *together*—"

Hathor and Cal had crept forward, Cal shuffling because his hands were still bound behind him. They stood behind Bith unnoticed, though retainers and guards pressed closer. Hathor nodded at Cal. The boy girded his loins, waited for a pause and then spoke as quietly as he could into Bith's ear. "Mistress, wouldst you and Exalted *Schlein* . . ."

Schlein, who'd obviously been planning his next attack on Bith, snapped his head around. "How *dare* you! Interrupt *us*? Guards! Take these two out and kill them! Drain their blood and prepare them for the fire!"

Hathor's and Cal's eyes flew wide open. Bith leapt up from her seat and waved her arms. "*Kill* my retainers? How dare *you*! No one kills my staff but *me*!"

In his turn Schlein leapt up, rocking his heavy gold throne. He stabbed out a hand and had slapped into it the hilt of a great jeweled sword that glittered in the torchlight. "I *dare*! You forget your place and position! No witch woman can resist *me*, mistress of the sacred arts or not! Guards! I say *kill* these two and roast them! They'll grace our table and Morea herself shall eat their hearts!"

Bith rotated her hands and rattled a short arcane phrase like a curse. Crushing something in her left hand, she reached up and put her right hand on the sword hilt. She smiled sweetly up into Schlein's face and the giant paused, uncertain. Then a column of flame shot up the blade of his sword and ignited the tent.

Dusty and dry from a thousand suns, the sheet of canvas became a sheet of flame within a heartbeat. Schlein howled and dropped his sword. The adventurers smelt scorched flesh. Bith jumped away from his swinging paw and bumped into Cal. The tent flooded with smoke and the screams of fifty dark minions. Schlein howled curses and called a dozen orders at once that no one heeded. Cal called to Bith, who stood six inches away, *"What do we do?"*

"What else? We run!"

Everyone else was doing the same. A torrent of fetid flesh pushed and shoved and screamed to get out the doorway of the tent, shoving others to progress to safety. It was impossible to see in the eye-smarting smoke. The stench of the room, the heat, and the smoke left nothing to breathe, and the party's lungs cried for air. Hathor kept a heavy hand on his two friends as he half-helped, half-dragged them towards a wall. Blackness gaped where someone had picked up the side of the tent. Hathor brushed at rumps with his axe and shouted for his friends to follow.

They popped outside into what now seemed pure, sweet, night air. They had collected two deep breaths when Bith called, "Come on! This way!"

The girl tucked her cloak up and bolted. She ran past the front of the tent and towards the slope and the distant wall. Hathor took off after her with long dog-like lopes of his bowed legs. Cal struggled to keep his balance as he ran.

"Hey, hold it! I'm still tied!"

Bith whirled, chirped a word, and Cal's bonds fell away as if cut with a knife. Pins and needles shot fire up his arms. He waggled his hands to get some life in them as he ran after the whippet Bith and her sheepdog Hathor, who handed him back his sword and shield.

Confusion was king around the leaders' tents. Guards, retainers, servants, women, and soldiers ran hither and thither on whatever errands they chose to pursue. They ran toward or away from the tents as their whim took them. People called for buckets, for blood, for battle, and for booty. Men waved swords in the air and shouted without knowing why. Orcs shrilled and slapped one another in their fear. Dogs barked.

Bith pulled her hood up and ducked her head. She twisted and turned among the crowd unnoticed. Hathor nudged or threatened people with his axe, but did not hit anyone for fear of getting bogged down in a fight. Cal put an ugly grimace on his scarred face and made no eye contact. Strung thin and constantly moving, they dodged and darted their way to the front line.

Then they were in the clear. Cal looked up. Two hundred feet away, up a forty-five degree slope, was the first wall. It was lined with more helmets now, and more torches. He panted, "Do we just run up there?"

Bith was hunkered down, trying to look small. She snapped, "What else would you have us do?"

Cal looked right and left. "I see no archers down here, but the defenders up there will probably nail us before we get half way. We're caught between two forces."

"But we're friends."

The boy gasped, "Yes, but the people up *there* don't know that! They'd probably shoot first and wonder later."

"Well, we can't stay *here*!"

Hathor grunted agreement.

Cal bit his lip. "You're right, but . . . All right, try this. Hathor and I will go abreast. You go before us."

"Why me?"

"Don't argue, damn it! Pull back your hood so they can see you're a human woman—girl. Then they won't shoot, I hope."

For the first time Bith noticed just how many rotting bodies there were on the slopes, and how most of them were festooned with arrows. She hesitated before she said, "All right, let's try it. I don't want to go back to Schlein."

"Me neither," Hathor and Cal said in unison.

Bith pulled back her hood. Her face was flushed and lovely in the flickering firelight. "Here we go!"

Together the three mounted the slope.

They were halfway when a shout sounded behind them. The shout was picked up to carry throughout the army. The trio imagined they could hear the booming voice of Schlein thundering above everyone else. Cal called, "Keep going! Don't look around! That costs time!" They scrabbled with their hands up the flinty slope.

A black arrow hit the slope wide of them. It came from behind. "Don't stop!" Cal shouted. "Orcs are lousy shots!" With that something knocked off his leather helmet. He let it tumble down the slope.

Bith's yellow boot slipped on the scree and she fell and banged her face. Blood started from a scrape on her chin. Cal and Hathor both reached for her but she shook her hands at them. "Never mind! Climb! We're almost there!"

And they were. Another thirty feet would bring them to the foot of the wall. Of course, getting over it was another concern, but even so Cal shouted, "We're going to make it! *Hel-lo up there—*"

His voice was cut off as something grabbed his boot and slammed him to a halt. He spun, clawing for his sword. In the black night against the grey slope, black shapes scuttled among the still ones. A swarm of large orcs were after them— and were upon them.

The orc attached to Cal clutched his boot in one hand and a jagged knife in the other. With an animal howl he raised his arm to plunge down the knife. Cal kicked him in the face with his free foot. That orc fell over backwards into another and the two skittered a dozen feet down the slope. Then Cal was up with his antique sword and swinging.

He swopped overhand for the head of the next advancing orc, but instead lost his footing on the treacherous slope and fell himself, hard on his rump. Bith bleated behind him: he must have just missed her with the backswing of the sword. Hathor roared and pitched a rock that caught another orc in the chest. The creatures paused in their ascent. Three humans with weapons in hand faced them from the advantage of height. There was no way to carry the attack. Instead the monsters settled for shouting and howling and chucking rocks of their own. Cal tried to keep his guard up and rise at the same time, but he didn't dare: he'd pitch headlong and be among them in seconds. Bith shouted too but did nothing else, since she couldn't touch an enemy to spell him. The only other spell she could think of was a light spell, which was not a good idea. Steel-headed arrows struck sparks all around them. Rotten shots or not, enough shafts sent their way would find a mark.

Something—a thrown axe—bounced off Cal's shield. The blow knocked him off balance. Hathor hooted and shuffled his way even as a giant black shape rose before him. An orc had a war axe raised high, ready to split Cal in half. The boy winced involuntarily. This was going to hurt.

A *zop!* sounded, and a crunching noise. The shape fell over backwards to crash on the slope. Then another arrow buzzed, and another, all striking targets. These arrows came from behind the adventurers—from atop the wall.

The orcs howled with rage and disappointment, then took to their heels as a shower of red-fletched arrows fell among them. Hathor, Cal, and Bith risked a glance over their shoulders to see—a ladder!

"Come on!" a mustached man called from the wall. He waved his gauntlet wide. "Quick! Before they change their minds! Get up!"

The three got. The orcs howled loudly but without conviction. Probably, Cal thought, they planned to storm the castle in the next few days. They'd have their revenge then.

Then he was behind the wall and things didn't seem so very bad.

The castle defenders were all good folk and true, men and women with blond hair and clear blue eyes. There were about a hundred and fifty of them all together, all warriors.

The mustached leader introduced himself as Barin, house carl of the kingdom. "Welcome to Cairngorm, friends! What's left of it, anyway. We didn't know what to make of you lot coming up that hill. Thought you were some suicide squad driven mad to attack, or something. We've seen stranger sights along these walls. How ever did you get through that army?"

"You were right. We're suiciders," Cal told him with a soldier's black humor. "And I'm not sure how we did it."

"It was Hathor did it," Bith replied. The three stood on the wall and looked out at the dark valley spread before them. It looked much the same as the view from the opposite side. There were enemies thicker than locusts as far as they could see. "He pretended to be delivering us as prisoners. It got us through."

Barin signalled to a younger man for a torch. He held it up close and studied each one of the three. He peered especially at Hathor. "You'd be a—troll, now wouldn't you, son?"

Hathor grinned and the man stepped back from the fangs. "Yessir. Good troll."

"Never was there a stouter heart, or more honest," Bith added.

"Pulled our tails out of the fire," Cal agreed. His voice was overly gay. "We were for the stew pot. Mercury and Mob! Good job, Hathor! But don't ask me to do it again."

Hathor grinned so his fangs shone. His face was ugly in the torchlight without his battered hat to obscure it. "No. Cal was right. Was bad idea."

"But we're here," Bith breathed. She glanced back at the boiling army of monsters and suddenly had to sit down. Cal and Hathor joined her.

Barin snapped his fingers, a dull sound with his gauntlets on. "Forgive me my manners. You must be fell tired. Farin, fetch some wine, will ye? There's a dear. That's one good thing about the end of a siege. We get to kill the livestock and pillage the cellar. Fresh meat and all the wine we can soak up." He smacked his lips.

The weary adventurers were given flagons of honeyed wine and black bread, roast meat and cheese. "We've broached casks and sampled wine until we're pickled. Good for these cold nights, it is. We've even watered the goats with wine. Flavors the meat and saves trips to the well. We ain't leavin' nothing for the orcs."

Cal wolfed a huge chunk of meat, washed it down with wine, and then asked, "S'good. Bith, what were you and Ugly there—Schlein—arguing about? Did he really think you were your mother? That can't be right."

Bith huddled small as she ate. "No, that's what he thought. A lot of people mistake me for my mother."

"How can they? Doesn't she look—older?"

Bith shook her head and her dark hair shimmered. "No. She keeps her looks with spells. It costs other people theirs, but she keeps them. She's that way."

Cal asked, "Is that why you're in no hurry to get home?"

Bith didn't reply.

Sergeant Barin cleared his throat. "What I want to know— not that I've followed anything you've said thus far—is why you've fought your way into this castle. This place is doomed, you know."

Bith sniffed and raised her scraped chin. Cal thought she looked glad for a distraction. "We're here to speak to your leader. The chief mage. We—uhh—have an important message for him."

Barin shook his head. The ends of his scruffy mustache waggled. "That's too bad. He ain't here."

"He's not?"

"Nope." Others shook their heads around them. The defenders of the castle all had the same gestures. They all looked alike, like an extended family. "No, ma'am. He went up into his tower one night and never came down. There's been no sign of him since."

"He's deserted us," a woman proclaimed.

Barin shook his head some more. "We don't know that, daughter. He could have gotten into some mischief. He could have been trying some spell to save us all and had it backfire, for all we know. We mustn't speak ill of our lord."

"Nor the dead."

Barin just shook his head.

Cal looked along the wall and to the castle and the dark mountains beyond. The moon was up, and it cast a glow upon the upper peaks. "Why defend, then? Why not just pull out?"

Barin frowned. "No reason, really. 'Cept this is our home. We've lived here going back so many generations no one knows when we came, or where from. We're hanging on as long as possible. The bastards haven't made any serious moves towards us yet. Mostly just noise and mock advances for the young 'uns. They're still gathering here in the valley, spilling out of the damned cloud like bees swarmin' on a summer's day. We can bide a bit. Maybe Criegsten will come back with some plan. There's always hope. But any road, if he don't, we'll just slip over the mountains at night. We know the hills and the caves and no amount of orcs can stop us getting out."

"I wish we'd known the back route coming in," Cal mumbled. He asked for more food and was given it. The defenders watched them incuriously, like cows. Only Barin had any intelligence in his pocked and seamed face.

"What about—" Bith started. She stopped and looked sideways at her companions, who nodded. "What about a sword, a fabulous sword? Is it still here, or has—what was his name?—your master taken it?"

Barin nodded his head. "Criegsten of Cairngorm. Lord Criegsten sometimes. Master of Multhothy, he called himself, though he never did tell us where Multhothy was. We asked him often enough, around the fires late in the winter, when he was in his cups, about it, Multhothy that is, but he never told us. It was a secret, he said. He liked secrets, he did. Likes 'em, I should say.''

"The sword?" Bith prompted.

"Oh, that's right, you asked about the sword. Forgive me. I'm a garrulous old man surrounded by children who've heard it all before. That's what comes of being uncle to every blooded being within five leagues. It's nice to see some new faces, let me tell you. You must be the first brown-haired wench inside these walls in three generations."

"The sword?"

"Oh, yes. Yes, it's here. Up—" he turned and lifted his arm to point high, high—"*way* up there. In his room. Hangs in the air, it does. We wouldn't touch it."

"Hangs in the air?" Cal asked.

"A simple enough spell," Bith told him. She asked Barin, "May we see it? We promise not to touch it."

'Well," Barin rasped his stubbly chin with his horsehide glove. "I don't know. I suppose so, seeing as how you've come all this long way, through that bunch. I suppose. Soon as you've finished your food I'll show you. Er, no, I'll have Erin show you. There are four hundred seventeen steps up to that eyre."

Bith set her wooden cup on the stone wall. "We're done. Aren't we, Cal, Hathor?"

Cal the Prepared and Hathor the Ever-Hungry each snatched up as much food as they could and stuffed it into their shirts. They wiped bread crumbs off their chins and hefted their weapons. "Right. Whatever you say, Bith. Lead on."

Barin fished out of his pockets a ring of three keys, all brass. He pointed out the biggest one to Erin as he gave it to her. "Escort them up to Criegsten's keep to see this sword, but don't let them touch it. You understand? No one's to touch it. Them were Criegsten's words. His final words to us, maybe." The trio promised they wouldn't touch the sword or anything else.

And off they went on the last leg of their long journey.

The hill rode even steeper up to the second, smaller wall. Cal opined the inhabitants must be born with one leg shorter than the other. He paused to check the valley floor once again. The orcan army roiled and bubbled, but there seemed no sign of imminent attack. Their guide, Erin, growled. "Them were the best fields in the northern reaches. Used to be a river bottom. Ten feet of topsoil. Now they'll never grow anything again, we're thinking."

They passed through the gate and into the midst of the small village. Like the inhabitants, the tiny houses all looked alike. Even the yellow dogs that came out to bark at them all looked alike. Cal smiled and reached out to pat one. He had seen villages like this before: he'd grown up in one.

Either Cal's show of interest or the task of being a guide set Erin to talking. She told them about Cairngorm in a monotonous drone. The party discerned more from the way she talked than from the actual words.

Like most frontier settlements, the people were not brilliant. They survived by hard work and hardship. Between the short growing season, the isolation, the raids by animals and enemies, the land gave up its produce sparingly, and to survive the people had become like the land. They went into the fields with a hoe and a spear. Children learned to churn butter and hunt deer, to card wool and chop wood, to cut wheat and kill bandits. People knew their jobs and were set in their ways. Yet if the land made them hard, it also made them content, proud of their ability to survive and even prosper in the wilderness. They guarded what they gathered jealously, but once someone was "family" they showered him or her with generosity. They laughed silently at the same old tired jokes.

Of the wizard, Erin could tell them that Criegsten arrived from "the outside" about thirty years ago. He was very wise, they decided. (Bith sniffed. Anyone who could *read* would seem a *genius* to this lot.) He was very old. (That made sense to Cal. He'd heard those who used magic either lived a very long or a very short life.) Criegsten kept to himself, moved into the vacant castle alone, but helped whenever anyone asked. (Hathor liked that.) Why he'd "deserted them in their hour of need" Erin couldn't understand, but her voice was more hurt than angry.

The people had been here forever, she declared, but not perhaps for much longer. Raids by "orcs" (they called all their enemies orcs, even the giants) had intensified in the last few years. Several outlying families had been slaughtered. Everyone had had to relocate inside the walls. The Mistwall, once just a smear on the horizon, had advanced to within a stone's throw. It had been halted, thanks to Criegsten's enchanting ''the magic sword'' and setting it up as a barrier. But forty days ago orcs had begun to spill from the Mistwall. The people resisted their every advance. There were four hundred Cairngormers all told, more than two hundred able-bodied warriors. But four hundred could not resist four thousand with more arriving daily. The end of Cairngorm was not far off.

They came to the foot of the castle.

Seen up close, it was small, as northern castles tended to be. It was a multitude of kinks and crannies, spires and crooks and doubled ramparts that no one needed, with a deceptively small core. It was also more crumbly than they had supposed. It was carved from the same flint that made up the slope. It seemed strong, except that the tower did indeed hang over the cliff further than any mason could fashion. Three natives guarded the single door. Their guide accepted a torch and led them inside.

It was up, up, up, and up some more. They walked up hundreds of steps, each worn with a deep dish in the center. The interior of the castle was very plain, mostly cut-stone walls with no ornamentation other than old wooden shields and faded banners. The light of the torch dipped and bobbed, sparkled on mica flecks, frightened mice and birds in nests. Bith thought this a dreary place to be a woman. Hathor wondered why humans went to the trouble of building above ground when caves were ready made and more varied. Cal walked with a catch in his throat, for the place reminded him of home.

Up they went, nose to tail, up winding stairs and straight ones, across balconies and through arched doorways, and up again. Finally they turned into a tiny twisted stairwell where Hathor's shoulders brushed the walls. They stopped on a landing. Erin faced a door with an ornate brass lock. Bith took the torch and held it above her head, for no one could pass. The warrior woman fumbled with the key and then turned the tumblers with an eerie screech.

The room they entered was black, but it took on an eldritch glow as they advanced with the torch. Erin lit torches in iron sconces. The party filed into a fairly large room, a space bigger than the public room of most inns. Scarred tables lined three walls and two tables stood in the center. Wooden boxes and tin pails full of dusty animal parts or greasy liquids stood on the floor. Beakers and vials and burnt trays and candles and books littered the tables. Poles and flags and other junk filled the corners. The rafters that stretched high into the conical roof were hung with multitudinous dusty things: a stuffed owl, a net full of sea shells, a horse tail, a thin bone fully six feet long. The stubs and wax of a thousand candles were stuck to everything. The room was scented heavily with brimstone and charred wood, saltpeter and fermented leather, formaldehyde and mint, cabbage and dust.

Erin pointed across the room. Illuminated by a queer fairy glow, the adventurers could see a huge arch that lead out onto a tiny balcony. The balcony overlooked the Mistwall and nothing else.

At the mouth of the arch, half in, half out of the room, a slim black cross was silhouetted against that roiling rain-bowed wall.

A sword hung in mid-air.

The runesword.

CHAPTER
8

"Don't touch it," Bith said.

Cal had immediately stepped over to the sword. Now he squatted for a better look at it. "Why not?"

"It's spelled. To touch it might banish the spell."

The warrior woman Erin said, "You're not going to touch anything anyway." She rapped the haft of her spear on the stone floor for emphasis.

Cal lit a candle from a torch so he could peer at the sword. The thing was beautiful, the most beautiful artifact he'd ever seen, weapon or otherwise.

The sword was outwardly very plain, but it had lines as perfect as a virgin's body. The pommel was a round emblem with a rune engraved on each side. The handle was wrapped with gold wire. The crosshilt tapered in slim lines to a pair of matching knobs, each again etched with a rune. The blade was slim both in thickness and width—not much thicker than a knife blade, no wider than three fingers. It looked to be as long as Cal's arm: the perfect length, he thought. There was no chasing on the shining shank, but there were runes written far down the blade around the cutting edge. The letters were nothing Cal had ever seen before. Straight here, curlicued there, linked and separate. The edge of the blade was so fine the boy could not even see it.

Bith came over and peered close at the sword's engravings. Cal could see the freckles on her nose reflected in the blade's surface. He asked her, "Can you read the words?"

"They're not words, they're runes."

"What's the difference?"

"Words are made of letters, which are abstract lines that represents sounds. Runes are pictures. You don't read them as much as you interpret them. They carry more power than words, too."

"Why?"

"Because. Let's see . . . The one here on the pommel, that would be the most powerful one because it's closest to the heart. It looks like a mountain. See the snow on the peak? Or maybe it's sunlight. A mountain might mean power, or solidity. Or it might stand for the home of a god, or the god himself. Or a country or empire. Or masculinity."

The boy held the candle close. "How can one picture stand for so many things?"

The girl sat back on her haunches, balanced on her yellow boots. "It probably doesn't. A picture, or symbol, has different meanings in different cultures. Look at an owl, for instance. To one people it might mean wisdom. To another it might mean death is imminent. Or it might just symbolize night. You can't know what meaning the picture carries unless you know the stories that go with it, what people think of it. I don't even know if these are dwarf runes or human runes. Or something else."

Cal sighed. "I get the idea, sort of. Anything else?"

Bith pointed to a rune on the hilt. "This is a wing."

"Means flight?"

"Or speed. Or all of a bird's powers: toughness, far sight. This looks like an eye next to it, so it probably does mean far sight. . . . This looks like a deer, maybe for fleetness. I don't recognize any others. The mountain is significant, though. Maybe this sword's name is Mountaintop or Mountain of Light or—"

"*Mountain of Light?* Wow! *Is* that its name?"

"I told you, I don't know."

Cal crept closer to the sword and Bith waved him back lest he tumble onto it. He said, ''We could ask Vili.''

''*You* ask Vili.''

Cal did, calling the god's name, offering his own worn sword, peering into the magic one. At one point they thought they detected a flicker within the shining surface of the rune-sword, but the god did not appear. Erin watched them uneasily.

Bith said, ''If Vili is around here, or in there, he's probably too weak to manifest himself. All the power from the sword—and Vili himself—would go into holding back the Mistwall. Vili is trapped inside an artifact of his own making, not an uncommon fault of people who dabble in magic.''

A snore startled them. Hathor had lain down on the stone floor. The girl got up and walked off to look at the rest of the room.

Cal sat on his hams and stared at the sword. His hands itched to pluck up the sword and make a practice swing. A strong blade with a long reach, it would cleave the air and anything else effortlessly. The gold wire around the handle and the fat button pommel would give it weight and heft and a good counterbalance. The polished crosshilt would feel like silk along the fingers. Mountain of Light! My! but he wanted this sword! With a weapon like this a man could do anything—slay a dragon, lead an army, conquer the world!

How long the boy stayed there, staring at the sword, he didn't know, but he started when someone touched his shoulder.

Bith yawned, ''Let's go, Cal.''

''Go?''

''Yes, go.'' Bith—who had bags under her eyes—nodded towards the door. Three more Cairngormers had joined Erin. ''They want us out of here. I'm about to drop anyway.''

''Nonsense,'' Cal replied, but he swayed on his feet. ''Well, maybe a short rest. Say, why don't—''

''You sleep here next to the sword? Forget it.''

Cal frowned. ''What, can you read minds, too?''

''I can read yours.'' She plucked at his sleeve. ''Let's go before they drag us out. I want to try sleeping in a real bed for once. It's been weeks.''

Cal huffed, but he was too tired to argue. It had been a

long day and a longer night. He and Bith routed Hathor.
Together they were escorted to temporary sleeping quarters.
The last thing Cal muttered was, "I wonder when we'll see
Endril again."

Bith tossed on a stormy sea. Waves threw her from wave
crest to trough, curled over and crashed down to bury her.
No matter how many spells she tried she was helpless,
knocked under the water a hundred times only to surface
again, snatch a breath of air, and go back down. The water
was black and white. Fish sailed overhead. Suddenly a huge
white sea worm burst from a wave alongside her. Its black
maw drove straight for her. She couldn't move. She was
pinned against the sea. The mouth bit her in half. . . .

Morea's daughter jerked awake. Someone was shaking her
shoulder. She tried to roll over and almost fell from the bed.
She was tangled in blue blankets.

It was a bright autumn morning. Frost rimmed the edge of
a cut-stone window and sparkled in the light. Erin, the tall,
blond, and dull warrior, had been the one shaking her.

Bith kicked the last of the covers loose and sat up. She
wiped her forehead and found sweat.

The Cairngorm woman said, "We've captured someone at
the castle gate!"

"Hunh, what? Someone?" Bith panted, couldn't catch her
breath. "Can you be a little more—specific?"

The woman's brow clouded. "We've captured someone at
the castle gate."

Bith tried, "Yes?"

"It's a tall man, dead white, with a short bow. He says—"

"Bow? All in green? He's ours."

The woman blinked.

Bith held the covers to her breast. "I'll be right there. Just
give me a moment, please."

Alone, the girl poured water from an ewer into a bowl and
rinsed her face. The nightmares were back. After sinking
deliciously into a real bed and clean blankets, here she'd
awoken practically on the floor, her mind conjuring demons.
She wondered if the dreams meant anything. Not that she
could remember them. She combed her hair and looked out
the window. Down in the valley, orcs continued to spill from

the Mistwall. There were thousands of them. Nightmares asleep and awake, she thought. It wasn't fair. She wondered if her mother was ever bothered by nightmares. And if she ever wondered where her daughter was . . .

Bith shuddered. She flapped her clothing in the air by way of cleaning it, and joined Erin.

In the main hall of the castle, a trio of natives stood with drawn swords. In their center was a loose-limbed Endril. He greeted Bith with a nonchalant wave.

Cal and Hathor were brought in. When all three vouched for the elf the guard dispersed, but they didn't go far. The humans, troll, and elf were invited to sit down at a long table laid with a hearty breakfast. Barin came in, escorted by a half dozen look-alike family members, and the meal began. There was oatmeal and raisins, cold tongue and cold shoulder, small beer and cakes. The party ate well in the strained atmosphere. Clearly the presence of the elf upset people.

Bith tore bread and asked, "All right, Master Elf, how *did* you gain the inside of these walls?"

"I walked."

Bith sniffed delicately. "I suppose my question was poorly aimed. Our real question is, why could you just 'walk' when we could not?"

Endril stared at her innocently with his pale blue eyes. "You could not have followed the way I came."

"And why not?"

Endril almost shrugged. "No human could."

Cal blew out his breath and reached for more beer. The soldier wanted to chastize the elf for walking off so abruptly, for leaving them in the lurch, for not telling them more. But he held his tongue. It would accomplish nothing. Besides, the elf seemed even quieter and more reserved than usual. Could one of the fair folk be melancholy? And even for an elf, Endril looked very pale, as if he'd been wounded. Cal said, "Never mind, Bith. We should be glad he's back."

Bith shook her head but agreed. The castle defenders shook their heads around them. The breakfast talk moved to the state of the orcan army. It was largely dormant in the bright sun, Barin told them. The monsters might try a push to-night—they used the dark for their own purposes. Barin said, "The Dark Army was stirred by your passage the way mud puppies are aroused by a stick.'' The elders of Cairngorm were trying to decide whether it was time to send the old people and the children into the hills.

They had finished their meal and were talking when a soldier ran into the hall. "Come quickly!"

"What is it?"

"Hurry!"

Everyone pressed out the door. Something was happening beyond the outermost wall. Some commotion. A block of orcs and others—looking like spiders again from this height—were rushing the walls. No, they were pursuing someone, pegging arrows and spears at a tall figure who sprinted before them. The arrows found their mark but bounced off. Finally the grey figure—in a pointed helmet?—attained the wall. He disappeared for a moment, then reappeared as he vaulted over. He dropped into a knot of castle defenders.

Endril said, " 'Tis our companion, the giant."

Cal snorted. "Backbreaker? I thought we'd seen the last of him. Where's he been?"

The party could see the grey stone giant—it had been his pointed head they'd seen and not a helmet—wave his long arms in earnest conversation with the smaller blond humans. Finally the lot of them turned and pointed up the hill, and the giant stepped from their ranks. He loped up the hills in great strides, no more discommoded than a hare, and joined them before the gate.

No one greeted the giant. Cal reflected that the others must be as uncomfortable with Backbreaker as he was. He was just too—sinister, alien. Powerful? The boy asked, "What kept you?"

The giant called Mountain Back Breaker lifted his raptor's hands. "I fell in with some other giants. They wanted to talk to me. It's been a long time since I met kin."

Cal scratched the scar on his upper lip. "I didn't see any big fellows like you last night."

The monster lifted his hands again.

The boy asked, "What did they have to say to you?"

"Much. Nothing. Talk of the big people. My father died. I have been away a long time."

Nobody could top that. Cal rubbed his scar. "Well . . . Let's get back to the sword."

Endril said, "Yes, let us. I have yet to see this monument."

They filed into the castle and climbed the myriad stone steps to the tower.

Cal ran directly to the sword. In the morning light it glittered like a jewel.

"Don't touch it." Endril's admonishment cut into his reverie.

Cal reflected the elf had been with them for only ten minutes and already he was giving orders again. "Can't I even breathe on it?"

"No," Bith cut in. "Nor drool either. It's hexed. Don't you be."

Endril said, "See here." He stepped to the balcony and signalled the boy to follow. The elf pointed down.

Down, down, down, so far and so far underfoot that Cal's knees turned to water, was the floor of a dry canyon. The boy had to grip the edge of the low balcony—small comfort— but Endril looked over as unconcernedly as a bird. "Do you still doubt that the object of our quest here holds up this balcony? Certainly no natural or contrived strut keeps this shelf in place. Touch that sword and it may be your last act, short of screaming, before hitting the bottom of this gorge."

Cal glanced up at the Mistwall. They could see the far wall of the chasm, but the cloud started just above it. It was the only thing in sight, really. Seen up this close, the closest they had come to it, the wall had a maddening and hypnotic quality. The colors that made up the wall roiled not in circles, but rather tumbled upwards and yet downwards at the same time, like a rainbow waterfall gone mad. It drew the eye and held it like some massive fire—a fire racing to consume the watcher. Endril touched his shoulder and Cal shook his head. He averted his eyes downwards but saw only space. He backed into the room.

Endril followed. "Somehow this sword also holds the Mistwall at bay. Recall you our view from across the valley? And see there and there? The wall has a belly sucked in with its midpoint *here*."

"It must be very powerful, then," Cal said.

Bith spoke behind them. "Powerful, yes. But like a fire, it's too hot to grasp without tongs."

Cal looked at the two, then at the sword before them. It was unreal the way it hung, a foot above the floor, touching nothing. "But you're just guessing about the sword. If I did pick it up, nothing at all might happen."

Endril nodded in that maddening way he had. Then he flinched as some twinge touched him. He'd limped considerably coming up the stairs. Cal suspected his right leg had been wounded recently. The elf cleared a bench of books and sat down gingerly. He continued. "True. But then, you might not be able to move it at all. It might be rooted in that spot as if driven into anvil and stone."

Cal stared at the sword in helpless frustration. "I want to find *some* way to get my hands on it."

"Let us look then, and see what we find. To break a spell we need the spell maker. Let us find the wizard, or the wizard's words."

Erin barked, "You'll not touch a thing! Barin said so!"

Endril turned on her with gentle eyes and gentle voice. "Would you have us find your wizard?"

"Barin said—"

Bith mumbled under her breath for some time. Now she reached out a soft hand and touched the warrior woman's shoulder. Erin shivered and stared at the magic user—stared as a bird stares at a snake.

"Erin," Bith's voice was silk on glass, "We're . . . your . . . friends . . . aren't we?"

"Y-y-yes."

"Good. That's good. Friends are nice. Now, why don't . . . you go ask Barin . . . if . . . *we* . . . can help find your . . . wizard? That's what you want, isn't it?"

"Y-yes."

"Good. Good. Go ask Barin."

The soldier woman turned and clomped off down the steps. Bith sighed. Endril nodded to her. Cal frowned. "I didn't know you had—what do they call it?—suggestion powers."

The mage lifted her pert nose. "I have a lot of powers."

"You better not use that spell on me, or any of the rest of us."

Bith made a face in imitation of his serious one. Cal frowned deeper and the girl laughed. Hathor grinned a toothy grin.

Endril waggled a hand at the room. "Bith, let us see what other powers you command. There was a magic user in this room at one time and now there is none. Can you discern whence he's gone, and how?"

Bith bit her lower lip as she looked around at the mess. Every table, every space underneath, every corner, every nook and cranny was littered or stuffed with junk. Finally she said, "I can't guarantee anything. There may be some sign or script as to where he's gone. But he could just as easily have fallen over the balcony drunk. Or been spirited away. I'll try, but it will take time."

The elf said, "We have time. Some little anyway. Try as you may."

"All right. First things first. Why don't you all stand by the doorway?" The elf, the soldier, the troll, and the giant shuffled through the crowded room out of her way. Backbreaker had to crouch, with knuckles on the floor to keep from hitting his head in the rafters.

Bith fished in a pouch and came up with a double pinch of something. She pushed her sleeves up and stuck her fingers in the air. "Watch for anything that glows," she said, and began a sonorous chant that built quickly.

> *"Come to me, things unseen,*
> *You've the pulse, I the mean,*
> *Now I scry the ways inside,*
> *Unto to me let no spark hide!"*

Bith repeated the phrases until she had the cadence just right. Then she snapped her hands to flick the magic dust into the air.

The men gasped as—just for a moment—objects in the room lit up. Green, blue, gold, orange, red, white, a dozen things flashed on and off in an eyeblink. Most of all, the sword winked like a glimpse through a furnace door—bright yellow, white hot, searing on the eyeballs. Then the show was over. The restored room was dull and grey by comparison.

The magic user stood pursing her lips.

Cal said, "That was fabulous, Bith! I've never seen anything like it! Do you do that often?"

Bith was distracted. "What? Oh, that was nothing. I expected more."

"More?"

She put her hands on her hips. "Yes, a lot more. With this many objects in the room, so little magic. It's odd . . ." She ended with a sniff.

"It's had some effect," Endril commented. He watched the roiling mass of the Mistwall.

"Is it getting closer?"

"No. But it's moving more fiercely, as if agitated."

Cal asked, "Could your spelling have done that?"

Bith drummed her fingers on the back of a chair. "I don't know . . . Well, what *next*?"

None of them had an answer. In the silence there came the sound of shuffling on the stairs and hoarse breathing. Soon Barin appeared at the door. He staggered into the room and immediately took a chair. Erin came in behind him and helped him sit.

"Odin and Isis, I'm too old for this trip!" he croaked. "I could almost let the Dark Ones have this castle. How did old Criegsten *do* it? He must have had magic in his legs."

Bith continued to scan the room with her hands on hips. "That might have been one place."

The sergeant rubbed his mustache. "That Criegsten. He was a queer sort. I always thought a lot of his tricks were smoke and mirrors, and knowing his audience was simple. Have you any clue as to where he went?"

Everyone shook their heads. Bith said, "We haven't made an intensive search yet. We were, uh, wondering how to proceed. Have I your permission to poke around in here?"

Cal piped up, "Can we, for instance, take up yon sword?"

Barin waved a hand as he fought for breath. "Touch whatever you want—except that sword. Criegsten said it was the only thing holding up the castle, for what his word was worth. I have to admit some of the underpinnings in the hall look awful dicey. Sure something's holding up this pile of rock, and it ain't money nor faith. No, go ahead and fool with whatever you want, except the sword. Take it all. We're none of us magic users and can't use it. The Dark Army'll just get it."

Bith's frown did not go away, but she rubbed her hands. A

mage turned loose in a wizard's cave was like a wild boar in a marketplace. The girl hunted for sacks.

Endril murmured, "Let us remember our purpose here, Bith. To learn the whereabouts of this Criegsten and to see if indeed we can take the sword with us." His companions blinked at the last phrase until they remembered the outsiders in the room. The Cairngormers might not take kindly to the idea of destroying the sword. "We can load bags while you look. Find some trace of a spell, or record in a book. Or a doorway or portal. Or means of escape."

Bith pointed. "Cal, Thor, would you move all the open books to this table, please? And find a crate for the closed ones? Endril, sort through that stuff and remove all the prosaic gear, please. Let's see. Barin, can you tell me, sir, when was the last time you saw Criegsten?"

"The last time? Oh, that would be . . . Well, what's today? When did the army first start to leave the wall?"

"It was twenty-some days ago," Erin supplied.

Barin squinted. "Was it? But I had dinner with him just the other night. . . ."

"It was before the full moon, Father."

Bith asked, "Could he have left the castle without your people knowing it?"

Erin asked, "Walking, you mean?"

"Or flying? Did he fly?"

"Not that I ever saw."

Bith chewed the end of her thumb as she looked around. Cal and Hathor were gingerly moving books as if they might explode. Backbreaker had sunk into a corner to doze. Endril stood on the balcony and watched the Mistwall and the sky. The tips of his lank white hair flickered in the breeze. The magic user said to no one in particular, "I see nothing big enough for a portal. No mirror or tapestry. No throne. Hathor thought this mountain was honeycombed with tunnels. Is that true?"

Erin sniffed and put a hand on her guardian's shoulder. The old man was asleep. "True enough. It's part of our escape route. We keep them clear and check them often. There are naught but bats and worms down there. The tunnels wander up and down. Most are useless. We collapsed some long ago.

None go down to the valley, so the orcs can't attack from underground."

Bith had turned to the books that lay open on the tables. There were over a dozen of them, all different sizes with pages odd-shaped and mismatched, stained and mouse-gnawed. The parchment pages were largely blank. Here and there were tiny lines or scratches or drawings inscribed in faded ink.

Bith wet her fingers and gingerly touched the edge of one book. When nothing happened she raised the page and crooked her head to peer at it with the light behind.

"What are you doing?" Cal asked her.

"Hmmm?"

"What are you looking for? There's nothing there."

Bith brushed the page and peered with her nose no more than an inch off the page. She mused, "Maybe. He *was* the secretive type. . . ."

"Hunh?"

"What?" Bith looked up. "What do you want?"

"*What* are you looking at?"

"I'm looking for rebuses."

"What?"

Bith frowned. "Honestly, haven't you learned anything? Do you know how to read?"

Cal's flush answered the question, but he snapped, "I know better than to stare at blank pages like some stupid hypnotized chicken!"

Bith's frown turned to confusion. "What do you mean, 'hypnotized chicken?' They've no brain."

"Now whose education is lacking?"

Erin said from across the room. "He means when you draw a line in the dust from a chicken's nose."

"Chickens don't have noses," Hathor said. He was chewing on some root he'd found.

"Beaks, then."

"Why," Cal ground his teeth, "are you poring over those blank pages?"

"These? They're not blank."

Hathor came over and stared close. *Munch, munch, munch.* The root had the consistency of a chair leg. "Naked."

Bith looked down. "What?"

Cal stepped past the troll and jabbed a grimy finger, pinning flat the page in Bith's hand. "Where—are—the—words?"

The girl brightened. "Oh! They're right here. They're just sealed."

"Sealed?"

"Masked."

"You mean, invisible?"

Bith shook her black hair. "Well, it looks like it, though it isn't, really. They have a conceal spell on them."

"Can *you* see them?"

"Oh, no. No one can until the spell is lifted. At least, I don't think anyone can. No, I can't. I just have to decide which ones to unseal, is all."

"And how do you decide that?"

"You read these little rebuses here, if that's what they are."

It was Cal's turn to peer close. "These little squiggly lines? That's just spider scratching, or art, or something, ain't it?"

Bith shook her glossy head again. "No, no, no. They're little words or phrases twisted to make a drawing. They're called rebuses. Like when you're first learning your letters and the tutor writes the word 'reindeer' all twisted so it makes a little picture of a reindeer, starting at the tail and making the legs and finally the horns. It's to help you remember the word. You see them all the time, on cave walls or doorways or blades and such. Don't you?"

Cal shook his head. "No. Wait. Is that what's on the blade there?"

"What? No, no. Those are runes."

Cal sighed. He pointed to the page again. "Why don't those pages look like any writing I've ever seen before?"

"I told you, these are *rebuses*. Mages use them all the time to note what spell is really on the page once it's unsealed. Look here, see this one? It looks like an olive branch, but really it has the word 'peace' written into it. So it's probably some kind of friend spell. See?"

Cal peered closely, as did Hathor. (*Crunch, cranch* in Cal's ear.) Cal did notice that the etching on the olive branch seemed oddly un-barklike. He conceded, "Well, maybe. But a friend spell won't do us any good."

"But it might not be a friend spell. Surely you don't be-

lieve everything you read, do you?'' Bith waved a breezy
hand at the man and troll's glassy stare. ''Don't you see? It
might be a trick. This page might contain a hate spell, or a
love potion. You can write any rebus you want, after all. Or
the page might really *be* blank, and this is just the page he
intended to inscribe a friend spell on later. Or it could just
be a description of some artifact he knew of that had a friend
spell, or just anything at all.''

Cal rubbed his forehead. Hathor scratched his ear with his
root. Bith went on. ''See this? This page refers to another
page somewhere else. The book is full of cross-references to
confuse people. Or there might be two masks on the same
page, one covering another. Or three. Or it might be trapped.
There are spells to hold, you know.''

''What good is that?''

''To protect your work from snoopers. A stranger might
unmask a page and start reading. Surprise! he trips a hold
spell. That freezes him like a statue—he stands there until
the writer unfreezes him.''

Cal burst out, ''That's awful! You could *die* waiting for
someone to come back!''

Bith shrugged. ''Of course. Many have. Why do you think
every magic user's den has at least one skull lying around?
He or she didn't find that in the middle of the road.'' Everyone in the room except the girl looked around. There were
three skulls and one jawbone showing in the room. ''Or the
page could blind you, or drive you mad, poison you slow or
fast, or just kill you outright with a lightning bolt.''

Cal and Hathor backed away from the table.

The girl gave a merry laugh. ''I don't think we have to
worry about that here. Much, anyway.'' She turned and
flipped that book shut and tossed it to the back of the table.
She pulled another close as Cal and Hathor retreated across
the room.

''Gorm and Ghast,'' Cal muttered. ''I'd take a clean sword
thrust on the battlefield rather than pore over these things.
It's like shoving your hand into a box of serpents.''

Bith looked up and was surprised to find herself alone at
the table. ''Oh, come now, it's not that bad. There are tricks
you learn to protect yourself, protections that you wear or
carry in your pockets.''

"Do you have any?"

"Some. Of course, you never know if they're going to work against a particular spell. An enchanter will never sell you a protection against another spell of his own making. That would be foolish. But there's probably nothing in these books that can hurt me. Actually, if something does spring at me, I'll know I'm close to what we want."

"Hell of way to find out," Cal muttered.

Hathor agreed. "That like pulling down rock to see if it fall on you."

Bith murmured, "Umm hmm."

From the opposite wall Cal called, "But can you find what we want in one of those books?"

Endril spoke from beside him, his voice so quiet the boy and troll jumped. "There's no guarantee the books can tell us anything about where Criegsten has gone, or why. That's just a starting point. After the books she may have to investigate all these artifacts separately, then search the room itself."

Cal looked around at the jumble. "That could take *weeks*!"

The elf nodded. "Years, more likely, to find all the secrets in this room. And then probably not all of them, or even half. Mortals are too short-lived to learn much."

Cal gritted his teeth and said nothing.

Bith laughed again. "Don't you worry, Endril. I'll have what we need pretty soon. Within a day."

Hathor finished the root with a crack that set all their teeth on edge. "I go look around," he announced. "Look at caves."

Cal watched the girl's slim back, bent over the books, and the elf's bland face, ageless and unseamed. "I'll go with you," he said. "And find something to do."

"Check the state of the Dark Army," Endril told him. "You have a soldier's eye. See if they're massing for an attack or a cutting-out expedition."

"They're not going to wait any weeks, that's for sure." Cal muttered as he followed the troll down the stairs. Back-breaker had left the room some time earlier. Assisted by Erin, Barin awoke and dragged himself out of his chair to make his creaky way down the stairs. Endril and Bith were left in the room. The elf walked to the edge of the balcony. He stood with his toes projecting through the stiles until they hung over the chasm beneath. He stared at the Mistwall as if staring could penetrate its depths.

Alone in the room, Bith closed another book and stacked it against the wall.

Days passed.

By the end of the first day Bith had pored over every book twice. Cal had taken another long nap and then polished his antique sword. He came in often to gaze at the runesword. When he crouched low and the room was still he imagined he could hear it singing. Endril watched the Mistwall from the balcony or was gone. No one knew where. Hathor and Backbreaker were likewise absent.

By the end of the second day Bith had thrown three books out the window.

Cal practiced swordfighting with some of the young men and women, but most were busy packing and putting food by. Endril wandered the hills behind the town. Hathor and Backbreaker were still gone.

By the end of the third day Bith was throwing artifacts off the balcony, some of which glowed even as she threw them.

Cal chafed at the lack of work and fighting. He borrowed a heavy bow and took potshots at the Dark Army. He argued with Endril that they should "*do* something." The elf ignored him and dried flowers on a flat stone. Hathor and Backbreaker poked among the hills. The defenders of the castle asked Cal which side the troll and giant were on.

By the end of the fourth day Bith was setting fire to artifacts before throwing them out the window. Cal and Endril wondered if they should ask her why, but decided not to.

Cal noticed that no one else was issuing forth from the Mistwall. Did that mean the Dark Army was complete? The force seemed to be massing, stirring. The Cairngormers were almost ready to flee. Cal announced that if nothing happened soon he was leaving with the castle defenders, but he was going to snatch the sword off the balcony just before leaving. Endril said nothing. Hathor and Backbreaker came back and reported there were caves under the hillside "full of bats and nothing else."

By the end of the fifth day the men voted to disturb Bith.

What they found was not encouraging. The room was almost empty. Bith was haggard, with grey bags under her eyes, stained hands, and a white-hot temper.

"*Wrong?* I'll tell you what's *wrong!*" she shrilled. "That lying old fossil Criegsten was a *fake!* He was a fraud and an *idiot!* *Look* at this stuff!" There wasn't much left to look at: a stuffed owl, brass candlesticks, a box of odd metal parts, a few books, some other things. "This is *junk! Trash! Humbug!*"

The men asked, "What?"

"He faked everything! There's not a magic spell in one of these books that would work, or that a child couldn't do with his eyes closed! And these *things!* Residual magic as old as the hills! My grandmother's *shoes* had more—" The girl paused to snatch up the stuffed owl, march to the open window, and pitch it off the balcony. "—more magic and were more interesting than these—trinkets! And he claimed to have forged the *runesword!* *He* took credit for *dwarven* work! He couldn't conjure a homunculus from a quart of *demon* blood!" She paused for breath and huffed, "Barin was right. All Criegsten ever did was *cheat!*"

Cal, Hathor, and Backbreaker looked around the room and didn't know what to say. Endril tried. "All you say is no doubt true, good Bith. With all your knowledge, you would know. But how is it the runesword hangs in the air?"

The girl waved a tired hand. "Oh, that. Anyone can do that. Once the object's in place it stays there until disturbed."

"But it does keep the Mistwall at bay?"

Bith sighed. She peered in the sword's direction. "Yes, it must. I can find no notes on it. Nothing. He hasn't written any fresh notes—*lies*—in years. But he did prop it up there. I don't even know where he got the sword, for that matter."

"Barin doesn't know either."

The magic user sniffed. "He probably *stole* it from some blind beggar."

Cal asked, "Can we move it, then?"

Bith flapped her arms. "*NO!* Not until we know what will happen! You want to get us all killed? You want this place to drop out from under us? Or have the Mistwall slam down on us? Or something worse—lightning, blindness, who knows what?"

The elf offered, "But—"

"I *told* you, there's no discussion of it anywhere. And I don't know where the fool disappeared to either, not that I *want* to find him. There's no mention of a portal or a teleport spell or a carpet or walking hole or *anything*!"

At their back someone spoke. It was Erin, obviously come to find out what the commotion was about. "Did you look in the cellars?"

Everyone turned. "What?"

The woman stammered as everyone stared at her. "I—I asked if you'd—looked in the cellars. Just before he disappeared Lord Criegsten spent much time in a corner of the cellar. He wouldn't let us near, and we—"

Very quietly, very icily, Bith said, "Please show me."

Not much later Cal, Endril, and Hathor stood with her in a small set of chambers deep in the heart of the castle. The rooms were tiny with rounded ceilings, carved from rock before the castle above had been assembled. The light of torches was absorbed by dry bare walls. The floor underfoot was slippery with dust and grime. There was nothing in the room except a rotted tapestry nailed to the wall.

The girl ranted some more. "*Here!* Bast, Bathsheba, and Baal, why didn't somebody *tell* me about this room *earlier*?" Bith waved her arms until the sleeves of her shirt flapped like wings. "How am I supposed to *learn* anything if *people* don't *tell* me about these things in the *first* place?"

Backbreaker, too tall for the room, hung back in the stairwell. Erin stood behind him. "You never asked, you know," she put forth from the darkness. "You just wanted to see his room in the tower, and we let you—"

Bith pushed up her sleeves with stained fingers. "Oh, shut up. I'll *bet* this is where he went."

She reached out and snatched down the tapestry. Unfortunately she hauled down with it a sheet of dust and mold that set them all hacking and coughing. They had to retreat to the stairwell. Bith rubbed her eyes with dirty hands, which made them itch abominably. When they could go back into the room, a stark pale wall stood behind the remnants of the tapestry.

"Look you—*hack*—there," she announced. And sneezed.

"Looks like a wall," Cal said.

Bith swore. "Idiot."

With a grand gesture she wet her fingertips and traced a wide circle on the wall. Then she rolled out a short chant, her detect spell. The wall shimmered like water, then the circle turned black.

"See? It's a hole."

"Worm hole," Hathor said. He had a parsnip in his hand which he munched on.

Bith *tsk*ed. "No, no, no. It's not a worm hole. It's too big. It's a portal hole, made with magic. A sort of melting spell that turns the rock into a gas. Slow but powerful. You need fifty pounds of holed cheese to even start it."

Hathor walked to the five-foot hole and stuck his head in. *Munch, munch.* "It's worm hole."

"We'll see. Fetch torches."

"Finally!" Cal leapt up the stairs. "Action!"

A few minutes later they had three torches. Cal strapped his scabbard and shield across his back to keep his legs free. Hathor shed his bearskin and carried his felling axe. Endril held his short bow with an arrow alongside it. Backbreaker went unarmed as ever.

Cal looked in the hole. "Hathor, why don't you go first? You're used to mucking around in caves, and you can see in the dark, right?"

"Yeah."

"I'll go second. Endril can bring up the—"

"I'll go first," Bith interrupted.

"What?"

"I found this portal, I'll go first. It might be magic-trapped. Get out of my way."

Cal stepped aside. The girl stepped to the hole and lifted her foot high to enter, careful with the torch near her hair. The boy shrugged and pointed Hathor after her. Cal went next, followed by Endril and Backbreaker. Erin watched them go.

The hole went straight for about fifteen feet, then slowly bent to the right and down. The bottom was like a trough, so they had to walk with one foot placed in front of the other. The floor was not smooth, but rippled like the bottom of a quick-moving stream. Hathor crouched on two bare feet and his one free hand. Cal had to stoop: almost immediately he developed a crick in his neck. He envied the troll, who moved as easily as a monkey. He could not hear the cat-quiet elf behind him. He did hear Backbreaker's grainy skin rasp along the cave walls. The giant probably had to crawl on all fours.

Around the bend and down they went. The descent was gradual at first, then slanted farther. Any more slant would force them to cling to the walls. That would be difficult, since the floor was slimy in spots. The light was strange, a mixture of bright flashes of torch and sudden black shadows when someone occluded one or more. The only sound was the scrape of leather or giant skin on a wall.

They had no idea how far they crept. At one point they passed through an intersection of tunnels. The side passage went up and down, very steep. Cal asked about it.

Bith called from up front, "A powerful mage could fly through these tunnels."

"But I thought Criegsten was a fake. And why would anyone melt their way through a mountain when they could just walk away from the castle?"

"I don't know. Perhaps he wanted to be mysterious."

Cal muttered, "Perhaps he was crazy."

The floor's slant became steeper. Cal could feel his toes jam as his hobnails tried to bite. The ceiling rose and became rougher as they entered part of a natural cavern. Bith gave a grunt of disgust.

"What is it?" Cal called.

"It's—*ugh*—some mess of grey gunk. A lot of it."

"Worm shit," came Hathor's voice.

"Will you *stop*? It's not ——"

Her scream filled the cavern and pierced their ears.

CHAPTER
9

The thing coming at Bith was an enormous white ring with a serrated edge around a gaping hole. The hole was big enough to swallow the girl easily.

The worm (Bith had the fleeting thought that she'd been *dead* wrong) completely filled the tunnel they stood in. It should have—the worm had drilled it. The worm was a mountain of white flesh; its maw just went on and on with receding rings.

Bith stifled another scream. She didn't have time for another spell, and couldn't have touched the worm if she wanted to. She simply chucked her torch down its throat and ducked.

The flaming brand flew into the worm's maw and disappeared. The beast didn't even slow down. All Bith had done was blind herself temporarily. At least she wouldn't see that mouth close shut on her and snap her in two. She squinched up her face and felt another scream escaping.

She'd forgotten she was not alone. A hand snagged her tunic and jerked her backwards. More hands landed and carried her straight back. Bith felt as if she had tumbled off a cliff and fallen into friendly branches. Then the hands on her were cool, dry, and scaly. Backbreaker loomed above, eyes luminous in the dark.

By the light of the giant's eyes and a sputtering torch Bith saw the men attack. Cal's poor sword and Endril's slim one winked and disappeared and shone again like summer lightning. For a second the girl's lonely heart sang as she thought they were leaping to defend her. But no, they were just saving themselves as well. The men flanked the troll with practiced precision. The worm rippled towards them like a loathsome tide.

The attack was Hathor's. The troll raised his felling axe in both hands. At home in the tunnels, he knew just how high he could heave it and not hit the ceiling. His hairy arms swelled as the steel head rose, bobbed, and then *chunked* into the worm's lip.

The worm stopped. Hathor struck again. Up went the arms and the long axe haft and then *down* with a meaty smack. One more blow whacked a hunk out of the monster's maw. A white slab as big as an inn table writhed with its own life on the round tunnel floor. Hathor was shouting as he swung, lustily howling in trollish, the noise like thunder. Cal shouted too with the meaningless oaths of a soldier and even Endril sang in a clear ringing tone.

The worm had stopped, even retreated a fraction, and the three warriors advanced. Hathor twisted the next blow, sank it sideways, and a larger chunk of worm flapped and fell away. The maw was half gone, and white pus dripped where it had been hacked. Hathor had swivelled to whack at the right side when something black engulfed the five of them.

Bith felt something wet and cold and infinitely disgusting slap her in the face. It immediately began to burn and itch. And it crawled. With a shriek she clawed at herself to get it off. The goo smeared everywhere, and everywhere it landed it burned and crawled. She shrieked again until she got some in her mouth, and that alone shut her up. Flailing her hands down her body, she located a clean section of her tunic tails and wiped her face clean, spitting and spitting again and again and damning herself for ever going down any damned tunnel. As she scraped her ears clean she heard a new kind of shout.

"Hathor!" It was Cal. "HATHOR! Where *are* you?"

"Gone," Endril's voice was clear and inhumanly calm. "It's taken him away."

"Well, for—" Cal's suggestions after that were unhelpful.

Only the cat-shine of Backbreaker's eyes gave them any light, and that a deceptive one. Endril called for a light. Cal fumbled with a torch and burned himself relighting it. He picked up his sword from the floor, unmindful of the glop clinging to it. Bith shuddered from head to toe as the black stuff all around continued to move.

"What *is* this?"

"Never mind!" Cal snapped. "We have to go after Thor!"

"But what *happened*?"

Endril finished mopping black goo from his face. "It vomited this—discharge of slime at us. A defense like a skunk's, I reckon. Then it snatched up our troll."

Tears started in Bith's eyes. "Hathor is *eaten*?"

Endril shook his head. "Swallowed, mayhap, not consumed. He'll more likely to suffocate if we don't—"

"Then *let's*!" Cal snapped. And he trotted off down the tunnel with torch and sword. Bith and Endril and Backbreaker trotted to catch up with him, slipping and sliding on the slimy smooth floor.

The tunnel hooked sharply right—Bith wondered how a worm could eat through rock like cheese—then the light disappeared. They heard a *"Whoop!"* that trailed off and ended with a thud. Endril slid to a stop, but not soon enough. The tunnel floor took a sudden bend downwards, and the elf was too far along. His slick soft boots had no purchase on the floor and he followed Cal. His final words were, "Your sword, boy! Put down your—" *Thud.*

Bith snagged a dry patch of wall and stopped, breathless. The stone giant hovered behind her like a rock outcrop. She listened. The soft sound of swearing came up the tunnel, in man's tongue and elven. So they were safe.

Or were they? Left in the dark, Bith crept forward a hair more and peered at the opening. She stood on a lip of stone and sensed a vastness out in the black before her. A breeze, cold and musty, trickled past her cheek.

"Cal, Endril, are you all right?"

"Aye," came the elf's voice from the darkness below.

Cal got his torch lit yet again. Its soft flare showed their surroundings. Bith and Cal gasped.

The tunnel had emptied into a larger cavern. A luminous sheen—moss or slime or foxfire—reflected the torchlight like a bronze mirror. This underground world was not brown dirt or grey stone, but a luscious soft red with yellow streaks that chased each other in maddening swirls. Stalactites dripped stone from the lofty and irregular ceiling. The floor of the cavern had been covered with stalagmites, but these were broken off and crushed underfoot. Just as well, Bith realized, or Cal and Endril might have been impaled. The cavern stretched away in two directions, maybe sixty feet high, maybe thirty feet wide. The worm hole—she felt a tightening in her chest: she'd been so *sure* there was no worm—continued on the opposite side of the cavern, high up, as if a god had threaded a giant needle through the mountain.

Cal held the torch high and the red-yellow light of the cave shimmered in a thousand thousand facets. "No sign of Hathor. No, wait."

The torchlight shimmied and bobbed and danced. Then Cal said, "Here's his axe."

Bith leant even further forward, in danger of losing her footing. She wondered how she'd get down to the men—they were almost twenty feet below her. Backbreaker still stood just behind her, immobile. She called, "Is there blood?"

Endril had joined Cal. The elf took the torch. "I don't know. Let me look—"

The firelight was suddenly magnified a hundred times, as if someone had ripped off the roof of the cavern. A giant white form, big as a sailing ship, spurted from the worm hole opposite. Cal yelled, Endril shrilled, and Bith froze as the worm returned. It was the same one—could there be more than one?—for it bore the hack marks around its mouth. The worm poured from the hole like a cataract of water, straight for the opposite hole where Bith stood. The girl shuffled her feet, slipped, whimpered.

Something—Backbreaker—shoved her from behind. She tumbled from the tunnel.

The worm's mouth dilated.

Bith fell. Inside.

The girl shrieked as the edges of the mouth passed her. Then the light was gone as the throat snapped shut.

Bump, thump, clump, wham! Bith fetched up against a cold wall. The surface under her—then next to her, then above her—twisted like a bed in a nightmare. Her hands found some ridge and she grabbed hard. The roof, also ridged, banged against the back of her head. She was going to be crushed in the throat of a giant worm! Bith found herself praying and crying and wishing she were back in her mother's castle, sitting on the balcony with her cats and looking out over the misty lake. But she remembered her mother and how she had mocked her daughter's weak stomach, and Bith hung on and gritted her teeth. If for no other reason than to show her mother up, she had to survive.

And in fact, she wasn't dead yet. Or even close to it. As the seconds passed she found herself still clinging to one ridge, held in place by the other. Nothing else happened. The worm was still moving, undulating like a ship at sea, but the ride was smooth. Bith tried to take stock. She fought down panic by concentrating on spells. Which one could get her out of here? Any of them? Fireballs? Glow? Levitate? Ignite! Yes, surely this—flesh—would burn if she got the spell off right. But how would she breathe in the smoke? And imagine the stench!

The worm took a dive downward. Bith felt her hair falling down her back. Was it stuffy in here already? Would she suffocate before she could get off a spell? It was so *black*! Something flopped across her hands and she recoiled from the touch. It was hairy, like a big spider. But warm. And the smell was familiar.

Carefully she unpried one aching hand and put it out for the object. It was soft and grimy with—hard nails? It was a hand? A foot! Hathor's!

"Thor! *Thor!*" the girl cried, "I'm so glad to find you! I— Thor?"

She tugged at the foot. It fell limply from her grasp. Was he dead? Had the troll suffocated? No, he was too tough to die. And too nice. The girl let go to lock both hands onto the foot. She dug her fingers in alongside the ropy tendon and felt. Yes, there was a pulse! It would be all right. Unless they both suffocated. Or were crushed, or swallowed further, or drowned in black slime.

The worm dropped with a stomach-wrenching lurch. It bucked and twisted and rolled on its back until Bith's brain shook in its pan. She tried to think of what to do, but was too dizzy and weak. Then suddenly the beast shuddered all through its frame. And she could—see—light?

A gash in the worm's side opened and light spilled in. The gash shut and the blackness returned. Then it cracked open again and stayed that way. Something slim and shining penetrated the crack.

A voice called, "Bith! Are you in there? *Bith!*" It was Cal.

"Here," the girl squeaked. She gathered her breath and shouted, "Here!"

An arm holding a torch shoved inside, followed by Endril's head. "There you are. And Thor. Would you like to come out?"

Bith gasped. She had to press with her back to get free of the embrace of the dead worm. Then she crawled over Hathor's body and was helped through the split. She pointed Cal and Endril back to the troll and they tugged him free.

The girl clung to the elf while the boy dragged the troll to a level spot on the cavern floor. Bith looked around. The giant worm lay on the floor of the elongated cavern, as huge, white, and repulsive as the Mistwall itself. It was dead white with heavy creases at intervals where the segments joined. There was twenty feet of it showing in the cavern and more inside the tunnel beyond—she had no idea how long it really was. The thing twitched feebly, the spasms making it jump three feet at a time. The gash that Endril and Cal had hacked in the side—Bith wondered how they had known where to hack and not cut their fellow adventurers—oozed white pulp like tree sap. Evidently the worm had snatched up Hathor, retreated, then come back and shot across the upper part of the cave to engulf Bith. She wondered if the thing had used an intelligence for that or had merely followed blind instinct and sucked up everything in sight. She looked at the monster worm and felt her knees go weak.

"We were lucky to get you free," the elf said quietly. "It was suspended over our heads. Cal leaped up and struck. He must have hit something vital. It almost fell on us."

Bith opened her mouth, but only a squeak came out.

Aside from being out cold and unbelievably filthy—as they all were—the troll seemed unharmed. They patted his cheeks and pumped his chest and after a few moments he came to. He worked his face in a goggle-eyed fishy way before he sat up.

"Where's my axe?" he asked.

Cal gave it to him. Hathor lay back down with it clutched to his chest.

"Do we bury you now?" the boy asked.

The troll opened one eye. "Don't like worms to eat me."

Everyone laughed with relief. Cal quipped, "He probably didn't like you much, either. I'm surprised he didn't puke you up."

"Washed my feet. Taste good."

"Think," said Endril, "how this experience has increased our knowledge by leaps and bounds. Now you two know how a worm feels when fed to a fish."

"I think I'll become a vegetarian like Hathor here." Bith giggled. "I'll stick to corn and roots and mushrooms."

"And dogs," Cal added.

They all laughed at that, but the laughing died down as they noticed a rumbling that built and built like a storm coming in overhead.

"What's that? An earthquake?"

Endril was up and reaching for Hathor. "We should move, I think. This worm—"

Wasn't dead. It must have been only stunned. For suddenly it gave a massive hump in the middle. A long clean split appeared far down its body, away from the gash. The giant frame jerked, once, twice. Then with a nerve-shattering rip the still-living segment of body separated from the dead section. The however-many feet of invisible body tore free and disappeared into the tunnel, but not before leaving something behind.

The party of adventurers howled as the central artery of the worm squirted a waterfall of black glop into the cavern. The same crawling sticky filth that had been shot at them earlier now returned in an avalanche. Too late they tried to dodge out of the way. The ichor spilled all over their upraised arms and down their necks. Blinded, they couldn't see the torrent that hit them, but they could feel it. Endril managed to wipe his eyes clean and push at them. "Run! Go that way!"

Stumbling, cursing, scratching, the party banged into stalagmites and slipped on patches of slime until they clunked into a wall at the end of the cavern.

The swearing went on for some time in various languages. Pinned in the corner, Bith clawed her face clear, though she thought bitterly she'd never feel clean again.

A whiff of fresh air wafted around them from yet another worm hole in the wall. Only Cal had a torch. He'd juggled shield and sword and torch since they'd gotten inside this mountain. He made to strike it alight with flint and steel yet again but Bith stopped him.

The cavern did indeed end here, tapering away to a juncture of floor and ceiling. The girl moved to the hole and stuck her head inside. The hole sloped downwards, and far, far down, she thought she could see a sheen of reflected light. Or maybe it was just spots before her eyes caused by the intense darkness. She pointed out the hole to her companions.

Cal grunted. Endril said nothing. The boy got the torch burning and held it high. The entire floor of the cavern was no longer red and yellow but black and squirming. The carpet of whatever it was—what was it, anyway? Bith held her sleeve up to her face. By the intermittent light she could make out the black goo. It was a combination of tiny, tiny insects and their residue. Mites, of some sort, and the crud they generated. A colony of parasites living in the intestines of the worm. Bith shuddered and scrubbed some more.

Endril said, "We're safe for the moment."

Bith snapped, "I can't *believe* we survived an attack by a giant worm only to be trapped in the corner by *bugs*."

"We haven't had the best luck, or judgement," Endril admitted.

Bith continued, "And we're no closer to this damned wizard. He could have gone anywhere! Why didn't you tell us about these caves, Hathor?"

The troll shrugged. "Did. Backbreaker and I explore. Found bats and nothing else."

"What about this worm?"

Another shrug. "Worms move fast. Go miles in a day

looking for food. Saw hole but didn't see worm. He came back. Sorry.''

The girl sighed. ''Oh, I'm sorry, Thor. It's not your fault. We were just surprised, is all. *Oogh.* I *hate* bugs!''

''Hey, what happened to Backbreaker anyway?'' Cal asked. ''He disappears more often than Endril here.''

Bith pointed. ''He was up there—behind me. He tried to pull me back when the worm lunged. No, wait a moment. He pushed me.''

''Pushed you?''

The magic user thought hard. ''I think so. I think . . . he tried to push me clear of the worm's maw.''

''Or into it?'' Cal asked.

''Now why would you say that?''

The boy shrugged and waggled his sword. ''I don't know, but I haven't trusted him since the day he signed on with us. He's been pretty chummy with Hathor here, though.''

Hathor shrugged again. ''He just follow me. Not talk much. I not like him either.''

Bith combed her crusted hair with her fingers. ''Well, never mind. He'll turn up again. Like a bad penny.''

''Are these insects coming at us?'' That was Endril.

''And how,'' said Cal. ''Let's try this hole. Thor?''

The troll twisted among them easily—Bith recalled he could see in the dark—and stuck his head down the hole. ''Hunh. Goes to bottom of ravine, must be. Smell fresh air, big fog wall. Water, too.''

''Clean water?''

''Yep, spill from inside mountain. I go?''

''Go.''

The troll hopped into the round passage. He set both hands and feet against the circumference and scuttled away like a spider. The other three waited in the circle of firelight. It was quiet. The puddles of bugs gave off a slight hissing-crunching sound, like surf on a gravel beach.

After a while Hathor's voice carried up from the hole, sounding hollow and distant. *''Hoy! Come here. Found something.''*

Cal called down, *''Whaaaattt?''*

A pause. *''You see. Something good.''*

''Good?'' Bith asked.

Cal shrugged. "Better there than here." He snuffed out the torch, tightened his gear, and entered the tunnel. Bith climbed up behind him. Her leather-soled boots slipped on the smooth floor. Endril came last.

Cal was muttering ahead. "The slope gets steeper."

"What?" Bith asked.

"I said, the slope—*whoa! WHOOOOOAAAA!*"

"*Cal!*"

Cal was gone. The girl and the elf froze. They heard only a faint banging and scraping and a stream of receding profanity. Bith inched forward and saw where the tunnel did dip, smoothly but almost straight down before heading up again. The sheen of light was brighter now, strong enough for her to see her hands. She called, "Cal! Cal! Are you all right?"

Silence.

"Ca-"

"*I'm fine.*" The voice came from far away. "*Come on ahead, but do it on your—rump.*"

"My what?"

"*Slide. You'll be fine.*"

Bith looked back at Endril. The elf waved an elegant hand. Bith sighed and sat down carefully. She drew on her gloves and tucked her hood over her head. Then she scooted forward an inch, then another, then—she was sliding!

Like Cal, she let out a *Whoo!* as she slid and banged and swooped around corners. The ride was rough and scary, but exhilirating too. Down and down she went, faster and faster, sliding on her tunic and cloak with occasional braking with her hands. She wondered if she'd fetch up against some wall, but recalled that Cal had survived.

Then suddenly she rounded a corner and the light blinded her. The tunnel ended and she flew into space with a bleat. But strong arms caught her and set her down gently on a rocky slope.

Peering between her hands, Bith took a step and staggered. The strong hands—they were Cal's—tugged her aside. She got her vision back just in time to see Endril shoot from the hole above her and crash onto the shale slope.

Bith turned to Cal. "Why didn't you catch *him*?"

Cal grinned at her. His teeth were white in a face black with slime and dust. "What fun would that be?"

The elf sat up rubbing his elbow and the back of his head. He got his eyesight back and located his companions.

The crowd looked around. They were indeed where Hathor had said: at the bottom of the chasm behind the castle. Rock walls loomed on two sides. The Mistwall roiled above one side in its queer U-shape. Above the other, the tower balcony projected at a dizzying height. If they walked to the left far enough they would enter the valley. To the right, the canyon narrowed as it wound into the hills. The floor of the chasm was fallen rock, some sparse grasses and scrubby trees. It was also littered with the stuff Bith had pitched off the balcony in days past.

The girl put one hand on the wall and looked up. "We came all the way from up *there*?"

Cal grunted. "Yep. We have to go back up, too."

"Why do you say that?"

"Come here. Look what Thor found."

Hathor was hunched over farther down the slope. He squatted awkwardly, like a crippled duck, and took small steps sideways. Bith put her feet carefully lest she fall.

Bith called, "Hathor! Hey, Hathor! What's the big idea of letting us tumble down the slope?"

The troll turned curiously. Cal laughed. "*He* didn't slide. He walked. But a human can't do it the way he did."

Bith sighed anew. "I keep forgetting how disparate we all are."

"Disparate?"

"Different. We've nothing in common, really."

"Except that we're all mad as hares in spring."

Bith laughed. "There is that."

Hathor stood up when they arrived. He grinned his wolf's grin. "Fun?"

Bith rubbed her backside. "Fun. Oh, yes. I can't wait to do it again."

Cal said, "Look what we found."

Hathor handed her a slim bar of silver. The girl accepted it and weighed it in her hand. It was about eighteen inches long and slim as her finger. It was round on the ends and entirely smooth. Something about its heft tickled her memory. She bobbed it in the air a few times. It felt somehow alive, as if it were fluid and not solid. More quicksilver than silver, she thought.

"It's a wand."

Cal nodded. "That's what we thought. And look here." He held up a small metal bracket.

"A belt buckle?"

"Unh, unh. Too small. I'd say it's a shoe buckle."

Endril came close and looked without touching. He stroked his pointed chin.

Hathor had resumed his scavenging. He suddenly grunted and stooped and came up with some white nuggets. He poured them into Bith's other hand. She peered. "They're—teeth."

Endril murmured, "Human."

The girl chirped. "Ah! I was right! The old fool fell off the balcony drunk and scavengers ate him."

Cal shook his head. "Try again."

Bith just looked confused.

Cal asked her gently, "What happened to you in the tunnels?"

"What happened to me? I got covered in muck."

"Before that."

"I got—swallowed by a worm."

"And?"

"Why are you asking me all these questions? You and Endril cut me loose. Me and Hathor."

"Right. Now suppose you were a wizard being clever and poking around in a bunch of caves. And you got snatched up, swallowed by a giant worm. And you pass out from lack of air, like Hathor did. Then what happens to you?"

Bith stared at the small white teeth in her palm. Then she recoiled and dropped them. They rattled on the shale. *"Yuck! Ugh! Yew! That's disgusting!"*

Cal nodded. "Sure is."

Endril picked up a tooth and looked close at it. "So the magician was swallowed and digested, and all that survived were his teeth."

"And the metal. It all passed out the worm's back end and rattled out that hole. Down to here."

Bith was rubbing the palm of her hand against her filthy pants. She had not, however, dropped the silver wand. Endril tossed the tooth over his shoulder. "So much for finding our magician."

"In one piece, anyway. We're stuck with the problem of taking the sword by ourselves."

Endril said gently, "We are to *destroy* the sword, Cal."

"Well, maybe."

Bith looked up at the Mistwall, over at the castle balcony, and both ways down the ravine. She asked bleakly, "Why don't we just walk down this canyon and keep going?"

Endril stroked his chin. Cal stirred the fallen teeth with the toe of his boot. Hathor walked back to their party with another scrap of metal. It was a crumpled badge cut in the shape of a crescent moon, made for sewing on clothing. Cal offered to hold it, since it was silver.

Hathor scratched his neck. "Wash?" he asked.

Bith shook her head. "Oh, yes, the water. Lead us to it! Please."

The water was farther down the canyon. It was no more than a trickle that spilled from the rocks and emptied onto the shale. A twin line of tough green chased it across the rocks. The people took turns scooping water in their hands. They mopped their faces and necks and scraped the gunk off their clothing. They drank their fill and felt much better. Eventually they sat down in a circle of rocks and propped their backs as comfortably as possible. Even with the Mistwall looming over them the sun was warm and pleasant. Cal produced jerked meat from a pouch. Hathor shared his ubiquitous roots. The four munched and chewed and talked over their dilemma.

"Well," said the soldier philosophically, "at least we learned where the wizard went. He came to a bad end."

"Ouch," said Bith.

"Yep, he's been passed to a better place."

"Stop it."

"Yessir, he should have had a more noble outcome . . ."

"Cal!"

The boy ripped jerky with his teeth. His fingernails were as black as Hathor's. "Does this mean I can pluck the sword up and run with it?"

"No, it doesn't mean that."

"How about if I promise to run *fast*? Very, very fast."

"Can you run faster than the roof can collapse?"

"Sure."

"It is not just the castle that concerns us," Endril said. "We must think of the Mistwall. I am sure if we touch the sword it will envelop the castle, maybe the whole valley. We cannot allow that. We need time for both ourselves and the defenders to get clear. No one goes into the Mistwall and returns, as so I've heard." He stopped and the three males looked at Bith. "Well, almost no one."

Cal countered, "What about those orcs and other beasties? If they come out of the Mistwall they must be able to go back into it. I say it's grandmothers' tales to frighten children. It's just a bank of fog you can walk in and out of. It just stinks, is all. Right, Bith?"

"No. The smell of evil gets into your head and poisons you. You'd become one of them before you saw daylight again."

"Not me."

Endril said, "Let us hope we not test it. The student might not survive the lesson."

Hathor said, "Bith should grab sword, jump off balcony. Fly down here."

"I can't fly."

"Oh."

"Suppose we tie a rope to it, then throw the rope off the balcony," Cal offered. "Then we come down here and jerk the rope."

Bith shook her head. Her grimy hair flopped around her face. "You don't understand. It's balanced there as if on its point. One touch will undo the spell. I think. Or, as I said before, you may not even be able to move it, as if it were fixed in stone. There may not be a solution to this problem. . . . I don't know. We're just going round in circles."

"Circling or no," Endril said, "we must see that sword does not fall into the hands of the Dark Lord. Whoever or whatever he is, having even a minor god like Vili under his thumb would give him power too awful to consider."

Cal rose and stretched his legs. "I'd be willing to just grab it and run. Give me a clear shot down those stairs and stay out of my way. We'll see what collapses first."

Bith snapped, "How many times do we have to say it! You *can't*—"

Hathor interrupted them both, "Where sun go?"

"Eh?" The party looked up.

"The Mistwall," Endril whispered. "It's moving."

It was. Whereas before they could look and see clear sky above the face of the fog, now they are looking at the bottom of it. The greenish smokey cloud had drifted across the canyon. Even as they watched, the balcony grew dimmer, harder to see through the mist.

"How can that be?" Cal asked.

The elf stared up at the castle, his long face somber as an eagle's. "Perhaps it's time. The Dark Lord's forces are in place. Perhaps one big push of magic is enough to engulf the castle. Or perhaps someone's moved the sword."

"Moved the sword? No, I want the sword!"

Bith retorted, "Cal, we've *told* you! You can't have it! You're obsessed with the thing."

The soldier shook his head. "No, I'm not! I just want a chance to hold it once before we destroy it."

"Hist! Listen!" said the elf. He had his head cocked like a dog.

Hathor grunted, but the two humans could hear nothing. "Now what?"

"Storm," said Hathor.

"Not a storm," Endril corrected. "Shouting. War cries. The Dark Army *is* attacking."

"We've got to get up to the tower!" Bith said.

Cal hitched up his belt. "Which way?"

Bith looked around. "Not up that tunnel. Hathor is the only one can scale that."

The troll hefted his axe. "Know another way. Backbreaker and me find it."

Bith asked, "What do you suppose that giant's *up* to, anyway?"

Cal snorted. "Who cares? Let's go."

Hathor led the way, though he went in the direction opposite they would have guessed. He led them up the canyon away from the castle, past the spring. From there he mounted a tumble of stone and crawled onto a ledge. He reached down a mighty arm and pulled the others after him. Two more lifts brought them to a cave.

"It's good we have you, Thor," Bith panted. "We couldn't climb this ourselves."

Hathor grinned. "Easy. Come. Quick way back."

The way was easy enough, if long. They negotiated an old riverbed, then a series of switchbacks. They went underground half the time, through caves or along ledges the rest. Occasionally they walked the bottom of a sharp cleft that had no rocks to impede them. Hathor explained this was part of the back way the defenders had mentioned as their evacuation route, which they kept clear of debris. "Met scouts in here when walked these past days."

They met someone now. Hathor hushed them and pulled them back into a niche. This spot was a wide track with rock walls that almost met overhead. Cal snuffed out the torch in the sand underfoot. The party froze and listened. Soon they all heard it, a reassuring sound: a chattering like a flock of magpies. Children calling to their friends, entreating their parents to be carried, singing and laughing. Hathor stepped out and raised a horny hand.

The families of Cairngorm were well equipped to travel. Each man, woman, and child bore a pack and cloak and carried something in their hand. Several led donkeys piled with sacks of food and firewood and tents and geese tied by the feet. At the sight of the party the children squealed and ran to their mothers. The warrior men and women hefted their axes and swords, then let them drop. "Friend Hathor, Bith, Cal, Endril! Advance," called a tall man in front. He was, as with all the rest, blond and blue-eyed and shaggy-maned.

"What transpires on the wall?" Endril asked.

"The enemy rises in a wave to sweep over Cairngorm. Not all the arrows in the world could hold them back. It looks like a black carpet thrown against us. We could see it coming all morning. They left their normal camp activities after breakfast and drifted to the tents. Someone tall gave a speech for a long time. Then they turned and swept upon us not three hours ago. Barin didn't even try to hold the first wall. We shot our lot and fell back. We are the first wave to leave, with the children and mothers and elders. The rest hang back to make sure none are left and see we are not overtaken."

"The castle still stands?" the elf asked.

"Aye, for now, but not much longer. 'Tis a sad day," he told them, his voice grown hoarse, "By nightfall Cairngorm will be gone from the face of the earth. But not from our minds or hearts. Eh, good people?"

The crowd raised their weapons and their voices in a lusty cheer that rang against the walls. But the silence that followed was just as loud.

"Go then, good people, and may the spirits guide you on your way," Endril told them. "Yours is not the first village to fall under the Mistwall's deadly embrace, nor shall it be the last. But like all bad storms, it will blow away eventually and leave the earth fresh and clean."

The yellow-haired people nodded, but their faces were sober. Without many more words they passed by the party and down the slope towards the unknown.

The party of four were quiet when again they stood alone. Cal asked Endril, "Do you believe that stuff about the Mistwall being rolled back some day?"

Endril replied, "All things come to an end. All. But a land may lie dead at the bottom of the sea for a millennium before it feels the sun again, and a lot of beings come and go in darkness during that time."

"That's very encouraging, Endril," Cal told him bitterly. "You're as uplifting as a lark."

"Live some," the elf replied, "before you judge."

On that sour note the party trudged uphill towards their goal.

"Stop here," Hathor said after they had gone another few hundred yards.

Cal asked, "Why?" The way before them was another stretch of cave, open and clear.

"Secret." The troll pointed to a dark space way above head height. He crouched down with his hands against the wall and motioned someone to get on his back. "Climb."

Endril did as the troll suggested. Hathor straightened his powerful legs and the elf snagged the ledge. He swung up light as a squirrel into the space.

"It opens up," they heard him say, "into another passage."

Hathor grinned and squatted again. "Shortcut to castle. Backbreaker and me find."

Cal helped Bith onto Hathor's back. He said, "The castle defenders don't know it's here?"

"Nope. No one go in for years."

When Cal was on the ledge he reached down and offered his hand to pull Hathor up. He wished he'd offered his left hand instead of his right because his shoulder creaked in its socket. The troll was *heavy*.

The four brushed aside ancient cobwebs and peered down the tunnel. Cal said, "It's *black*. Looks hand-hewn."

"Goes under wall."

"What wall?"

"Castle wall, big one." The troll sketched a circle around his waist.

"The *outer bailey* wall? That surrounds *everything*?"

"Yup. Old tunnel to valley floor. River bed, I think. But big stones on other side. We couldn't move."

"But how—"

"Side tunnel goes to castle. Come."

"He's right, Cal," Bith interrupted. "Enough talk. Let's go."

"But I can't believe the people who live here don't—"

"Come *on*!"

Hathor had taken the lead again, without benefit of torch. Cal strove to light his as they shuffled along in the intense blackness. He dropped his flint and couldn't find it, then gave up as the rest of the party left him behind. Bith gasped as she stumbled. Endril and Hathor, in the lead, had no trouble seeing. Cal brought up the rear, as usual. This was his preferred position, one a soldier takes pride in holding, but today he could have done without it. It was tiring being a second-class citizen in the dark behind trolls and elves. He stumbled often over fallen rock.

Suddenly the boy plowed into Bith's back as she banged into Hathor. Endril had somehow gotten out of the way. Cal sputtered but the troll shushed him. *"Listen!"*

Cal listened. "I don't hear any—"

"Rawwwwwwwwwwrrrrrrr!!!!!!" The shout all but knocked

Cal and Bith over. The sound was deafening in the close cave, goose-pimply in its unhuman basso.

It was Hathor who had shouted. A battle cry. He was charging down the tunnel and swinging his axe at some flickering light ahead. He added a very human, *"Follow!"* Endril, Cal, and Bith followed, with their ears ringing and their blood pounding, towards what they knew not.

Hathor screamed around a corner into a maelstrom of hairy faces and jagged weapons and flickering torches. Cal and Bith had only a second to register the scene.

In a three-way juncture of tunnel stood a knot of orcs, evil humans, and piglets. The humans alone carried birch torches. Fresh-sharpened steel shone on the edges of war spears, battleaxes, mattoxes, and short swords. All else was black or hair or dirty grease, the smell of which filled their nostrils. Past the first knot—there had to be twelve enemies within arm's reach—a long dim line of more evil soldiers trailed off into the dark of the leftmost tunnel. Every evil face was turned towards them in astonishment.

Standing tall amid the group, stooped by the low ceiling, was Mountain Back Breaker.

Cal grabbed Bith's shoulder to pull her behind him. Endril dove to the right to avoid the troll's backswing.

"Elf! Elf!" shouted a chorus.

Hathor howled again and swung his felling axe high. The troll's howl was echoed by a dozen throats. The axe flew in a murderous arc and plowed into the first three enemy soldiers.

Blood sprayed in the air, scattering the firelight in all directions.

CHAPTER
10

There were three enemies down on the dusty floor of the cave. The troll's broad axe had severed one man's arm: he lay on the floor screaming as blood gouted from a stump. An orc had fallen back showing lungs through split ribs. A piglet was dead from a smashed head. The others—orcs, men, and all—pressed backwards momentarily from the horror of the attack.

Hathor kept them staggered. He was spattered with others' blood. His face was a fanged and screaming mouth. And his axe swung back and forth as if he were cutting wheat. Minions of the Dark Army clawed and fell over each other to get out of the way.

Cal stood frozen as he tried desperately to guess what was going on. That a whole troop of dark soldiers could be here, sneaking to the castle through these tunnels, when only Backbreaker and Hathor had known the tunnels were here, had to mean that—

"Backbreaker's *betrayed* us! The *bastard*!" Cal's voice shook with rage. "He's opened the tunnel for them! I'll fix *him*!" He changed his grip on his sword to wade into the attack. Behind Bith began to chant.

'No,'' interjected Endril, his voice inhumanly calm. He caught the boy's leather sleeve in a strong grip and dragged him sideways.

Cal's boots skidded. He jerked a vicious elbow. ''What are you *doing*?''

The elf didn't answer. He shoved the boy up the tunnel towards the castle, then grabbed Bith with the other hand and moved her. The palms of her hands were luminous and smoking. She shook his hand off and continued her spell.

''Hathor's bought us time,'' Endril explained. ''We're in the proper tunnel now. *Thor! Join us!*''

''Elf!'' a voice screeched. ''Kill elf!''

During this short interval Hathor had felled another five soldiers. His swings were wild and uncontrolled as he threw all his strength into them. Now he stopped suddenly and backed up, turned and crashed into Bith.

The girl staggered and recovered, then ducked past the troll back towards the enemy. ''Stand clear!''

Bith slapped her hands on the bodies of two dead orcs. Her fingers had to be flat or she'd blow her fingernails off. Raw energy churned from her heart, rushed down her arms like a boiling cataract, then left her palms in a blinding flash.

With a *whoosh!* twin jets of flame gushed from her palms. The tiny intersection lit up. Fire crackled and spat as hair, leather, wood, and skin ignited. The flame was blinding, the stink appalling. Cal controlled the urge to retch. Endril barked, ''Run!'' and they ran.

With Hathor in the lead and Endril behind, the party gathered speed and pelted along in the dark. The two humans never were sure who was where. All they knew was that it was very dark. They held a hand in front of their faces for protection. The howls and screams were left behind.

Hathor called back, ''Good spell.''

''I just wish I could shoot fireballs from a distance!'' the girl gasped.

On they ran. The humans missed their footing often but thankfully never fell. As their breath began to burn in their lungs Hathor warned, ''Slow! Wall here!''

He trotted and stopped. Cal rearranged his baldric. Bith panted and leaned on the wall. Endril pressed past them to help Hathor.

"What is it? A door?"

"Wood wall. Break through."

There came a grunt and then a *crash!* of splintered wood. Hathor kicked again with his bare feet. He ducked through the hole. A strong vinegary smell surrounded them. Cal groped with his hands and thumped up against something solid and round. Bith and Endril followed.

The elf turned immediately. "Bith, can you do your fire spell again?"

"Huhh? What? I guess so, yes. Where are we?"

Wood clattered. Endril found Bith's hand and set it gently on a pile of kindling. "Fire this." The girl fumbled out another firefly (her last, she reckoned) and gasped the ignite spell. The fire crackled into life.

They were in yet another part of the cellar beneath the castle. The wine cellar. Huge barrels and hogsheads taller than a man lay on their side, some tapped with bungs, some obviously empty. A stairwell was at the far end of the chamber. The wall they had broached from the other side was made of white-washed planks laid sideways. It made up a wall—a false wall—behind two barrels.

Endril reached out and shoved at a barrel. It didn't move. He shoved another and it rocked. "Empty. Cal, grab hold and we'll roll it in front of the hole.

Hathor had run to the stairwell, presumably to scout. The elf and boy got the barrel off its stand and wrestled it in front of the hole to the tunnels.

Bith frowned at the smallness of the blaze. She rubbed her palms, which were painfully red. "I'm sorry, that's all I can do right now."

Endril fanned at the small blaze with his hat. "It will suffice. Would we had some brandy."

Cal the soldier had done some scouting of his own. "Maybe we do. This can't hurt, anyway." He held up a small glass bottle from a sideboard.

Endril pointed at the tiny blaze. Cal whipped the bottle against the stone ceiling. It shattered and rained liquid onto the barrel. Flame leaped and licked up its side. Cal threw three more bottles—"It's a shame to waste this!!"—and got the blaze roaring. Smoke filled the low room and made them cough. The three shuffled to the stairs and ascended. After they had passed the thick door Endril slammed it shut, but there was no lock to engage.

They were in a short, sunken corridor that slanted up to the rest of the cellar rooms. They could see light at the top. Voices sounded. Then down the corridor stepped three Cairngormers bristling with weaponry.

The closest man swiveled his shield in their direction and took a firmer grip on his short sword. "Where the devil did *you* come from?"

Endril nodded. "Yon wine cellar. There's a passage beyond the back wall full of your enemy."

"There be no passage through that cellar. We'd know of it." The three, two men and a woman, shuffled their feet to get elbow room and a better look at their opponents. They were black with muck and grey with cobwebs. Hathor, with blood across his face and chest, was a particularly unsettling figure.

"You don't or you'd have blocked it," Endril corrected. "My troll discovered it just these past days. And now a horde of orcs are in it and coming fast."

"I don't think so. I think we better take you to Barin—" Hathor cocked an ear. "They here."

With a *smash!* the wine cellar door burst open. Orcs howled and screamed and gibbered as they flooded out the door.

The adventurers were gone. They bolted past the natives, who fell in close behind.

In the catacombs under the castle stood the rest of Cairngorm's army. The blond men and women warriors—more than two hundred of them—had gathered together, said goodbye to their homes and fields, and marched in orderly retreat into the cellar. The dark had finally come. Some had cried, some had sworn, some were silent. Many had grumbled over a missed fight.

Now as the screaming orcs came into sight a howl of equal rage and intensity welled up from the natives. Weapons shot into the air. The orcan invaders and the human defenders had glared at each other across two stone walls and a stretch of no man's land for a long time, and all were eager, glad even with a fierce joy, to close and hack and maim and kill. The noise threatened to shatter eardrums as the battle was on.

Vili's adventurers were caught square in the middle.

Cal shouted, "Form up! Make a wedge! Form up!"

He yelled for effect and planted himself in the leftmost position. Hathor fell in beside him. Endril flanked on the right, further away from the troll in the center, for Hathor was right-handed and swung his axe from that side. The elf had a wall at his right as a giant stone shield. Bith was behind them. Their practice on the plains paid off now. This "wedge," as they called it, was a tight unit that could withstand attack on three sides, with a magician for backup.

The formation centered around the axeman. A strong fighter with an axe was a terrible thing in battle, for he could knock down enemies like wheat. An axeman could smash through any defense, go where he wanted, and stop anything: it was sergeants with axes that surrounded a king on the field. Yet an axeman needed swordsmen to watch and protect him from a sudden thrust, for he needed both hands on his weapon and he carried no shield. His swordsmen were in turn safe as long as they stayed close (but not too close). With a magician behind them to weave spells and confuse the enemy, the formation was almost invincible.

The party's arrival timed with the first charge by the Cairngormen, and they matched up on the end of a battle line that snaked through the twisted cellar. They held the enemy at bay. Maddened orcs saw too late the giant troll and his axe, and their howls turned to cries of anguish just before Hathor smashed through their shields and shoulders and heads. Anyone reaching in with a blade to pink the troll received a thrust in the throat or eye from Endril's waspish sting, or a good honest shot from Cal Talienson's poor but burnished blade. It was not long before Hathor had a knee-high pile of bodies before him.

The shouting and the clash of armor was frightening, and the stone rooms were hot. Sweat ran in their eyes. Cal shouted, "Look there! I'd like to stab that son of a bitch!" Past pillars and stone walls they could see Backbreaker. The giant used no weapons but his fists, which he flailed high in the air and brought down on human defenders like twin sledgehammers.

"I'd like to do *something*!" Bith shouted from her cramped position behind the soldier.

"Conjure some water!" Hathor panted. He feinted a swipe at a knot of glaring orcs.

"No time." That was Endril, calm as ever. The elf hopped forward and spitted a man through the heart. Cal wondered if, since a pitched battle couldn't excite him, anything could. "We needs get upstairs and quickly. After—"

"The sword, we know!" Cal interrupted. "How do we get there?"

"We know the castle. These orcs do not," Endril said. It seemed strange to be discussing orcs when the very same were jabbing at them from five feet away, but such was war. He pointed his dripping sword to a passageway thirty feet down the wall. "*That* portal takes us up a back stair to the main hall. Let us go thither."

Cal grunted. They couldn't just back out and leave a hole in the ranks, but the battle seemed to be shifting away from them. It was hard to tell in the darkened cellars. Hathor's pile of bodies was almost a hill the enemy had to climb. And the Cairngormers wanted to be away down a far passage anyway. The boy hitched up his belt and made sure of his footing on the blood-slippery stone. "Right! We can disengage! Let's—"

Hathor interrupted, "Company!"

A pack of four savage men, blond and blue-eyed servants of the Dark Lord, had just arrived in the cellars ready for war. Their eyes lighted at the sight of three males and one *woman*. With a hoarse shout they raised shining weapons high. In a steady line, and without dropping their defense, they slid over the pile of bodies. They had swords or short bill-hooks and square shields bound with iron. They wore copper-studded armor and iron helmets. Larger and stronger than most men, they had obviously practiced as a unit themselves. They laughed horribly and taunted their victims as they closed.

They got a surprise.

"Only four?" Cal jibed, and he added a string of epithets to insult their manhood that made Bith blush. It was calculated to make the men mad, and it worked. The end man roared and left the line to strike the boy down from superior height.

Cal expected that and countered. Instead of drawing his shield close to absorb the blow, he flung it wide and high.

The brute balked momentarily as the edge of the shield clipped the underside of his arm. *"Ha!"* Cal barked. Too late the barbarian whipped his own shield around to hit Cal in the face. The boy had made one expert stab at the bottom of the leather armor. The man was pierced through the gut without realizing it. Cal only had to fend him off until his strength departed and he died.

Endril had his metal glove and his slim, balanced blade. He crouched low, dangerous as a mountain cat. His end man advanced warily. It looked too easy. It was. As he roared for a traditional attack he learned how difficult it is to kill an elf.

Endril's attack came not in the center, but to the outside. Where this man expected a blow on his shield, Endril side-stepped and slashed the man on the outside of his weapon arm. The black blade cut like a fish knife, and it opened red flesh to show white bone along half his forearm. Another flicker, and the underside of the arm was cut clean through. The man's arm was effectively sawn through except for the bone. Blood began to blossom as if from a split wineskin. Aghast, the man back-stepped and twisted his head to look. Endril ended his life with a surgical stab just below the ear.

The two men in the middle concentrated on the axeman before them, for they had done this before. While the first baited the troll, trying to elicit a rash stroke, the other cocked his sword arm behind him, the trap hidden by his shield. If the first barbarian could get the axeman to overreach or stumble forward—for nothing threw a man off-balance more than to slash with an axe and strike nothing—his companion would take both arms off with one hard blow. But Hathor could not be baited. As the man before him ducked in and weaved back, Hathor started to swing but held it. Yet each time the man stepped in he threatened to stab Hathor. Three times this happened, in and out, the man actually laughing at his prowess, while his companion waited. Once Hathor stumbled and the man got in a lick that pinked his shoulder, just missing the ear. Hathor looked for his companion swordsmen, but they were still engaged. Even Bith was gone from his peripheral vision. He ground his fangs and muttered trollish oaths under his breath. The second man kicked out with a steel-toed boot and clipped his knee. It didn't hurt, but it distracted. Another thrust by either would put Hathor off-balance or push him back and he'd be done.

Then suddenly the first man made to hop forward and could not. He tried to get back and couldn't. Shielding himself, he glanced at his feet to see what he was stuck in. There was nothing. His feet weren't even touching the ground.

He yelped some oath. His companion looked confused. The first man was taller, suspended in the air a foot. And rising. He windmilled his legs and began to tilt backwards. Flailing only made him spin more. Soon he was horizontal, facing the ceiling. He howled. His companion, both hands full, dithered around and finally decided to tow his friend clear of the fight. He kept his shield up and snaked a sword hand into his friend's belt. In that moment Hathor struck.

The troll threw back his axe and swung hard, knowing he'd connect. The axe hummed and hit the men with a meaty *whack!* The air-borne barbarian lost his right leg below the knee. Knocked clear, he spun out across the room in a dizzying circle, jetting blood. His companion stayed where he was, an axe head buried in his chest. Hathor stood at the end of the hickory haft and watched the man's face turn from red to white. Then the fellow's eyes rolled up in his head and he dropped in place. So deeply was the axe buried that Hathor had to brace his foot on the body to wrench it loose. The severed leg lay between them.

The troll turned to find Bith sunk on her haunches. Her hands hung limp beside her. Sweat lined her brow.

"Was that you?"

The girl gulped and nodded. "I'm not supposed—to be able to levitate—anything more than I can—lift. And I didn't have to—*touch* him!"

"You save my life."

"Did I? I was—only trying to help."

Cal straightened and shoved his man clear. He toppled onto the stone floor with a crash. "Only *four*?" the boy roared. "*Come on*, the rest of you! *Come on!*"

Endril's hand on his collar arrested him. He towed Cal away from the fight. "Let us go."

The fight had moved away into other parts of the cellar. Cairngorm was making an orderly retreat. Only dead natives and dying marauders were left behind. The party herded themselves out the door and up a set of stairs. Endril led.

On the second set of stairs they came up behind two orcs who jabbered to one another. They never heard the elf. He lanced the two of them and pitched them like bales of hay over the heads of the party to smash on the steps below. "Always blathering when they should be fighting," the elf commented.

These stairs brought them to the foyer before the main hall. In the hall itself a troop of something-or-others overturned tables, smashed candlesticks, and set fire to tapestries. The beasts were fat underground dwellers, pasty and slug-like, with bloated faces and sparse white hair. They shrilled when they saw the adventurers pass the door. The first one around the corner got his long nose sliced off by Cal. That one disappeared to be replaced by another who also stuck his nose out and also got it sliced off. The soldier put his back to the door and waited with a cocked arm for the next.

"Come *on*, Cal!" Bith called down from the stairs.

"I'll hold the bridge!" the boy called.

"No, you won't!" Endril barked.

Cal gave a soldier's reply, short and sweet. He added, "You can't tell *me* what to do!"

The other three had paused on the wide stairs. Endril said, "You come now or I'll hoist you over my shoulder!"

Bith called, "And we'll get the runesword and you won't!"

The boy groused. He checked the doorway again—he could hear clucking inside—then bolted away and up the steps. It was well he did, for in the next instant a dozen slugs charged around the corner with slender spears. They ran so fast and so clumsily they clanged the iron tips against the wall Cal had vacated. They looked around stupidly and finally spotted the party disappearing up the stairwell. They squealed and gave chase.

In a short while the adventurers had knocked aside a few more looters and gained the wizard's tower. But at the top of the narrow stairwell they found the door closed and the key missing from the brass lock. Endril slammed against the door without budging it.

"Bith," Endril said, "can you dismantle this door?"

The girl peered past him to see. "Umm, I guess so. I can, uhh, use a fire spell, or an enlarge. Or maybe a—uhh—"

"Never mind. Step you back. Thor, knock it down."

"I'll mind those—whatever they are," Cal called.

Bith said, "I'll go with you."

It didn't take long for Hathor to hack out the lock in the old wooden door. Endril called Cal and Bith to him. Threats had kept the slugs at bay. The party stepped into the wizard's chamber. It seemed to the humans like years since they had been there last, but in fact it had been only early morning. The room was darker now for the Mistwall blotted out the sun. It was hard to say whether the fog seeped inside the balcony or not.

Hathor and Cal dumped a sturdy table and set it before the ruined door. They wedged junk into the stone floor to hold it in place. They turned and found Bith and Endril looking at the runesword. It hung in pristine beauty, suspended like a diamond in mid-air.

Cal joined them. He stared at the perfect sword. "What now?"

"I don't know," Bith said.

Nor did any of them.

A hammering sounded on the door along with a squealing of slugs and deeper hum of something big. The door and the table bracing it creaked.

"Well," said Cal, "do *something*!"

"That's very helpful, Cal," Bith snapped. "What would you have us do?"

The boy waved his hands. "We're supposed to destroy it, right? So how do we do that?"

"I don't know."

"Nor I," put in Endril.

Cal swept an arm around the room. "Days and days of reading all those books and you can't find a spell to ruin a sword?"

"I told you! There was no mention of the sword!"

Cal leaned closer for a look. Bith said, "Don't touch it."

"Bith, to destroy it we have to touch it first, don't we? Look, they forge swords in coal fires. Can't your fire spell melt it?"

"No. It wouldn't be hot enough."

"All right, wouldn't it just break if we slammed it against the floor? I've seen swords break from lesser blows, especially if they're cold."

"I doubt that would work."

"What if we throw if off the balcony? Anything would break falling from that height onto rocks."

"Maybe . . ."

Hathor too had hunkered down for a look. "That not work."

"How do you know?"

"You can tell. Read steel. Tough," the troll shrugged. Then he grunted. "What that there?"

"Where?" Everyone peered close.

"There. Look like Vili."

The four people put their heads together to squint at the blade. Was it imagination, or was there a face deep in the steel, as of someone reflected in a foggy mirror, or seen through smoky glass?

"It's Vili," agreed the elf. "He's saying something."

"What?"

"I don't know. I can't make it out."

Cal said, "He probably wants us to sacrifice ourselves to his glory."

The door jumped in the frame. Someone must have brought up a pole to use as a ram. Another thump elicited a splintering sound. The door would not sustain many more blows.

"Well, *what* are we going to *do*?" Cal asked again.

Bith fluttered her hands in the air. Endril stood loose-limbed and stroked his chin. Hathor brought out a stone and quickly stropped his axe blade.

The door shattered into a dozen pieces. The table got knocked aside. The pole used to batter it down was chucked inside. A confusing jumble showed blades and armor, white hair and black pug noses, shaggy heads and iron helmets. A trio of chittering slugs were ejected into the room, presumably to draw fire. Behind them came a phalanx of tall orcs and humans, at least five of each, careful and slow with weapons foremost.

Hathor stampeded forward with his axe at port arms. Endril whipped out his slim, black blade and took a stance to his left. Cal raised his worn sword and shield.

The orcs and humans grunted as they surveyed the room and the three defenders before them. A barbarian pointed out the shining sword to his partner. The slugs picked themselves up and scurried to one side. The largest orc, a black monster with notches in his ears and white scars etched on his face, waved left and right for the line to fan out. A wide attack was called for.

The defenders could see the battle would be swift and short. In the silence before the storm Endril said, "Bith, do what you will."

"But I don't know what to do!" the girl wailed.

The maulers took a step forward. They gripped and re-gripped the haft of their weapons. The leader grunted something in orcish.

Cal said, "I know what to do."

Without turning around he took three long steps backwards onto the balcony. He tossed his old sword aside and caught the pommel of the runesword.

The suspended weapon came away as easily as if a squire had handed it to him. As everyone in the room watched the boy took a small practice swing, then a wider one. The sword was alive. Cal could feel it. In one second he came to know that sword more intimately than he'd ever known anyone or anything before. It was feather light in his hand, yet it had a deadly, quivering weight in the nose that would carry through any obstacle. The balance was perfect, better than an empty hand. A man would never be betrayed and pulled off-balance, never tire from swinging it. In a stark moment of frozen time Cal knew everything there was to know about swordsman-ship, about fighting, about living, about dying. When he moved the shining blade, it hummed ancient runes of power. The songs sang in his head like lightning on a winter's day. With this sword he was a master.

In slow motion Caltus Talienson brought the blade around to face his enemies. None had moved. Nothing in the room had moved since he'd touched the sword.

Cal could see everything clearly, in the tiniest detail: the curled legs on a flea on the wrist of a red-haired man, traces of worn engraving on the sword of the gnoll before him, a drop of sweat at the tip of an orc's mustache. He could see every flaw in their armor, every notch in every blade, every weakness and hesitation. He could hear the hearbeats of his foes and his friends. He could feel the stone floor under his boots shift in its bed.

Still no one moved.

As lightly as a butterfly preening its wing, Cal swept the sword behind him. The runes sang to him, rang in his ears. He could hear a choir of angels urge him on from distant hilltops. And inside him rose a bubble, a wave, a flood, a shout.

Cal roared, *"VILI!"* at the top of his lungs. Then he was moving faster than the wind. He was upon the enemy.

The first assailant was a man with blond braids who wore studded leather. He carried a gnarly spear set with obsidian behind the long steel blade. Before the man could blink, Vili's sword swiped through the man's shoulder, his spear, and his chest with no more trouble than cutting a flower. The man hadn't even fallen before Cal attacked the next. This was an orc, grey-skinned and black-haired, wiry but tall. Cal's returning backswing caught him at the neck and took off his head neatly. Before that blood could spurt Cal completed a loop and killed the next orc as he tried to flinch out of the way.

A long spear came at him from the second rank. Cal watched it come. He tossed his shield away because it hampered him. With his bare hand, he pushed the man's wooden spear aside, caught it and pulled. He thrust the runesword straight into the belly of the owner, twisted the blade to free it, and drew it back. The dying man's hand stabbed out to punch him and Cal jumped forward. He drove his shoulder into the man and bowled him backwards into his fellows who crowded the top of the stair. As they fell in a tangle Cal was already spinning to the left, careful to always swing the sword away from himself, seeing everything, reveling in his power.

The red-haired man with the fleas tried to run, but Vili's sword flicked across his back, splitting his wire-laced armor and severing his spine. The man folded in half. His scream sounded to Cal like a cow lowing in the fog. The master swordsman completed his spin and found three more enemies staring at him with wide eyes and open mouths. Cal laughed again. They too would go down like wheat before Vili's scythe. The sword was thirsty, and gods like a blood sacrifice, the more the better. Vili's handmaidens sang from the clouds and filled the chamber with music. The runes built in his mind, revealing all the answers mankind could ask and many more beside. Cal was more than a man now. He was like a god himself.

To his friends he was a blur. At the first shuffle from the orcs Hathor had readied a blow, but in another second he'd had to jump back out of Cal's way lest he catch a taste of the humming blade. Endril had also moved back. Bith put her hands to her mouth and tried to stifle a scream. It was frightening to see Cal this way. The boy had taken three short steps since meeting the enemy, and he'd killed three men at every step. He moved faster than a rabbit before a hound, faster than a windstorm breaking branches in a forest, faster than an eagle pouncing. The runesword whipped through the air like a hummingbird. Blood geysered into the air, bringing a smell like hot metal. The clash of arms and armor was horrendous as the sword blade cut through steel and copper and iron. Broken weapons ricocheted off the walls like hail. The dying screamed or burbled or prayed and the living shrieked and cursed. Cal danced and spun, cut and thrust, hacked his way clear, jumped into another group of living enemies and turned them into dying men.

Hearing the noise of the battle, more orcs crowded from the stairs into the room, lusting after battle and blood. They received only a quick death from a blade they barely saw. Soon Cal the master swordsman could barely set his feet down on the stone floor. Attackers were writhing bodies on the floor and the boy was standing on them, yet he didn't notice. Nor did he notice as an orc jabbed a spear into his back above the kidneys—the orc simply died a second later. A slug smashed a bludgeon into Cal's kneecap to no effect. One huge barbarian got in a sword thrust to Cal's groin, but the only reply was a jab through the jaw into the brain. Still Cal killed with the blade, tireless and unstoppable.

"Venus and Vulcan, they're killing him!" Bith bawled.

"He kill them," Hathor corrected. "All of them."

The three had retreated to the balcony. Endril took his eyes off the majestic Cal and looked around. "And us besides. Note you how the mist closes in."

"Yes," Bith said with a hand to her face. "It *stinks*!"

"It's more deadly than just poison," Endril agreed. "It will overwhelm us soon. Moving the sword has indeed unleashed it."

The air was seemingly gone from the room. In its place was the greenish vapor of the Mistwall, a smell of low tide and swamp gas and things newly dead. It thickened the air so that even Cal, no more than fifteen feet away, was hard to see.

Bith suddenly felt a trickle of something on her head. She looked up and got dust in her eyes. What? . . . Then she realized what it meant: if dust was filtering out from stone that had sat in one place for many hundred years . . . she tried to say something but could only squeak as . . .

The balcony creaked ominously. It was only a mild grinding, but the noise froze the three of them. Then the handrail at either side disappeared, separated from the building, gone in the fog without a sound.

Bith jumped into the room to stand on the spot the runesword had occupied. This brought her closer to the fighting, the screaming, the splash of blood and crunch of bone and flesh. A dead orc stared up at her with wide yellow eyes. A dying man leaked blood at her feet. She bit her knuckles. The whole mess had happened so fast, within seconds. The orcs had burst through the door, Cal had turned into a superman with the runesword in his hand, and now the tower threatened to collapse. Panic overwhelmed her. Bith covered her eyes and prayed to be home with her mother.

Hathor barked out, "No!"

A gray mass came through the door by stepping on and over soldiers. He was too tall for the doorway and had to duck. Then Backbreaker's pointed head reared above the crowd. He was covered from the neck down with blood and his hands dripped gore. He even had blood in his mouth where he had bitten people. People, Bith thought, the brave defenders of Cairngorm. How could they ever have trusted this monster?

Backbreaker, if that was his true name, gobbled orders in some arcane language. But the orcs and humans in the room did not respond. In mindless procession they had poured up the stairs to attack whoever was in the room, only to find, three at a time, that a boy with a sword proved unkillable.

Cal was still jumping, dancing, swiping, calm and cool and altogether unhuman. He cut down men and skewered orcs and backslashed gnolls, all with a savage joy. Then he saw Backbreaker and his eyes flashed. The girl and the troll and the elf saw his reaction clearly. The old Cal was still inside somewhere. With a howl their friend threw himself at the traitorous giant.

Backbreaker had seen enough to know he must avoid the sword. Quickly he seized a villain in each hand and threw them like dolls at Cal. The swordsman swiped one in half with the unbelievably sharp sword, but he was bowled over by the other. As Cal went down Backbreaker threw another victim on top of him. Then a half a dozen enemies closed in with spears and knives. They were eager to kill this slashing wonder, eager to carry a piece of him away to show their comrades.

Hathor howled and leapt at the pile of bodies. He sank his axe blade in a man's back, but two more took that one's place. Endril protected the troll by cutting an orc's wrist to the bone. Then the elf dragged the girl forward.

"Come," he said in a calm voice that cut through the noise, "arms will not suffice. We need a spell."

Bith's legs quivered so badly she thought she'd fall. This wasn't adventure: it was death, death, death everywhere! "A sp-spell? *What* spell? I *can't*!"

Endril continued to drag her towards the melee when all she wanted was to run away. "Any. A good one." Then he slashed another thing's shoulder—Bith couldn't even tell one race from another in the writhing, pitching pile of bodies— and kicked the unfortunate aside. Backbreaker stood in the doorway and pointed and cursed and gibbered like a demon.

The elf stooped, poking flesh randomly with his sword. He trapped an arm against the stone floor. It was Cal's free hand. Bith wondered that he was still alive. The boy's hand writhed to claw and tear even as the rest of him was buried. Above Hathor shouted again and again as he fought to free Cal from the mess. Endril snatched Bith's hand and forced it onto Cal's.

Bith's mind rattled around inside her skull. A spell to help Cal, to save all of them? Why her? Why couldn't it be someone else? Why hadn't she just gone home? A howl from Hathor rocked her backwards and she almost lost the hand.

Blood squirted from somewhere and splashed on her breast and her hair. They would all be awash in blood soon. They'd spill theirs onto the stone floor of a wizard's crumbing castle if she didn't do something.

But *what*?

CHAPTER
11

Bith pressed her hands to the side of her head only to find they were smeared with blood. She wracked her brain and wept openly. Which spell? What could do any good?

Cal was buried alive. If only he could push them off, if he were stronger, like hulking Hathor—

She had it.

Fumbling in her belt pouch with one hand, fumbling with the other to hold Cal's hand, she dug out an acorn and pressed it tight against his palm. Cal's hand squeezed it.

> *"Grow, thing, grow, fast not slow,*
> *Fill thy vision onto the sky,*
> *In slipping your bonds and going beyond,*
> *You rise, the largest of all the rest."*

Had Bith had time to consider, she may have selected another spell. Confuse, or invisibility, perhaps even levitate. But she forgot. She had never done an enlarge spell on a human before, just dogs and cats and birds. And she had forgotten that ever since she'd passed through the Mistwall into the free lands, her spells worked twice or ten times better than they ever had. Or that Cal was already under a spell, a divine enchantment that made him strong and brave and vitally aware. Or that he was holding onto a sword that embodied the powers of a god.

She remembered all this and more in a moment, though. For Cal's hand—all anyone could see—suddenly ballooned to the size of a troll's. Then to the size of an ogre's. Then a giant's. Then . . .

The pile of bodies that had swamped Cal was rising. Endril took Bith's hand and urged her back. Hathor retreated with them. They watched with open mouths.

Cal's enemies, who had thought to be in control, were confused. They jabbered and looked around and banged their heads on the rafters. Some were too slow. Living and dead alike were caught amidst rafter-junk and pressed against the ceiling. Enemy carcasses gave off a ghastly crunching sound. A boot as big as a barrel suddenly popped out of the pile to the right. Then a great hairy head like a brown haystack appeared at the other end. A column of steel showed among black and red shapes. It was wider than a bench, longer than a coffin. It had runes carved on it.

The floor leaned dangerously now. The whole tower was tilting towards the chasm. Endril and Hathor and Bith looked to their only escape. It was through the tiny doorway that was blocked by a dozen orcs, a screaming Backbreaker, and Cal's expanding form. Bith watched a gap between two flagstones gape like a fish's mouth. The balcony crumpled and disappeared behind them. "We've got to get out of here!"

"There he go!" Hathor shouted.

Cal the giant emerged from underneath his enemies. They spilled off him like leaves. Men cursed. Orcs whimpered. Everyone fell back. Backbreaker barked at the horde to stay put, but Cal was taller than Backbreaker just sitting up. The young giant banged his head against the far wall, cracking it. He put out a bleary hand and shoved it away. Daylight spilled into the room. Everyone, friend and enemy, shrieked and bolted for the stairs as the tower shuddered.

"Come!" Endril called. He caught Bith's upper arm and charged with his sword out straight. Hathor put both hands on his axe handle and used it as a bar to shove people aside.

The tip of Endril's sword caught the traitorous Backbreaker

square in the open mouth. The monster jumped with surprise at a blow that should have killed him. He snatched at the elf but could not reach. Endril paused only long enough for Hathor to knock two men down the stairs, then he slung Bith like a bag of clothes after the troll. The elf produced a long white knife and slashed at the giant's ribs, but the blade skipped off. Backbreaker reached again as Endril bounded away and down the stair.

The last thing they heard from the room was a trio of screams and a crunching noise. Then the stairs lurched as a gobbling growl of stone sounded. Sunlight spilled down the stairwell.

Bith yelled, "What?—"

Endril had his back to her, for he faced up the stairs. "The tower is gone."

"What? Oh, *no*! Where's Cal?"

Endril said nothing. He only urged them downwards. "Hurry. The rest of the castle may follow."

"But where's *Cal*?"

"He's *dead*! Move!"

Bith trotted along with one hand on Hathor's shoulder. With the other she wiped away tears. "It's my fault. My fault . . ."

Hathor kicked retreating orcs headlong down the steps. They had practically a free path. Bith noticed for the first time the troll was wounded in many spots. He had been pinked in the neck, chopped in his red hair, sliced on the arm. He limped from a leg wound that ran blood all the way to his broad bare feet. But he never complained.

A roar behind made her turn. Endril was a dozen steps above her, skipping backwards light as a squirrel. He still had his slim black sword in his right hand, his impervious glove on his left with the white knife. Backbreaker was after him like a personal demon. He screamed and piped and hooted and howled with the noise of a thousand mad dogs. He slashed with his talons at Endril's face and arms, but always the elf moved nimbly out of the way. Almost always. His sleeves were in tatters, and Bith guessed the fair skin underneath was too. After what seemed an age they all reached the bottom of the stairs. Hathor slid in front of Bith and raised his axe in the air. Backbreaker, not ten steps up, looked as large and as fierce as a crazed dragon.

"Go!" Endril called. "He's after Bith!"

"Me?"

"Go, *now*!"

Hathor shifted his axe, took Bith's fine and trembling hand in his own calloused hairy one, and pointed towards the sunlight of a distant door. "We go that way."

"But the Dark Army's out there!"

"In here too. Castle fall on us. Run!"

Enemies scampered past and ignored them. Blocks rained from the roof of the castle and thudded on the floor. Hathor half-carried the girl out to the dazzling light.

The space in front of the castle was clear and amazingly quiet. Ruins of the village smoldered, having been burned to the ground by the orcs. Many dead dark shapes lay scattered about, and a few fair ones. There were live dark shapes close by, too. A handful of gnolls and trolls stood well back from the castle so as not to be hit by falling rubble. Down the slopes the bulk of the army still clung to the valley floor like a carpet. Endril, Bith, and Hathor cast about for an escape route. The nearby marauders noticed the trio and grinned evilly. They shuffled towards the party. Then the color drained from their faces as they pointed past them towards the Mistwall.

"Form a circle," Endril warned.

Bith asked, "Wait . . . What are they pointing at?"

The three adventurers turned and looked.

Rising above the Mistwall, coming from the canyon behind the castle, something huge blotted out the setting sun.

Was it a tree, impossibly tall? Or some pillar of a mountain? Or a waterspout? It was too tall to be anything living. But it was.

It was Cal.

The boy that was their friend, that Bith had teased, that Endril had argued with, that Hathor had joked with, strode towards his enemies, ninety feet tall.

Bith marvelled at the vastness of the magic before her. Perhaps her magic had been enhanced by the runesword. Or perhaps it had been the presence of the dead magician in the tower room, the old faker who could not protect his people. Or maybe it was something within Cal. Whatever had done it, here he came, tall as a god.

Cal moved slowly, as if in a dream, but he covered ground like a cloud. His legs were thicker and taller than tree trunks. His clothes flapped in the breeze like a storm. His head was lost in the brightness of the autumn sky. A sound rolled out too, a sound like thunder. It was laughter from a true giant.

Cal marched full into the teeth of the Dark Lord's Dark Army.

BOOM, BOOM, BOOM. The valley shook under his footsteps. The army ran screaming. A boot as big as a house swept forward in slow motion. A pack of giants and ogres, no bigger than ants to this giant, scattered in terror as that boot crashed in their midst. Two were kicked a hundred feet. One disappeared under Cal's hobnailed sole. Then the other boot stamped down. Enemies gibbered and cowered and died. Men, gnolls, trolls, orcs, and a dozen other races ran and screamed and tripped over one another. They either died or they didn't as the giant's feet trod among them. They were helpless to save themselves.

A phalanx of something—they were too far for Bith and the others to see who they were—lifted bows under the shouts of an officer. A dozen skinny shapes released a flurry of arrows at the giant's head. The tiny shafts struck home in the giant's face, but they only made him turn. Cal lashed out with the runesword.

The mumble and grunt of runes was loud and weird, a chorus of the damned. The blade hummed through the air. The sword had grown along with its owner and was now a shining rainbow of death thirty feet long. Before the archers could move or even scream the blade overtook them. Like grasshoppers trapped among wheat they were scythed in half to rain in bloody gobbets. The laugh came again. It was a deeper rumble now, not the laugh of their friend Cal, Bith realized, but the laugh of a god come to earth to play. Vili was there, owning Cal's body and using it.

A fireball shot into the sky and sizzled by the giant's dark head. Cal swung around. Bith saw the source, too. A figure, the tall, golden, god-man Schlein, stood in front of his tent with both arms before him. Another electric charge coursed through him, sparkled along his arms, and shot into the sky to land in Cal's hair. It trailed flame up the side of his head, but the giant merely swiped at it with his hand and the fire went out. Angry, Cal-Vili took a step.

His left foot came down and blotted out another handful of soldiers. Then the right boot swung, slowly, inexorably. Schlein lost whatever spell he was mustering. A hundred banners and poles skittered aside before a worn leather toe. The leader of the Dark Army disappeared in a fireball just as the boot connected. Schlein's tent and the one behind it were kicked into the sky like a pig's bladder in some game. Bith saw a wink of gold disappear toward the mountains. At first she thought it was Schlein himself, somehow riding his fireball, then she realized it was his golden throne.

The giant Cal, or Vili, reached down with monstrous fingers towards the scorched spot where Schlein had disappeared. Bith could not see for what.

A grunt sounded behind her. The girl turned to find Hathor and Endril being pressed for their lives.

The traitor Backbreaker had burst out the door of Castle Cairngorm onto Bith and her companions. His grey statue's face was twisted and ugly, his mouth a gash, his eyes wild. Talons were raised high in the air like a bear's. He came off the bottom step with a tremendous leap designed to carry him through Endril and Hathor and onto Bith. Right at that moment, the girl was more frightened than she had ever been in her life.

Yet Endril and Hathor held like a stone wall. The troll swung his axe overhead in a man-killing blow that made him grunt. Endril lunged straight with his slim black sword for the monster's throat. The axe blade thudded onto Backbreaker's shoulder and bounced off. The slim black blade caught in the hollow of his throat and bent with a *crink*. But Backbreaker was rocked. Elf and troll followed up with more blows, but so did the giant.

His hands hissed through the air. One caught in Hathor's back like a net full of fishhooks. The troll was unprotected without his thick bearskin. He sucked wind as the claws were dragged forward and off his shoulder. Blood flowed from a half dozen weals. Endril, faster than the eye could follow, fended off the slash on his side with his metal glove. But the claws came back quicker than a cat's. Hathor dropped his axe and fumbled for it even as his own blood made his hands slippery. Endril slashed with his white knife, but every stripe yielded only a dulled edge. The giant's skin was as tough as soapstone.

Nor was Backbreaker their only attacker. The white slugs were back, gibbering and quaking. They did not join in the fight, but picked up stones to hurl. Bith noticed the stolid trolls rolling up the slope towards them. Another few minutes would find the three of them surrounded by a horde of evil ten deep.

Endril didn't look back as he called, "Bith! Run! Fly!"

"I won't leave you here!" she shouted, though her voice shook.

"It's you he's after! For the price on your head! Fly and he'll leave us!"

A price on her head? *Hers?* Bith could barely believe it. She certainly didn't believe that Backbreaker would give up the attack on Endril and Hathor if she fled. And she couldn't just leave her brave friends here to die, even if that fate befell her also. Should she try another enlarge spell, on Hathor? But Cal seemed to have lost his mind. And she didn't know if she had the energy for it—she might pass out from the effort. Here she was again, wondering what to do while people died around her. Why had she taken up her mother's profession? "I won't leave!" she called again, to give herself courage.

"Then summon Cal! We need him!"

"How?" she asked the air, for Endril was gone behind the giant. Dwarfed by his size and bulk, the elf resorted to pricking him in the back. Hathor had given up trying to regain his axe. Instead he dove forward and grappled the giant around the waist. Backbreaker roared for the first time in pain. Hathor had bitten him deep in the side with his white fangs. The giant responded by ripping deeper into the troll's back. The peasant smock parted like a spider's web, as did the tough skin beneath it.

Bith cried, "Stop that!" and raised both hands. Almost before she knew it her shoulders and arms tingled. A blast of fire shot from her hands and wreathed the giant's face. But the monster merely blinked and shook his head and reached for her again. He ignored the troll's bites, Endril's jabs, and his own blindness to get the girl. Bith had no choice. She turned and ran.

Right into the pack of trolls.

A brawny arm shot out and rapped her in the breastbone so hard she sat down. She gasped for air as a dozen calloused hands plucked at her shoulders, her hair, her legs. The trolls meant to carry her off bodily. Bith jabbed her arms out straight at the lead troll, but another troll knocked them aside and her spell fizzled, sparks dribbling from her fingertips. She lacked the power to light a candle anyway. Someone clamped her hands. Trollish heads blocked out the sky. Bith was helpless. She put her head back and screamed, *"Endril, I can't!"*

Fast as he was, so fast he could often see humans blinking and thinking, Endril the elf had nonetheless been knocked backwards by an elbow to the face from the giant Backbreaker. The stumble actually saved his life, for unbeknownst a gnoll had come up behind him to slip a spearpoint into his kidneys. Endril slashed backhand with his short knife and opened the doggish face from muzzle to jaw. The gnoll fell away and Endril got clear. He swept the horizon with his acute vision and missed nothing.

What he saw was both good and bad.

The Dark Army was gone. Only a rabble was left. A confused mob of villains skittered around the giant Cal's feet with no plan except to escape personal destruction. They ran up the valley, up to the walls, back towards the Mistwall. Anyone who stood still was squashed, any group that mustered an attack was either kicked out of existence or stomped on, or buried under a handful of soil and rock ripped from the walls around Cairngorm.

The giant had stomped in ever wider circles, and now he was far down the valley near the Mistwall. Even as Endril watched the giant reared back his head and blew a mighty breath that swept into the fog bank and pushed it back. Putrid colors roiled and coiled and bubbled anew as the cloud gave up land it had claimed. Cal—or Vili in his body—blew again and shoved the Mistwall back a quarter mile, then a half. Then he started a game of sending monsters home. Many of the evil ones near the wall had run for its shelter, and Cal helped them along. With seven-league strides he kicked a dozen monsters like toadstools so they disappeared into the foggy bank. Cal scooped up a handful of caterwauling men and orcs and gnolls on his sword and flipped them far over the top of the cloud. Then he stomped his feet hard, once, twice. He hopped into the air and came down with CRASH that shook the entire valley and rattled rocks from the teetering castle behind Endril. The whole structure slowly caved in on itself. The giant roared in delight at the consternation and destruction of the Dark Lord's army.

But while Cal was winning a one-man battle with the Dark Army, his three small companions were losing theirs. Hathor still clung to Backbreaker's waist, but it was only iron will that kept him there. His back was in shreds. Endril could scarcely believe he had any blood left to shed. Bith was buried somewhere under a pile of grasping trolls. She would be safe enough, he reckoned, since the price demanded her intact. But more enemies were encircling the three of them, and only a miracle could save them now. A miracle, or a god.

Endril fished under his cloak and drew out his short bow. With deft and long-practiced fingers he strung the unbreakable string and nocked an arrow. If ever he had to make a trick shot, it was now. He dodged the cowardly white monsters and drew back his arrow. He adjusted for the wind, aimed, held his breath, and loosed.

Whether it was the sharpness of the razor arrowhead, the strength of the draw, or the uncanny aim, Endril never knew. But it worked. The giant Cal smacked a hand to his brow. He rubbed at the sunken arrow as a normal man might massage a fly sting. He looked around for the source of the pain and saw his friends in trouble.

With a roar that rattled the hills Cal picked up his giant feet and crashed them down. With one stride he covered half the valley. With the next step he covered another quarter, with the third step, an eighth.

Endril slashed behind him with a knife to keep gnolls at bay. Bith was screaming a blue streak, using some of Cal's oaths, and Hathor was still biting Backbreaker as they tumbled on the ground. "Help is on the way!" the elf sang in a voice that pierced the wind.

"Helpppppppp!!!!!!!!!!" Bith squawled.

Endril looked down the valley again. Cal had arrived at the

first wall of Cairngorm. But instead of towering over it, he had to hop. Endril peered and blinked. Something was wrong.

Cal was shrinking. It was hard to tell, with so strange a perspective and looking down a hill at a wall, but the boy was definitely not ninety feet tall any more. He was still taller than the castle, but he had to put a hand on the wall to hop over it as a shepherd would vault a fence. Cal raced up the slope, covering less ground with every step. Endril groaned. At this rate he'd be normal-sized when he arrived. What had happened? Had Endril's arrow awakened the Cal inside the giant's body and negated the magic? Had pain countered the spell? Or was it simply wearing off? Whatever the cause, Endril prayed to his woodland gods that he hurry.

Cal climbed the hillside in ten-foot leaps. Endril sang again, and Backbreaker looked up from where he was mauling Hathor. Suddenly the giant shoved Hathor free. Here was something worth fighting. The traitor gave a bawl that pierced eardrums as he raised his hands high.

Cal was puffing when he arrived. He was still abnormally tall, as tall as Backbreaker. He was obviously befuddled as to exactly what was going on. But the boy held the sword as if it were a talisman. He faced the fearsome blood-soaked Backbreaker squarely.

The stone giant shrieked and leapt full at the boy. Cal sucked a deep breath, threw his arms back, and brought the sword forward.

With one mighty *crack* the runesword cleft the stone giant in half from pointed head to pointed crotch.

Backbreaker, it seemed, had no blood in him, but rather bile like molten metal. As his stone-cased body split a gout of liquid fire pinwheeled into the air. A gobbet splashed onto Cal's sleeve and immediately set it on fire. Molten caustic dribbled down the shank of the runesword and burned his gloves. More acid sizzled onto the ground, etching a hole in the flint slope and crisping the grass. The two halves of the body collapsed together and began to burn, fierce and hot as a blacksmith's forge, too hot to watch.

Cal dropped the runesword and frantically stripped off his horsehide gloves. Gnolls howled and slugs gibbered in fright at the flames. Endril slashed with his knife to get clear and to Bith's side. Hathor, exhausted and bloody, managed to roll over and sit up. The trolls holding Bith stood dumbfounded.

Then Cal himself howled. He had picked up the pommel of the sword. It had no blade, only a melted hunk no longer than his fingers. *"Oh, NO!"*

The pause that followed the giant's destruction lasted only a moment. The remains of Backbreaker made a bright and cheery blaze that shrank rapidly. The gnolls grunted queries among themselves. The slugs shuffled around the helpless Hathor. The trolls retained their grasp on Bith so she could not flee.

Endril summed up the situation. The trolls were the threat. There were more than ten of them, and they had Bith. Endril addressed them in their own tongue. "Will you loose the woman now? Schlein is gone, his army scattered. You have no one to ransom her to."

The leader of the trolls, a tall beast with yellow fangs and finger bones on a thong around his neck, glanced down into the valley. The Dark Army was still in chaos, but not as badly as they had been five minutes ago. Knots of black monsters, whipped by their superiors, advanced towards the wall. Someone had raised a few standards before the only standing tent. The valley floor might be littered with dead, and many black trails led back towards the now-distant Mistwall, but there were scores of enemies left. The troll chief nodded that way and barked, "We take her there. They pay us."

Endril flicked blood from his short knife. "She's one of us. She stays."

The troll leader glanced behind Endril. Hathor was on his feet, weaving and weaponless. Cal had thrown down the stub of the runesword. He hunted for another, but found none. Bith was on her back with at least five hairy feet pressing her flat.

The troll chief laughed harshly. "We kill you easy. Eat your livers."

Endril took a step forward. Bith squirmed and clawed at a trollish foot. Cal drew his dagger and handed Hathor his bloody axe. The two limped to join the elf. The three stalwarts stood together again, if only for a short time. The trolls hefted their clubs and spears and grinned at the easy prey.

Endril spit out one word between his teeth. "Try."

The wind flickered around them as they all stood frozen. It was a rising wind with a howl in its teeth.

Or was it the wind?

Cal glanced up the slope towards the castle Cairngorm. He put a tattered and burned sleeve to his forehead to wipe his eyes. The howl grew louder, more articulate, separate yet united.

Cal roared with laughter and the trolls frowned.

"Look!" the weary boy called. *"Look there! Oho! Look!"*

CHAPTER
12

Howling, shouting, banging their swords against their shields, cheering, singing, crying, the people of Cairngorm charged down the hill. They were fewer now, not many more than a hundred, but they came in a wave as if a thousand. Their noise was a war cry and a hymn and a shout of joy all rolled into one.

The sight of them decided the gnolls and slugs. With a whine and a squeal they bolted down the slope for the wall.

The trolls argued among themselves at this new turn. Half of the party watched for only a second, then turned and fled. Three others held Bith down as the leader barked. The troll next to him argued some point and was struck in the face. In that moment Endril leapt. One clean swipe of his knife opened the chief's throat. He died gurgling. The other three picked up their feet and ran. They didn't get far. The forefront of the Cairngormers' charge, the youngest and fleetest, overtook them and cut them to pieces.

By now the remnants of the Dark Army in the valley had noticed the charge, and with it all ambition fled. Ravaged by a giant, deprived of their leader, denied the safety of the Mistwall, and now attacked anew by a relentless and revitalized enemy, they broke. Throwing weapons to the wind and knocking down their brothers, the Dark Army left the field a scattered rabble. The thin trails leading to the Mistwall became a solid flood. At their heels came human men and women fighting for their native soil. They watered it now with alien blood.

The four champions of Vili watched the charge go by with immeasurable relief. Hathor fell over backwards, the last dregs of his awesome strength gone. Cal soon joined him on the ground. Bith was already there, and she made no effort to rise. And so even Endril sat down cross-legged with his friends. The air was cool and clear and quiet.

Hathor the troll lay on his back and mopped blood from his face with what was left of his peasant's tunic. Then he rummaged under his shirt and drew forth a dark root of some kind. Spitting on it to knock off the flecks of blood, he bit off a huge chunk and began to munch methodically. He counted the colors of the twilight sky.

Caltus Talienson, ex-master swordsmen, picked up the stub of the runesword. It had cooled, but it looked more like a melted candle than a sword. There was about nine inches of blade intact. He tapped the end against a rock to see if it broke. It didn't. With a sigh he brought out a whetstone and experimented with sharpening what blade was left.

Bith of the Lost Lands, daughter of Morea, straightened her wide yellow belt with the devil's head belt buckle. She rearranged the dozen pouches, buttoning down their tops or drawing their strings tight. She tucked the silver wand into her belt until it felt right. Then she pulled out a bone comb and tugged at the burrs and sticks in her glossy black hair.

Endril the elf set his crooked sword and his hands on his lap. He closed his eyes, let his face relax, and began a sonorous song that barely registered on human ears.

And so Erin Barinsdotter found them a while later, when the last of the Dark Army had been dispatched or driven beyond the Mistwall. Erin too crouched down. She regarded each of them in turn with her open and honest blue eyes.

Finally she said, "What happened?"

No one spoke and she repeated the question. Twice.

Cal put down his stone and sighed deeply. "That's a good question. I don't think I know. The last thing I remember . . ."

"We thought you were dead," Bith said. "I'm glad you weren't. . . ."

Slowly, piece by piece, the story was put together there on the sunny slope below the ruins of Castle Cairngorm. Bith explained how her already-augmented enlarge spell must have been further augmented by Cal's holding the runesword—or something. Endril speculated that either Vili had seized control of Cal's enormous body, or Cal's mind couldn't function well under the strain of running such a large form—or something. Hathor mentioned that Backbreaker was no giant, not with that fire inside him. He was—something else—the heat of which had been enough to slag even the magical runesword, which in turn had been the only thing capable of cutting his stony hide. Hathor guessed their traitorous partner had been a demon, honey-tongued and hollow-hearted. Bith asked about this "price" on her head, and Endril replied he didn't know for sure: he'd heard it bandied about by the trolls at some point. Presumably Schlein had put out a bounty after Bith demeaned him in front of his followers. Exactly what he wanted with Bith no one knew, Bith included.

They all agreed they would be crowbait had not the Cairngormers returned. Erin explained that they had just vanquished the foes in the cellars and escaped out a back tunnel when the Mistwall receded and they decided to return for a look. She thanked Cal profusely for that, since it seemed the Mistwall would be held at bay for some time now, maybe a few more years even, and they could remain and possibly find some permanent solution, or at least a decent place to retreat to. Cal said he couldn't take credit for much. He didn't remember a lot of it—as a giant his mind had been full of wonder and glory and strength but not a lot of sense.

Sometime during the discussion, Castle Cairngorm gave a quiet groan and slipped over the edge of the ravine. It shattered with a quiet huff and cloud of dust at the bottom. The rock shelf was left bare. Erin said the castle had been falling down for years anyway. The warrior woman left them after that to tend to wounded and start fires for some supper. The four companions were alone again.

Cal asked Hathor, "Don't those wounds hurt?"

The troll peered at his shoulders and forearms and hands, which were covered with more seeping gashes than skin. "Not much. Yours."

"I don't have—" Then Cal noticed that yes, he too was riddled with them, including a bee sting-like welt on his forehead he couldn't explain. But there was little pain. Scratches itched more than anything else. "These *should* be—"

"A reward," piped a tiny voice they all recognized, "for a sterling performance."

Cal held up the stub of runesword so they all could see. Vili's tiny face was like frost on the blade. A long face with a forked beard and mustache and long drawn eyebrows. A tricky face, like a fox's.

"This is our *reward*?" Cal asked. "A balm for wounds suffered in battle? We got them on *your* behalf."

"You fought on your own behalf," the tiny god told him. "We only demanded you destroy the sword. Good work."

"You're free with your compliments but little else," Bith chimed in. "Where's our *big* reward? Remember, 'Anything you want?' "

"Well . . ." squeaked Vili, "We can not grant just anything right now—"

"Nothing, he means," croaked Hathor.

"—We have not a lot of power remaining. The channel through the sword hath drained us. We fade already . . ."

It was true, his face was winking out like a reflection on a cloudy pool.

Endril said, "Convenient, how he fades when we have demands."

Cal shook the sword pommel. "That's for sure. Hey, you weasly little crumb. You stay right—"

Vili was gone.

"I'd like to be giant around him," Cal said, "and stomp him into the ground."

"Next time we drink him," Hathor said, "then piss him out onto fire."

Bith giggled and covered her mouth. Cal and Hathor laughed a deep belly laugh. Endril smiled.

"He'll be back soon enough, I warrant," the elf said.

"Remember he mentioned *swords*? This was only the first. They'll be others, and he'll be after us to destroy them too."

"Fat chance," said Cal. He held up the stub of a sword and then threw it away in disgust. It clanged far down the slope. "I just wish we had something to show for all this besides scars."

Bith pointed a slim and dirty finger. "Cal, what's that green thing sticking out of your shirt front?"

Cal tugged at it. "This? I don't know. What is it?" He tugged at the green cloth and it came free, a lump stitched with red. "Why it's—"

"Your father's banner!" Bith cried.

It was. Cal held the flag up. It was not large, only two feet by three, and simply made. A red eagle took off for the sky with a red fish in its beak, all against a green background.

"But how did I get this?" the boy asked.

Endril replied, "You must have picked it up from the banners before Schlein's tent. Yes, I remember seeing you stoop for something amidst your rampage."

Cal hung onto the flag. It snapped in the fresh wind like a real sea eagle, proud and free and glad to be back in the right hands.

Bith said, "There you are, Cal, there's the best something you could ask to carry away."

Cal couldn't speak. He hugged the banner to his chest and put his head down. Everyone else was silent for a moment.

Finally it was Bith who said, "Not bad for a stableboy. Few of them have their own personal banners to carry into battle."

Cal cleared his throat. His voice was still husky as he said, "And you're still a princess, even without an entourage."

Bith lifted her hands. "No entourage? Look at me. Surrounded by ancient and learned elves, sturdy, loyal trolls, and seasoned warriors. One of each, anyway."

"Yes, an unlikely entourage," Endril said. "A deposed princess, an errant knight, a gentle troll, a lost elf. Four more disparate beings I doubt you could find in this world, yet look at us. We've learned to work together and laugh together, to survive, to trust one another—'tis no mean feat. And we had one thing correct from the very start. We were meant to be four. Like the seasons, like the winds, like the quadrants of the sky. No more, no less.''

Cal stood up. He rocked a moment on his feet, but finally stood steady. ''And where are we four for next?''

The others stood up, Hathor with help. Bith replied, ''I'm not leaving this village until I've had a bath.''

''Of course, your highness,'' Cal quipped. ''And your entourage will be glad to fetch you hot water. We can use a few days to replace our tackle too. I need a new sword, and we must get Hathor some real clothes instead of those scarecrow rags.'' The troll grinned and poked Cal in the shoulder with a knotty finger. ''But where then?''

Endril stroked his chin. ''There's a forest to the north of here, a beech forest, not far from a waterfall and a small village. Lovely to see this time of year. Very peaceful.''

Cal glanced at the others and winked. ''And when, Endril old friend, were you last at this oh-so-lovely village?''

Endril returned his hand to his chin. ''It would have been some seasons ago, perhaps . . . two hundred and fifty?''

Cal, Bith, and Hathor all nodded. Then together they said, ''Why not?''

About the Author

Clayton Emery is 36 years old, happily married with a small son and a wife in medical school. He has been a dishwasher, a carpenter, a zookeeper, a farmhand, a surveyor, a teacher, and a volunteer firefighter, among other things. He writes computer manuals for a living and fiction when he can. His books include *The 4D Funhouse* with Earl Wajenberg; the *Tales of Robin Hood* series; and a forthcoming murder mystery, *A Man on a Flying Horse*. A displaced Yankee, he currently lives in Cincinnati.